THE FOUNTAIN OF LIVING WATERS

THE FOUNTAIN
OF LIVING WATERS

THE TYPOLOGY OF
THE WATERS OF LIFE
IN HERBERT, VAUGHAN,
AND TRAHERNE

DONALD R. DICKSON

UNIVERSITY OF MISSOURI PRESS

Columbia, 1987

Copyright © 1987 by
The Curators of the University of Missouri
University of Missouri Press, Columbia, Missouri 65211
Printed and bound in the United States of America

Library of Congress Cataloging-in-Publication Data

Dickson, Donald R.
   The fountain of living waters.

   Bibliography: p.
   Includes index.
      1. English poetry—Early modern, 1500–1700—History and
criticism. 2. Water in literature. 3. Water—Religious aspects.
4. Christian poetry, English—History and criticism. 5. Typology (Theology) in literature. 6. Herbert, George, 1593–
1633—Symbolism. 7. Vaughan, Henry, 1622–1695—Symbolism. 8. Traherne, Thomas, d. 1674—Symbolism. I. Title.
PR545.W34D5 1987 821'.4'0936 87–1656
ISBN 0-8262-0639-5 (alk. paper)

∞™ This paper meets the minimum requirements of
the American National Standard for Permanence of Paper
for Printed Library Materials, Z39.48, 1984.

All photographs were taken from originals held at
the University of Illinois Rare Book Room.

For my parents

Velma Patton Dickson
and
Vernon Richard Dickson

Des Menschen Seele
Gleicht dem Wasser:
Vom Himmel kommt es,
Zum Himmel steigt es,
Und wieder nieder
Zur Erde muß es,
Ewig wechselnd.

> Goethe, "Gesang der
> Geister über den Wassern"

ACKNOWLEDGMENTS

The task of honoring one's colleagues is always a happy one, made all the more pleasant when their advice and collegial support have been so instrumental in bringing this project to fruition. I am most indebted to my two teachers at Illinois who stood Janus-like at my side during my apprenticeship: the one always looking beyond my work, helping me see the real significance of literary studies; the other, with his keen eye fixed on the "dark backward and abysm of time," helping me to locate my work within the traditions of western thought. To U. Milo Kaufmann and John Block Friedman I owe much; so also, to my long-time friends and colleagues, Stephen M. Watt and F. Jefferson Hendricks.

Many have read the manuscript of this book and helped steer me clear of major errors. Paul A. Parrish, Jeffrey N. Cox, Harrison T. Meserole, Margaret J. M. Ezell, and David R. Anderson, among my colleagues at Texas A&M University, have proved invaluable over the years. Also John R. Roberts, Jr., Ted-Larry Pebworth, Dewey D. Wallace, Jr., and, most of all, Sidney Gottlieb were all generous with their time and learning.

A special debt of thanks is owed to N. Frederick Nash and Mary S. Ceibert, the Librarians of the University of Illinois Rare Book Room, who helped immeasurably by providing counsel on bibliographic matters. Funding to enable me to complete this project was provided first by the Graduate College of the University of Illinois and later by Texas A&M University. Some portions of this book have appeared elsewhere, and I wish to thank the editors of *Renaissance and Reformation*, *The John Donne Journal*, and *Explorations in Renaissance Culture* for permission to reprint parts of my earlier essays. Special thanks to my editorial assistant, Suzanne K. Boyer.

Throughout this study, in accordance with customary practice, I have normalized the Renaissance spelling of i-j and u-v and silently expanded abbreviations. All translations are my own unless otherwise noted; all references are taken from the Authorized Version of the Bible unless otherwise noted.

D. R. D.
College Station
May 1, 1987

CONTENTS

INTRODUCTION

One of the most powerfully engaging *topoi* in Elizabethan literature is the mysterious circulation of water within the earth (through underground rivers) or in the atmosphere as a metaphor for ascent.[1] Shakespeare, for example, invoked it when Hamlet, rankled by his mother's hasty marriage to Claudius, importunes the heavens to remove him from the world by exclaiming: "O that this too too sallied flesh would melt, / Thaw, and resolve itself into a dew!"[2] Similarly, Marlowe's Faustus hopes that he might be swallowed up in the "entrals" of a noxious cloud, which will ascend toward the heavens, to escape Mephostophilis:

> You Starres that raign'd at my nativity,
> Whose influence hath allotted death and hell;
> Now draw up *Faustus* like a foggy mist,
> Into the entrals of yon labouring cloud,
> That when you vomite forth into the aire,

1. In an important study, *Origin and Originality in Renaissance Literature: Versions of the Source*, David Quint also examined the *topos* of the source, the confluent origin of the rivers of the earth. He found the literary provenance for this *topos* in the Aristaeus-Orpheus epyllion that ends Virgil's *Fourth Georgic* and traced the influence of Virgil on such authors as Sannazaro, Tasso, Bruno, Rabelais, Spenser, and Milton. Quint's primary interest lies in the impulse toward orginality in Renaissance poetics; he took as his central figure the river Jordan, the type of the Logos, the primal creative agent. Though we explore some of the same biblical and classical materials, we differ on one central point: Protestant exegetes seem to have regarded the waters of life more as a figure for the radical transformation effected by the waters of grace than for the Logos, and hence they were more interested in the fact that putrid water was purified as it ascended from the bowels of the earth or that the universe was created out of the waters of the abyss in Genesis. This radical transformation had as its analogue the death and rebirth of the believer into the community of the saints.

2. William Shakespeare, *Hamlet*, in *The Riverside Shakespeare*, ed. G. Blakemore Evans (Boston: Houghton Mifflin, 1974), I.ii.129–30.

My limbes may issue from your smoky mouthes,
So that my soule may but ascend to heaven.[3]

The notion of dew returning to its heavenly source was as intriguing as the notion of the confluence of rivers within the earth. Poems embodying or depending structurally on the water-cycle are also quite common in the seventeenth century, especially in Herbert, Vaughan, and Traherne, and most readers no doubt will recall the most famous English poem on the subject, Marvell's "On a Drop of Dew." Unlike their Elizabethan forebears, though, these seventeenth-century devotional poets used the circulation of water in a consistent, even predictable fashion. Whether through the condensation and sublimation of dew or through the circuit of waters coursing within the earth, the endless circulation of water usually serves as a metaphor to present the descent of grace and regeneration of the soul and the consequent ascent or reintegration of the soul with its heavenly source. Though Marvell wrote so few lyrics that he is not usually considered in discussions of devotional poetry, "On a Drop of Dew" is so well-known and so perfect in its achievement that it provides a ready introduction to a study of the waters of life.

Marvell's meditative lyric focuses on the evanescence of a morning dewdrop, cradled within the petals of a rose, as the occasion to moralize on the transience of the soul on earth and to express the hope that the soul will ascend to its heavenly source. The poem compares the condition of the dewdrop to that of the soul, also separated from the heavenly realm; the first eighteen lines are given to the drop of dew, the second eighteen to the soul in a balanced, logical arrangement. Though critics have had little difficulty analyzing these lines, including the typological references to manna as a type of Christ invoked in the last four lines,[4] the recapitulative implications of the relationship between Christ as manna/dew and the soul as dewdrop have not been fully explained. The last four lines provide emotional and poetic closure by linking the conceit of the soul as drop of dew to a powerful biblical tradition, which allows a vast reservoir of meaning to surge into the poem. The implied analogy between "Manna's sacred Dew" and the soul as dewdrop introduces a crucial typological relationship to the notion of descent and ascent. Manna, a type of grace and of Christ, *distills,*

3. Christopher Marlowe, *Doctor Faustus,* in *The Complete Works of Christopher Marlowe,* ed. Fredson Bowers, 2 vols. (Cambridge: Cambridge University Press, 1973), V.ii.1950–56.

4. See Rosalie Colie, *"My Ecchoing Song": Andrew Marvell's Poetry of Criticism,* pp.

congeals, and *dissolves* as do the dewdrop and the soul. More important, the cycle of descent and ascent, which the manna epitomizes, is made possible by the power of the Sun, or Son, which the manna also foreshadows. Christ, in other words, is both an object of sublimation and the efficient cause of it. Unless we see how Christ as both manna and Sun validates the cyclical process of exhalation, distillation, congelation, and dissolution—upon which the three-fold analogy of dewdrop to soul to manna depends—we miss much of the brilliance and subtlety of the poem.

The first part of the poem describes a drop of dew that is delicately balanced on a rose petal. Even though the rose is frequently a symbol of beauty and perfection in the earthly garden, the thorns associated with it evoke the painful memory of the fall (Gen. 3:18). The drop of dew seeks restlessly to maintain its purity and separateness from the world while waiting for the sun to "exhale it back again." An appropriate object for Marvell's purposes here, the dewdrop like the soul has its origins in the heavens. Indeed, during the Renaissance, dew was thought to fall from the middle of the three regions that made up the earth's atmosphere (see Chapter 2 for a fuller discussion). Dew formed when watery vapor, drawn up into the air by the heat of the sun, condensed and fell as small drops. Generally this occurred at night when the warming rays of the sun no longer penetrated the atmosphere; any vapors would thus be cooled ("congealed" in common usage). Depending on the season, the watery vapor, or "meteor," formed hoarfrost or dew. The early morning rays of the sun were enough to "sublime" or "exhale" these drops back into the atmosphere, where they either formed clouds (depending on their relative grossness and the temperature) or were transformed into elemental fire (which was thought to exist above the region of the air).

Such is the hope of the dewdrop that the speaker observes. The time is early morning ("Orient Dew"), and the droplet—to use H. M. Margoliouth's paraphrase for line six—"closes in on itself all round"—because it fears contact with the grosser world.[5] It slights even the fair rose as it rolls restlessly, gazing upon the purer realm where it originated. Only the "pitty" of the "Sun" can save the

---

113–17; Ann E. Berthoff, *The Resolved Soul: A Study of Marvell's Major Poems,* pp. 27–30; Anthony Low, *Love's Architecture: Devotional Modes in Seventeenth-Century English Poetry,* pp. 238–41; and Michael Craze, *The Life and Lyrics of Andrew Marvell,* pp. 277–85.

5. *The Poems and Letters of Andrew Marvell,* 1:244.

dewdrop from being tainted through contact with the mutable realm.

> See how the Orient Dew,
> Shed from the Bosom of the Morn
>   Into the blowing Roses,
> Yet careless of its Mansion new;
> For the clear Region where 'twas born
>   Round in its self incloses:
>   And in its little Globes Extent,
> Frames as it can its native Element.
>   How it the purple flow'r does slight,
>   Scarce touching where it lyes,
>   But gazing back upon the Skies,
>   Shines with a mournful Light;
>   Like its own Tear,
> Because so long divided from the Sphear.
>   Restless it roules and unsecure,
>   Trembling lest it grow impure:
>   Till the warm Sun pitty it's Pain,
> And to the Skies exhale it back again.
>   So the Soul, that Drop, that Ray
> Of the clear Fountain of Eternal Day,
> Could it within the humane flow'r be seen,
>   Remembring still its former height,
>   Shuns the sweat leaves and blossoms green;
>   And, recollecting its own Light,
> Does, in its pure and circling thoughts, express
> The greater Heaven in an Heaven less.
>   In how coy a Figure wound,
>   Every way it turns away:
>   So the World excluding round,
>   Yet receiving in the Day.
>   Dark beneath, but bright above:
>   Here disdaining, there in Love.
>   How loose and easie hence to go:
>   How girt and ready to ascend.
>   Moving but on a point below,
>   It all about does upwards bend.

>   (ll. 1–36)

In the second half of the poem, using an analogical argument common to meditations on the creatures, Marvell then directs the reader to the relationship of the dew-cycle to the soul: just as the dewdrop "Round in its self incloses," so the soul, that "Drop . . .

within the humane flow'r," tries likewise to shun the mutable realm.
As one critic argues perceptively, Marvell's meditation narrows
inwardly as he "concentrates ever more fully on the single, self-
concentrated object."[6] Both the dewdrop and the soul reflect the
world, each fearing dissipation through direct contact. Marvell has
quite simply revealed a set of correspondences between the spherical dewdrop, whose "little Globes Extent" mirrors the "Sphear"
from which it is divided, and the soul, which "in its pure and
circling thoughts" mirrors "The greater Heaven in an Heaven less."

Some critics view the logic of this correspondence in terms of the
tenets of Neoplatonism.[7] In his *Enneads*, Plotinus provided explanations for the metaphors and images used in "On a Drop of Dew"
to describe the descent and ascent of the soul. One of his favorite
images of the One was the fountain of light, from which the many
emanate, and he characterized the natural movement of the soul
about this fountain of light as circular.[8] The farther the soul moves
from the fountain of light into the realm of matter, the more inhibited the soul becomes in its efforts to "recollect its own Light," in
order to maintain the purity of its "circling thoughts." The play of
light and shade on the dewdrop (the light it reflects is said to be
"mournful," that is, both full of morning light and piteous) underscores the anxiety of the soul, balancing itself precariously on only
a single point of its circumference. The soul is "dark" where it
touches the rose and "bright" where the light from the heavens can
penetrate. Yet the veneer of Platonism in this poem should not
conceal from us the profoundly Christian lesson that the speaker
reveals in his meditation. As some critics have noted, the description of the soul as a drop or ray "Of the clear Fountain of Eternal
Day" is a traditional Christian image. Scripture relates that mankind was created as an image of the divine and has the divine light
within.[9] Even so, Marvell portrayed the soul and the dewdrop as
impotent without the intervention of the Son. Both rely on the
"pitty" of the sun to draw them heavenward; neither is pure
enough to maintain its own integrity. The dewdrop is properly

---

6. Colie, p. 117.

7. See, for example, Barbara K. Lewalski, "Marvell as Religious Poet," in *Approaches to Marvell*, ed. C. A. Patrides, p. 261, who calls it "one of Marvell's most
Platonic poems," though she, too, notes its "profoundly Christian meaning."

8. Plotinus, *The Enneads*, pp. 417, 621.

9. Bruce King, *Marvell's Allegorical Poetry*, p. 30. See John 1:9, 8:12, and II Cor.
4:6 on biblical light imagery.

"mournful" because of its inability to affect its situation and because of its complex dependency on the sun, a fact that is explored
in the closing couplets.

Once the Christian element is acknowledged as the key to the
foreground of the poem, subtle biblical echoes can be detected in
the language of the first thirty-six lines. The "Orient Dew, / Shed
from the Bosom of the Morn" may suggest that the true source of
the soul is the "bosom" of God (John 1:18), whose return will be
from the east, the orient. "Mansion" in line four may recall the
description of heaven as a house with many mansions (John 14:2).
The "former height" (l. 22) can refer equally as well to the pre-
lapsarian state as to the pre-existence of the soul. The dewdrop is
also said to be "Like its own Tear." Because teardrops were usually
depicted as ovals, not spheres, in Renaissance emblem books,[10]
Marvell's insistence on the penitential aspect of the dewdrop—
especially when the poem's basic conceit depends on the sphericity
of the dewdrop, the soul, and the heavenly order—ought to be
regarded as important. Indeed, the notion of penitence and atonement is at the very core of the typological allusions introduced in
the last four lines to resolve the dilemma of both dewdrop and soul.

The Christian hope implicit in the first part of the poem—the
phrase "Till the warm Sun pitty it's Pain" has almost an evidential
value in the Renaissance—is made explicit in the final couplets:

> Such did the Manna's sacred Dew destil;
> White, and intire, though congeal'd and chill.
> Congeal'd on Earth: but does, dissolving, run
> Into the Glories of th' Almighty Sun.
>
> (ll. 37–40)

The logical connectives—see how the dew . . . so the soul . . . such
did the manna—indicate that the cyclical process presented by the
dew-cycle in the first thirty-six lines has been foreshadowed by
Christ, who himself also distils, congeals, and dissolves. Manna
symbolizes the true bread of life or grace (John 6:31), without
which spiritual regeneration is impossible. In Exodus, manna fell in
the desert hidden within a sacred dew to sustain the Israelites. As
"bread from heaven" (Exod. 16:4), manna is a type of Christ's
flesh, the body that is sacrificed to atone for man's transgressions
(John 6:31–35). Like the dew in Marvell's poem, manna is "White"

10. See, e.g., *Emblemata: Handbuch zur Sinnbildkunst des XVI und XVII Jahrhun-
derts*, eds. Arthur Henkel and Albrecht Schöne.

("it was like coriander seed, white," Exod. 16:31); it is "congeal'd and chill" ("as the hoar frost on the ground," 16:14); and it dissolves ("when the sun waxed hot, it melted," 16:21). One lesson that the reader garners from Marvell's meditation is that grace *descends* because of the sacrifice of the Son. The "mournful" dewdrop thus depends on Christ for its sublimation, as the soul depends on manna for sustenance and regeneration.

Marvell's poem, however, insists on a broader application of typology in these last lines.[11] The similarities between the exhalation, condensation, and (the hoped for) sublimation of the dewdrop, on the one hand, and the descent and ascent of the soul as "drop," on the other, also hold for Christ as the manna enveloped in sacred dew. Such a series has powerful typological implications. Christ assumes flesh to make possible the ascent of the soul. Christ descends like the dew, and though his body is immaculate ("White, and intire"), it is a human body ("congeal'd and chill"). Only by making sacrificial atonement can Christ unleash the metaphoric power of the Sun necessary to dissolve both himself as "sacred dew" and the soul as dewdrop. Though each Christian must try to imitate Christ, only the power of the sun/Son draws the drop of the soul heavenward. Left to itself, the soul is as impotent and as fragile as the droplet clinging to the petal. The soul should properly be penitent—"Like its own Tear"—but Christ's sacrifice is what allows the soul to dissolve and "run / Into the Glories of th' Almighty Sun."

"On a Drop of Dew" thus depends on a typological strategy that is far more complex than has been commonly acknowledged. Types were not identified merely as foreshadowings of Christ, but rather were understood as foreshadowing the full mystery of the Christian faith: that is, how each believer gains salvation by grace and through participation in Christ's atonement. Typology can be said to validate the conceit of the soul as drop of dew by establishing that Christ's life is truly the type or paradigm of the Christian's. Manna in the poem is not a simple type or foreshadowing of Christ as the bread of life. Rather, the pattern of Christ's life—descent and ascent as presented by the dew-cycle, with the dewdrop gazing

---

11. Patrick Cullen, in *Spenser, Marvell, and Renaissance Pastoral*, pp. 177–78, discusses the typology of the last four lines. While Cullen notes the parallels between the descent of manna and the sustained simile of the dewdrop, he does not pursue the recapitulative implications of this relationship, which in my view is the key to the poem's closure.

always at its source and striving to maintain its purity, capable of sublimation only by some outside agency—must become the type of the Christian's. Rosalie Colie is correct in arguing that Marvell did not break any new ground in his lyric poems:

> Marvell does not open for us—as Shakespeare does, and Milton, another poet who looked back over his shoulder at his own past—immense vistas of new poetic possibility. He does something quite different, boring deep into his own material to discover the concealed, to discard the outworn and useless, to re-animate with his intellectual energy traditions in his day fading into meaninglessness. . . . Marvell ends a great tradition, I think, with neither bang nor whimper, but with the scrupulous courtesy and grace that had carried the tradition so far, from Greece to seventeenth-century Europe.[12]

This is precisely what he accomplished in "On a Drop of Dew," a poem that is for the modern reader perhaps the best known example of a literary tradition that had been established firmly in 1633 with *The Temple*, refined in 1650 and 1655 with successive editions of *Silex Scintillans*, and also developed by Traherne in the Dobell Folio *Poems* (though unpublished until the twentieth century). While Marvell turned his hand only seldomly to religious lyrics, Herbert, Vaughan, and Traherne placed the typology of the waters of life in all its complexity in an important position in their major poetic works. The rich tradition of the imagery drawn from the typology of the waters of life did not die out, of course; we find it prominent in such a familiar hymn as "Rock of ages cleft for me." But as poetry became more public and less lyrical in the late seventeenth century, these devotional poets were tucked away in Palgrave and elsewhere until the twentieth century. It is not without significance that one of the early champions of the metaphysical poets, T. S. Eliot, employed the traditional associations of biblical water imagery in "The Waste Land."

The central aim of my study is to illuminate a major element in *The Temple*, *Silex Scintillans*, and the Dobell Folio *Poems* by examining the tradition out of which it grew in the biblical commentaries and the penchant for typology in the seventeenth century. Anyone engaged in the ongoing reassessment of Renaissance devotional literature must take account of the work of Barbara K. Lewalski, who has argued that the overwhelming emphasis on Scripture among English Protestants resulted in a distinctively

12. Colie, p. 4.

Protestant poetics, founded on biblical literary models and biblical modes of analysis.[13]

While all students of seventeenth-century literature are indebted to Lewalski for describing contemporary, Protestant influences on such religious poets as Herbert, Vaughan, and Traherne, the single-mindedness of her approach tends to rigidify the distinctions between the terms *Protestant* and *Catholic*. My own research has led me to a somewhat paradoxical conclusion about the "Protestant-ness" of the aesthetics of these poets. The emphasis given to typology as the primary figurative mode of the Bible does seem to distinguish Protestant poetics from medieval allegory. The reformers indeed believed that they were grounding their religious practices on the sure foundation of the Word by emphasizing biblical typology, which essentially represents an attempt to interpret Scripture using itself as its own key, by matching text with text to recover figurative levels of meaning. While there is some novelty and freshness in their methodology, paradoxically there is considerable continuity with the older tradition as well. Protestant commentators, seeking to free themselves from the arbitrary allegorizing of the Fathers, nonetheless returned to the text with a sophisticated methodology—involving a complex, threefold typology that closely resembled the traditional fourfold allegory. Studying a major biblical type—one that helps to structure the entire biblical narrative—is thus a fruitful ground for observing the continuities and discontinuities of cultural forms.

Herbert, Vaughan, and Traherne produced a body of poetry that revitalized the Christian salvation drama by using traditional biblical tropes in a more systematic and complex way (in accordance with Protestant theories of typology). Their common structuration of the metaphor of regeneration and ascent, of course, is based on the emanation and return (an implied circularity) of the waters of life in the Bible: just as water is the "agent" with which God created, sustains, and will restore the universe, so too is the water of life the agent of the believer's baptismal regeneration, sustenance by the dew of grace, and future restoration in the New Jerusalem. Underscoring the importance of the biblical water imagery that linked the creation and regeneration of the macrocosm to that of the microcosm (thus emphasizing what can be called eschatological typology) is the water imagery related to Christ himself. Through

13. Barbara K. Lewalski, *Protestant Poetics and the Seventeenth-Century Religious Lyric*, pp. 3–144.

the sacrifice at Calvary, Christ enables the dew of grace and the living waters of the sacraments to flow freely from the wound in his side. That the believers were regenerated by these waters, in fact that they produce rivers of living water (John 7:38) through typological imitation of Christ, was a phenomenon that intrigued theologians and poets in the seventeenth century. The typology of the waters of life also fascinated Herbert, Vaughan, and Traherne—even as it allowed Marvell to exercise his wit in the finely wrought "On a Drop of Dew."

For those who may be unfamiliar with the scientific basis of the metaphor of the water-cycle, Chapter 2 includes a brief account of Renaissance theories of the subterranean and atmospheric water-cycle. Also as background for the literary applications of the typology of the waters of life, Chapter 3 examines the intricacies of typological interpretive practices in the Renaissance; this chapter will also show that Protestants perceived a complex relationship among the major types of the waters of life. To accomplish this, we will examine the traditional interpretations of the major biblical events involving the waters of life: the creation of the universe out of the waters of the deep (Gen. 1:2), the rivers of living water issuing from Christ (John 4:10–14, 7:37–39), and the crystal fountain in the New Jerusalem (Rev. 22:1). Having established the background for this literary tradition and its metaphoric vehicle, we can then study the way Herbert, Vaughan, and Traherne employ the circularity of the waters of life in presenting the Christian paradigm for salvation.

❧[II]❧

THE WATER-CYCLE IN SEVENTEENTH-CENTURY SCIENCE

While the power and cogency of the metaphor of the circulation of the waters of life derived from biblical typology, the vehicle used to denote the metaphor comes from Renaissance science. For those unfamiliar with earlier theories of hydrology and meteorology, a brief account of the doctrine of the circularity of the waters of life may prove useful. Although I consider the hydrologic and mete- orologic cycles separately, the two are but a single manifestation of the great circle of perfection upon which the Renaissance notion of *harmonia* is based. The seemingly ceaseless ebb and flow of the waters in and around the earth—confirmed by observation, by the Bible, and by science—provided Herbert, Vaughan, and Traherne with an entire system of metaphors to depict the return of the soul to its heavenly source. Just as the "dew" of grace falls only to be drawn heavenward after it has given succor, and just as "living water" always returns to its source, so shall the soul travel back to God enveloped in and purified by the waters of life.

The Subterranean Water-Cycle

That pure water should spring from the earth and form into rivers to sustain mankind is a phenomenon that challenges the imagination. Throughout antiquity and into the Renaissance, near- ly all the important scientists and compilers of natural lore offered explanations of the origin of rivers and springs. To the modern mind most of these seem wrong-headed, lacking as they are in the basic concepts necessary to explain the hydrologic cycle in terms more consistent with our own mechanistic theories (for example, convection, vapor exchange, and dew point). Nearly all the ancient writers on the water-cycle assumed that the ocean (and the abyss) was the source and repository of fresh water, that subterranean passageways connected the abyss with the surface, and that the elements were converted into water within the earth. Given the overwhelming reliance on Aristotelian physics among earlier theorists, much of their writing seems mainly to rearrange pieces of a familiar puzzle. However, the nature of the subterranean water-cycle was still a matter of debate in the seventeenth century; in fact, the greatest *scrutator* of the abyss, Athanasius Kircher, was obliged to accommodate in some way the ideas of most of his predecessors in his syncretic *Mundus subterraneus* (1664). Since many writers, both ancient and modern, have examined the early theories on the origin of springs and rivers, we will only look at the most accessible and hence the most popular.[1]

Though Greek cosmology is actually quite pluralistic, with each theory opposed by a host of antithetical ones, the exigencies of textual transmission make the early Greek views seem harmonious.[2] Essentially, the Renaissance was presented with two major versions of the subterranean water-cycle, Plato's and Aristotle's, both of which were in part corroborated by the Bible. In the *Phaedo* Plato stated that all rivers constantly flow into Tartarus, a deep chasm within the earth that Homer speaks of in *The Iliad* as the begetter of all things; from Tartarus flows the great river Oceanus, which encircles the globe and forms the headwaters for all its rivers. This notion corresponds exactly to the usual interpretation of Ecclesiastes 1:7, a verse cited almost universally by Christian writers to explain the origins of springs and the circularity of water.

> All the rivers run into the sea; yet the sea is not full; unto the place from whence the rivers come, thither they return again.

1. For a more comprehensive history, see Frank D. Adams, *The Birth and Development of the Geological Sciences*; Asit K. Biswas, *History of Hydrology*; Yi-Fu Tuan, *The Hydrologic Cycle and the Wisdom of God: A Study in Geoteleology*. Also, the British Library possesses a volume of what appear to be theses written in the seventeenth century at German universities (Tracts, 537.g.34). All of these theses (some 37 total) dealt with the problem of the origin of fountains and other meteorological phenomena. Obviously, these questions were still very much at issue during this time.

2. G. E. Lloyd, "Greek Cosmology," in *Ancient Cosmologies*, ed. Carmen Blacker and Michael Loewe, p. 210.

The Geneva Bible gloss of Ecclesiastes 1:7, for example, reads, "The sea which compasseth all the earth, filleth the veines thereof, the which powre out springs and rivers into the sea againe."[3] Concerning the abyss, Plato wrote:

> For all the rivers flow together into this chasm and flow out of it again, and they have each the nature of the earth through which they flow. And the reason why all the streams flow in and out here is that this liquid matter has no bottom or foundation. So it oscillates and waves up and down, and the air and wind about it do the same. . . . And when the water retires to the region which we call the lower, it flows into the rivers there and fills them up, as if it were pumped into them; and when it leaves that region and comes back to this side, it fills the rivers here; and when the streams are filled they flow through the passages and through the earth and come to the various places to which their different paths lead, where they make seas and marshes, and rivers and springs.[4]

As is the case with most of Plato's scientific accounts, he is here transmitting the ideas of earlier thinkers. Thales of Miletus taught that not only does the universe originate from water but it ultimately returns to it in a great cycle. His disciple Anaximander also believed that the sea—which is the remainder of the primordial moisture that once covered the earth before the universe was formed—is the source of all rivers and all atmospheric meteors.[5] To many of the pre-Socratics, water was central to the mystery of the creation and sustenance of the earth, and Plato incorporated much of their wisdom in the *Phaedo*. However, the western world

3. *The Geneva Bible: A Facsimile of the 1560 Edition*, intro. Lloyd E. Berry, fol. 277[v].

4. Plato, *Phaedo*, 112a–112d, pp. 383–85. In the *Phaedo*, Plato also quoted Homer's description in *The Iliad* of "murky Tartarus, far, far away, where is the deepest gulf beneath the earth," (1:339) and of "Oceanus, from whom the gods are sprung" (2:81).

5. Charles H. Kahn, *Anaximander and the Origins of Greek Cosmology*, fragment 20, pp. 102–3. Hesiod also conceived of the origin of the cosmos in terms of a watery chaos much like that of Genesis. His *Theogony*, p. 87, l. 116, began with the familiar passage, "Verily at the first Chaos came to be." As Werner Karl explained in his dissertation, "Chaos und Tartaros in Hesiods Theogonie," Chaos here means vapor or sea mist: "Mit 'Chaos' bezeichnet Hesiod das Dunst- und Nebelmeer, das in dem einmaligen Weltprozeß zuerst entstanden ist und—nach der Konstituierung des geordneten Kosmos—in diesem seinen Platz zwischen Himmel und Erde einnimmt so Teil eines Ganzen wird." One other major source on the origin of the waters is the Aristaeus-Orpheus epyllion that ends Virgil's Fourth Georgic; see David Quint, *Origin and Originality in Renaissance Literature: Versions of the Source*, pp. 32–42.

knew only the Plato of the *Timaeus* directly through the translation and commentary prepared by Chalcidius in the fourth century A.D.[6] Until the Renaissance his notion of the abyss was preserved only through the Roman encyclopedists and through Aristotle.

Because Aristotle went to such lengths to refute the Platonic hydrologic cycle in addition to formulating an opposing theory, the *Meteorologica* must be counted as the *locus classicus* for views on the origins of springs.[7] That the abyss could be the fountainhead of springs and rivers seemed to him impossible due to the volume involved.

> But it is evident that if anyone tries to compute the volume of water constantly flowing each day and then to visualize a reservoir for it, he will see that to contain the whole yearly flow of water it will have to be as large as the earth in size or at any rate not much smaller. (349b, pp. 91–93)

Aristotle agreed that a portion comes from the circulation of waters from the subterranean reservoirs; that is, he accepted the existence of the abyss and the passageways that permit circulation. But he insisted that springs have other sources: especially, through the conversion of the elements into water. He argued that just as "cold condenses vaporous air into water above the earth, the cold beneath the earth must be presumed to produce the same effect. So not only does water form separately within the earth and flow from it, but the process is continuous" (349b, p. 93). Further, he believed that rain water filters through the surface of the earth and collects near mountains, "For mountains and high places act like a thick sponge overhanging the earth and make the water drip through and run together in small quantities in many places" (350a, p. 95). Rivers, he explained, were formed near large, cold mountains that could "sponge up" the largest quantities of water. Aristotle found, in all, three sources for springs (and the rivers that flow from them): the subterranean reservoirs, the conversion of air into water, and the filtration of rain water.

The Roman redactors of Greek science, especially Seneca and Pliny, were important sources on hydrology since their encyclopedias were far more accessible to medieval and Renaissance readers than the Greek sources they were based on. Seneca's *Naturales*

6. Plato, *Timaeus: a Calcidio translatus commentarioque instructus*, vol. 4.
7. Quotations will be cited internally from *Meteorologica*, trans. H. D. P. Lee.

quaestiones drew heavily on the *Meteorologica* for its hydrology.[8] He explained that sea water is circulated by "hidden routes" (*occulta itinera*) and that its salinity is removed by filtration (1:217); furthermore, he argued that air as well as earth is converted into water inside the earth (1:221–25). He did, however, take exception to Aristotle's notion that rain water contributes to the water-cycle. In a homely anecdote that later writers frequently repeated, Seneca stated that rain does not penetrate far enough to reach the caverns in the earth and so become part of the subterranean cycle:

> As a diligent vine-gardener myself I assure you that no rainfall is so heavy it wets the ground to a depth beyond ten feet. All the moisture is absorbed in the outer surface and does not get down to the lower levels. How, then, is rain able to supply an abundance to rivers since it only dampens the surface soil? (1:219)

Pliny's *Naturalis historia*, in addition to being a much quoted source on marvelous springs and rivers, also was the first to advance the accepted explanation of the mechanics of the cycle given in the *Phaedo*. The problem Pliny set out to solve was how water violates its natural tendency by "running uphill" as it circulates. This happens, he explained, because earth and water are joined in a "mutual embrace," earth being unable of itself to cohere without water and water being unable to remain still without earth to hold it up:

> The intention of the Artificer of nature must have been to unite earth and water in a mutual embrace, earth opening her bosom and water penetrating her entire frame by means of a network of veins radiating within and without, above and below, the water bursting out even at the tops of mountain ridges, to which it is driven and squeezed out by the weight of the earth, and spurts out like a jet of water from a pipe, and so far from being in danger of falling down that it leaps upward to all the loftiest elevations.[9]

Though his solution to the dilemma of water "running uphill" was later rejected, it does indicate how the mind must work to save appearances when tradition tells one a priori that something is so.

Of the medieval encyclopedists who carried on the tradition of Seneca and Pliny, the most widely read for over a thousand years was Isidore, Bishop of Seville. Owing to the fact that the notion of

8. Quotations will be cited internally from *Natural Questions,* trans. Thomas H. Corcoran.

9. Pliny, *Natural History,* trans. Horace Rackham, 1:301.

auctoritas was so powerful in the Middle Ages, Isidore is doubly significant, for not only did he himself become a prime authority on natural science, but in his *Etymologiarum liber* he made pagan science consistent with the greatest authority of his age, Scripture.[10] To Isidore the normative explanation of the origins of springs and the subterranean water cycle was Ecclesiastes 1:7. To make this possible, he explained, God created certain subterranean passageways about which the pagans had somehow known. All water flows into the abyss, the womb or matrix, and recirculates *per occultas venas*:

> *Abyssus*, profunditas aquarum impenetrabilis [est]: sive speluncae aquarum latentium, e quibus fontes et flumina procedunt; vel quae occulte subter eunt, unde et *Abyssus* dictus. Nam omnes aquae, sive torrentes, per occultas venas ad matricem abyssum revertuntur.
>
> (The *abyss* is an impenetrable depth of waters, or caves of hidden waters, from which fountains and rivers spring forth; or rather which pass secretly beneath, and because of this it is called the *abyss*. For all waters, or streams, return through the hidden passageways to the womb, to the abyss.)[11]

Beginning with Isidore, medieval compilers concerned themselves mainly with the abyss rather than with Aristotle's "conversion" or "rainwater" theories in explaining the circulation of the waters.[12] Bartholomaeus Anglicus was satisfied to quote Isidore outright: "*Abissus* is depnesse of water unsey, and therof cometh and springeth welles and ryvers. For oute of the depnesse comen alle waters, and tournen ageyne therto by pryve waies as to the modir of watir, as Ysider saith *libro xiii*."[13] Thus a modified Aristotelian view on the hydrologic cycle—one that accommodated the best of ancient thought with the Bible—prevailed throughout the Middle Ages.

In the year of his election to the Royal Society (1663), John Dryden summarized his century's attitude—the attitude of what Charles Singer calls the "insurgent century"—toward the Aristotelian approach to science:

    10. W. H. Stahl, *Roman Science*, pp. 214–15.

    11. Isidore, *Etymologiarum liber*, in *Patrologia Latina*, ed. J. P. Migne, 221 vols. (Paris, 1844–1864), 82, col. 489.

    12. Albertus Magnus, *Meteora*, was the important exception. His work expounded Aristotle's *Meteorologica* and rebutted any detractors. The *Meteora* gave special prominence to "rain-water" theories on the origin of fountains and to the notion of the abyss. In particular, see Book II, iii. 2–5, pp. 546–49.

    13. Bartholomaeus Anglicus, *On the Properties of Things*, 1:664.

> The longest Tyrrany that ever sway'd,
> Was that wherein our Ancestors betray'd
> Their free-born *Reason* to the *Stagirite*,
> And made his Torch their universal Light.
> So *Truth*, while onely one suppli'd the State,
> Grew scarce, and dear, and yet sophisticate,
> Until 'twas bought, like Emp'rique Wares, or Charms,
> Hard words seal'd up with *Aristotle's* Armes.
> from "To my Honour'd Friend, Dr Charleton"[14]

Because the seventeenth century saw the publication of Bacon's *Of the Proficiencie and Advancement of Learning* (1605) and Descartes' *Discours de la Methode* (1637), it is commonly designated as the age of inductive reasoning and scientific method. The "new" philosophy that was to call all in doubt, in Donne's famous phrase, was, however, not exactly new. It had its beginnings as early as Robert Grosseteste in the thirteenth century, who with his student Roger Bacon began rejecting ancient authority unless it could be corroborated by testing and observation. Their experimental science represents a genuine break with the medieval tradition of trusting the received wisdom of the *auctores* above all else. It is more correct to say that in the seventeenth century real advances in science became possible once the mathematical techniques were developed that enabled scientists to measure a world that had before been a qualitative one.[15]

Throughout the late Middle Ages and the Renaissance, a fledgling spirit of inquiry emerged in the work of scientists such as Georg Agricola, whom Thomas Lydiat at the time called that *diligentissimus scrutator subterraneorum*.[16] Agricola, skilled in observation by his training as a physician, abandoned the speculative theories of the scholastics for actual investigation. Hailed as the father of mineralogy and metallurgy, he spent much time in the mines of Bo-

---

14. *The Poems of John Dryden*, 1:32, ll. 1–8.

15. Charles Singer, *A Short History of Scientific Ideas to 1900*, pp. 218–88. See also A. C. Crombie, *Robert Grosseteste and the Origins of Experimental Science, 1100–1700*, pp. 44–60.

16. Thomas Lydiat, *Disquisitio physiologica de origine fontium*, p. 94. Lydiat was the official cosmographer and chronologer of Prince Henry, son of James I. He believed that the sea was the major source of spring water, a view for which Kircher was the spokesman. Lydiat was best known as an astronomer, and his *De origine* seemed to have made little impression on anyone save Edward Jorden, who mentioned him alongside of Agricola as an investigator of the subterranean world in *A Discourse of naturall Bathes and Minerall Waters*, p. 15.

hemia, then the greatest mining region in Europe, before rejecting the Aristotelian view that stones and gems were the products of planetary influences. Instead he argued that metals are formed from earth and water: subterranean fires of bitumen generate vapors that mix with earth to produce metals. Importantly, too, he emphasized that biblical accounts of a single "spontaneous creation" must be wrong because metals are constantly being formed in the earth. Agricola's work clearly indicated that theology no longer had a stranglehold on science and that a secular world view was in the offing.[17]

Because his work on metal formation featured underground waters, Agricola's *De ortu et causis subterraneorum* (1546) examined the nature of water vapors within the earth. He objected to various aspects of the classical theories on circulation for practical reasons: how could sea water rise to fountainheads when water is naturally heavy and how could either earth or air be converted into water? He was willing to accept, in coastal areas, the ocean as a source of springs because of the existence of saline springs near the shore and fresh water springs in the ocean itself. But he could find no supporting evidence for a mechanism that would allow the ocean to be the only source. He was even more adamant in refuting Seneca's and Aristotle's theories about the conversion of other elements into water.

According to Agricola, water was produced by the condensation of *exhalationes*, of which there are two kinds: *vapor*, which is hot and dry (*calida et sicca*), and *halitus*, which is hot and humid (*calidus et humidus*). When the aqueous *halitus* is refrigerated, it is converted into water. To convert the aerial vapor, however, its primary quality, dryness (*siccitas*), must first be changed. Agricola concluded, therefore, that water is only produced by the condensation of *halitus*, an aqueous exhalation, within the earth. Until this point in *De ortu*, he was simply applying Aristotelian physics with more rigor than the Stagirite. In explaining how this condensation and evaporation (to form the *halitus*) takes place, though, he introduced a new notion that was to engage the minds of investigators of the subterranean world for the next century. He attributed the evap-

17. See, e.g., the extensive editorial commentary on the formation of metals in Georg Agricola, *De Re Metallica*, pp. 46–53. Erwin Herlitzius, *Georgius Agricola 1494–1555: seine Weltanschauung und seine Leistung als Wegbereiter einer materialistischen Naturauffassung*, has the best study of Agricola's pioneering work in many fields and a useful bibliography.

oration of the waters within the earth (which enter through filtration of sea or rain water, or through rivers that passed underground) to subterranean fires burning on bitumen in certain areas within the earth. The evaporated water, *halitus*, rises through the hidden passageways, then condenses when it comes into contact with the cold rock of mountains. Simple experiments with a retort seemed to confirm this theory.[18] Subterranean fire was more important than water for Agricola's metallurgic studies, so the waters within the earth receive relatively scanty treatment; but his work on the subterranean world was to supply a crucial piece of evidence for the most extensive work on the abyss in the Renaissance.

Mundus subterraneus (1664), one of the great works of early science, came from the fertile pen of the Jesuit polymath Athanasius Kircher. A tome of nearly one thousand folio-size pages, it epitomized all that the ancient and early modern scientists knew about the subterranean world. The Royal Society received it enthusiastically within a year of its publication, and it later became a standard geological text. In the tradition of natural theology, Kircher prefaced his book on the origins of water, entitled *Lacuum, fluminum, fontium, natura & proprietate, eorumque ex subterraneis origine*, by quoting the normative explanation given in Ecclesiastes. For he said, "Haec ita certa sunt, ut de iis nulli unquam Sacri huius textus Interpreti dubitatio exorta fuerit" (These things are so certain, that concerning them no doubt has ever arisen to interpreters on this text).[19] The only objection to Ecclesiastes, he realized, is how water is elevated against its nature to the highest mountains. But he thought that he had the answers that eluded the highly abstract and metaphysical Aristotle, and, what is more, he could demonstrate the validity of his assertions with experiments and analogies.

First of all, he argued that the pressure caused by the flux and reflux of the tides, augmented by the winds, forces water through

18. Georg Agricola, *De ortu et causis subterraneorum libri V*, p. 10, wrote: "duae enim sunt exhalationum species: altera calida & humida, quam, distinctionis gratia, halitum nominare soleo: altera calida & sicca, quam vaporem. . . . halitus refrigeratus facile convertitur in aquam: at ex vapore aqua fieri non potest, ni utriusque qualitatis facta mutatio fuerit. non enim ex eo fit aer, nisi siccitas convertatur in contrariam qualitatem: nec ex aere gignitur aqua, nisi calor de ipso fuerit depulsus." He gave a detailed explanation of how clashing winds and burning coal produced the subterranean heat that transformed *halitus* into water in Book II of *De ortu*.

19. Kircher, *Mundus subterraneus*, 1:226. It was reviewed in the sixth number of the Royal Society's *Philosophical Transactions* (6 November 1665), 1:109–17. Parts of Kircher's work were translated into English as *The Vulcano's*.

the subterranean passageways because of the tremendous pressure of the sea's motion. That nature works in this way he proved by three different experiments involving capillary action.[20] Furthermore, he argued that there is a great fire in the center of the earth that feeds many smaller fires (here he seems to have been following Agricola's work on metallurgy). Figure 1 shows clearly the network of subterranean fires and the great storehouses or caverns of water within the earth, which he called *hydrophylacia*. Acting as a supplementary agent to the sea's pressure in circulating the waters, this central fire evaporates part of the water, which in turn rises through the passageways to the *hydrophylacia*, where it collects and condenses as a result of the change in temperature. The whole scheme is rendered in Figure 2, which shows how both hot and cold springs have their origin. The *calidus fons* (A) is fed by the underground passageway (L) that lies directly over the fires. Since it comes in contact with fire close to the surface, the water is still hot when it collects. The *frigidus fons* (B) is fed by *hydrophylacia* (P,V,X,Z) that are far from any fire, so the water is cold when it collects at the spring. The precision of his diagrams, the rigor of his experiments, and the persuasiveness of his analogies seem to have convinced most of seventeenth-century Europe that Kircher had penetrated deeply beneath the surface of appearances to discover the exact nature of the origins of springs and rivers.

As we have seen, the nature of the subterranean water-cycle was a matter of great interest. Kircher's view was, on the surface, just a rearrangement of earlier ideas, but it actually represents a signifi-

20. Kircher, 1:229, wrote: "Quo posito, certum quoque est, non sine admirabili naturae consilio factum esse, quod mare juxta Suppositionem secundam tot tempestatibus, tot ventorum statibus, tot descendentium nubium molibus prematur, fluxus denique refluxusque sui perpetua reciprocatione perenni inconstantia constantissimum sit." He went to great lengths to prove this point, using diagrams and analogies with retort experiments that had been previously understood and accepted. Though his ideas were anticipated by earlier writers, Kircher was the first to popularize them. Nicholas Gibbens, *Questions and Disputations concerning the holy scripture*, pp. 11–13, had proposed that springs were made by having the seas heaped together at the separation of the upper and lower waters during the second day, thus forcing water out of the mountains because of its weight. And Jorden, *Naturall Bathes,* pp. 18–20, used the analogy of Torricellian tubes to assert that sea water forces spring water to rise to the surface of the earth. To support this theory, Jorden recalled that Scripture (Job 38:8–10, Prov. 8:29, and Jer. 5:22) implied that the sea is higher than the earth, because the Lord fixed boundaries for the sea so that it would not overflow the land. See Andrew Willet, *Hexapla in Genesin*, pp. 6–8, for a review of the patristic commentary surrounding this problem.

Figure 1. The Subterranean Fire and Abyss (from Athanasius Kircher, *The Vulcano's,* no trans. [London, 1669], frontispiece).

cant advance in method with its scientific experiments and its analogies. A new spirit of inquiry was evident in the mid-seventeenth century; scientists, armed with more sophisticated apparatus and unfettered by a priori suppositions about the nature of the world, would put forth quite different explanations of the origin of springs and rivers in the generation after Kircher.[21] For the poets of the

21. Pierre Perrault, *De l'Origine des Fontaines* (Paris, 1674), was the first to measure rainfall and the amount of water carried off by a river. Others would follow his lead and soon the true relationship between rainfall and drainage was discovered. (Roughly six times more rain falls than water drains off the Seine.) See Adams, *The Birth and Development of the Geological Sciences,* pp. 445–60. By 1691 John Ray stated definitely that springs and rivers are fed by "distil'd" vapor or rain and not from the "fountains of the great abyss" (*The Wisdom of God,* p. 82). On the notion of the "circle of perfection," see Marjorie Hope Nicolson, *The Breaking of the Circle: Studies in the Effect of the "New Science" upon Seventeenth-Century Poetry,* pp. 47–80.

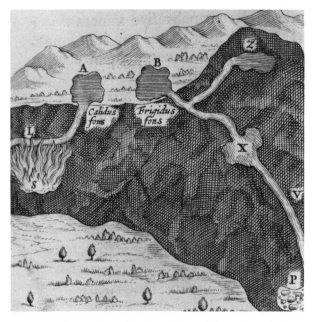

Figure 2. The Origin of Springs (from Athanasius Kircher,
Mundus subterraneus, 2 vols. in 1 [Amsterdam, 1664–1665],
I, 278).

early seventeenth century, however, the classical and biblical notion of the circulation of water—with its potent analogic relationship to the emanation and return of grace from God—was still the
powerful one.

The Atmospheric Water-Cycle

In light of the climatic importance of dew and rainfall in the arid
Middle East and its symbolic importance in the Bible, the ancient
Hebrews were surprisingly reticent on the subject of the origins of
dew. In Deuteronomy 32:2 we learn that rain and dew *fall* from
Heaven to the earth and that God's withholding dew is the most
terrible sign of disfavor because it blights the land (2 Sam. 1:21; 1
Kings 17:1; Hag. 1:10). Later, the Midrash offered only superficial,
albeit poetical, accounts of the "bottles" of dew and rain in the

heavens.[22] The ancient Greeks, on the other hand, were keen observers of *meteora*, and it was from the science of classical Greece that the Renaissance derived its knowledge of atmospheric phenomena. The word *meteor* in Greek meant literally "something raised up"; in the Renaissance the term referred to any "imperfect Mixtures condensed in the Ayr," which included such diverse phenomena as wind, clouds, mist, dew, lightning, comets, *draco volans, ignis fatuus*, and so forth.[23] The history of meteorology has been well recorded. To review the basic atmospheric water-cycle, we need only to look to Aristotle, since Renaissance meteorology was based almost exclusively on the *Meteorologica*. It was the basis for the handbooks of Seneca and Pliny, the primary sources on natural science in the early Middle Ages. By the beginning of the thirteenth century, Gerard of Cremona's Latin translation of the *Meteorologica* from Arabic sources was available; by 1259 Albertus Magnus had completed his influential commentary; by 1260 William of Moerbecke had made a direct translation of the *Meteorologica* from Greek manuscripts; and after the printing press made learning available to a wider audience, nearly 125 separate editions were published before 1601.[24]

Aristotle was the first to construct a theory that included all forms of meteors as part of a single, comprehensive process of elemental transformations. At the heart of his *Meteorologica*, indeed, at the heart of what I have been calling Aristotelian physics, was the notion of primary qualities that permitted the interconvertibility of the elements. Most modern descriptions of the Renaissance or medieval world view speak of all matter being composed of varying

22. See, e.g., Enoch 60:20 in *The Apocrypha and Pseudepigrapha of the Old Testament*, 2:225.

23. Benjamin Keach, *Tropologia: A Key to Open Scripture Metaphors,* 1:114; S. K. Heninger, *A Handbook of Renaissance Meteorology*, pp. 3–4.

24. Heninger, p. 10. Many have written on the history of meteorology. Otto Gilbert, *Die meteorologischen Theorien des griechischen Altertums*, is an excellent, though older, work on the subject. Gustav Hellman, *Denkmäler Mittelalterlicher Meteorologie,* is a collection of tracts on meteorology from the seventh through fourteenth centuries. Heninger's *Handbook* is very helpful, particularly for students of literature, because of the literary applications included with his discussion of theory. W. E. Knowles Middleton, *A History of the Theories of Rain and Other Forms of Precipitation*, is a comprehensive history of rain, though it is concerned primarily with a more "scientific " meteorology—i.e., meteorology after the invention of the barometer and other basic measuring instruments. Tuan's *Hydrologic Cycle* is also useful, particularly for eighteenth-century theories.

proportions of the four elements. It is actually more accurate to describe each of the four elements as combinations of two of the primary qualities: heat, cold, wetness, and dryness. In their natural positions (fire, air, and water were imagined to encircle the earth in great concentric rings), the elements buffered one another because of their antipathy to other primary qualities. Thus water, because it is "wet," was balanced by the "heat" of the air. Though each element had a natural place where it was found in the greatest concentration, all were constantly changing, one into the other; so fire and water were found within the earth, water and earth in the atmosphere, and so forth. For Aristotle maintained that "fire, air, water and earth are transformable one into another, and that each is potentially latent in the others, as is true of all other things that have a single common substratum underlying them into which they can in the last resort be resolved" (339b, p. 11). The common substratum was the primary quality they always share with another element.

That the elements were interconvertible was the basis for Aristotelian meteorology. Heat from the celestial region—both from the rotation of the spheres and the heat of the sun and stars—drew up "exhalations," the imperfect mixtures of the primary qualities.

> The exhalations that arise from the earth when it is heated by the sun must be not, as some think, of a single kind, but of two kinds; one is more vaporous in character, the other more windy, the vapour arising from the water within and upon the earth, while the exhalations from the earth itself, which is dry, are more like smoke. The windy exhalation being hot rises to the top, the more watery exhalation being heavy sinks below it. (341b, p. 29)

The "windy exhalations" (hot and dry) were sometimes ignited; sometimes their heat was "ejected" from them through contact with the colder air, giving rise to comets, shooting stars, the Milky Way, and other fiery impressions (341b–342b, pp. 29–39). The "watery exhalations," or "vapours" as they were commonly called in the Renaissance, "be as it were fumes or smokes, warme & moist, whiche will easely be resolved into water."[25] They produced rain, dew, mist, and so forth. These meteors were thought to be involved in the water-cycle.

What kind of meteor formed depended on two factors: the pro-

---

25. William Fulke, *A Goodly Gallerye . . . to behold the naturall causes of all kynde of Meteors*, fol. 2ʳ. See also, *Meteorologica*, 340a–341a, pp. 17–25, and 348b, p. 83.

portions in which the primary qualities were mixed and the prevailing temperature while they were rising. In their normal course upward, the exhalations passed through three stratified "regions" in the atmosphere. The uppermost region was the hottest by proximity to celestial fire and the heat given off by the revolving spheres. The lowest was also hot because of the reflection of the sun's rays off of the earth. The middle region was cold because of what Aristotle called *antiperistasis*: the cold was driven upward by the reflected heat of the sun's rays and imprisoned between the heat of the uppermost and lowest regions. William Cuningham explained this notion using a simple diagram (Figure 3):

> . . . the Aerie Region, is devidid into iii. parts, springing thorow Heate, and Colde: as the hier part of the Aere signified with A. being nere to the Orbe of the Fier, and is daylie carried about, (as Cometes and blasing Sterres ther ingendred, do apparantly declare.) and is made more hoote then the middle Region is: againe, the lower region next us, markid with C. is thorowe the reflextion of the Sonne beames rebounding from th'earth also made hoote, therefore the middle region B. beynge voide of heate, is alway coulde: yea and so much the coulder, howe muche the heate is more vehement in th'other two regions.[26]

Because they were lighter than the "vapours," the hot and dry "exhalations" ascended to their natural place, the uppermost region, where they formed comets, blazing stars, and other fiery impressions. The watery "exhalations," because they were grosser, never passed beyond the middle region. There, the cold condensed them into clouds. Some "vapours" never rose past the lowest region, especially those that formed late in the afternoon, and so they fell either as dew and mist or hoarfrost and ice, depending on the season.[27] Though some few disagreed with this schema, most accepted the notion of the three regions as the only logical explanation to account for the variety of meteors formed.[28]

The complete atmospheric water-cycle, then—according to the

26. William Cuningham, *The Cosmographical Glasse*, p. 42 [actually paginated as 45 by mistake].

27. This was the standard explanation. See, e.g., John Swan, *Speculum Mundi, or, a Glasse representing the Face of the World. . . . Whereunto is joyned an Hexameron*, p. 80.

28. Jorden, *Naturall Bathes*, pp. 8–10, did not believe in Aristotle's antiperistasis theory. He thought that air was naturally colder than water and hence produced snow, hail, ice, etc.; Aristotle held that air was "hot" and "moist" while water was "moist" and "cold."

Figure 3. The Three Regions of the Atmosphere (from
William Cuningham, *The Cosmographical Glasse* [London,
1559], p. 42).

Meteorologica and the host of texts and treatises based on it—was as
follows: the moisture about the earth

> is evaporated by the sun's rays and the other heat from above and rises
> upwards: but when the heat which caused it to rise leaves it, some
> being dispersed into the upper region, some being quenched by rising
> so high into the air above the earth, the vapour cools and condenses
> again as a result of the loss of heat and the height and turns from air
> into water: and having become water falls again onto the earth. (346b,
> pp. 69–71)

Just as water was circulated beneath the earth through the ocean to
the abyss and finally reached the earth as purified, fructifying
spring water, so too were the lighter vapors of the ocean and surface moisture drawn into the atmosphere and bestowed again as
purified, fructifying dew and rain.[29] When the hot and moist vapor

29. It is commonly supposed that the sun drew up only the purer and lighter
vapors of the sea, or that in drawing up vapors the salinity of sea water was purged.

rose all the way to the middle region, it condensed and formed a cloud—a wet and cold meteor that eventually produced rain. Dew was vapor "drawen up by the sunne in the daye tyme, whiche because it is not caried into the midle region of the ayre, abidyng in the lower region, by colde of the nyghte, is condensede into water, and falleth downe in verye smalle droppes," said William Fulke in perhaps the most widely read meteorological treatise in the Renaissance, *A Goodly Gallerye . . . of All Kynde of Meteors.*[30] The only real difference between the various watery meteors was a quantitative one: rain was the same as dew; snow the same as frost. The former were simply larger quantities of the latter (*Meteorologica*, 347b, p. 77).

By and large the Aristotelian atmospheric cycle was universally accepted until the end of the Renaissance. Cosmas Indicopleustes, a sixth-century Alexandrian monk, had the only variant explanation I have discovered. He believed that the angels drew vapors into the atmosphere: "God again provided rains for the good of the earth through the angelic powers, who with the utmost exertion bring them up from the sea into the clouds, and in obedience to the divine command discharge them wherever the divine command directs, for saith scripture by the prophet Amos: *He that calleth forth the water of the sea, and poureth it out over the face of the earth* (Amos ix,6)."[31] But for every Cosmas Indicopleustes, seemingly there were a thousand Isidores who stated succinctly: "Just so rains are begotten from the exhalation of the earth and the sea, which, when they have been elevated—either resolved by the sun or compressed by the force of the winds—are dropped onto earth."[32]

With the advent of quantitative meteorology, heralded by the Torricellian experiments in 1644 that led to the discovery of the barometer, the notion of the water-cycle began to change. By 1691 John Ray, the leading natural theologian of his time, scoffed at the idea of the abyss and its part in the great circulation of the waters. "I hope," he said, "those who bring up Springs and Rivers from the great *Abyss*, will not bring those Vapours, which unite into Drops, and descend in Rain from thence too."[33] The particular edge he

30. Fulke, *A Goodly Gallerye*, fol. 53ʳ.
31. Cosmas Indicopleustes, *Christian Topography*, p. 86.
32. Isidore, *Etymologiarum liber*, XIII.x, *Patrologia Latina*, vol. 82, col. 477: "Nascuntur enim de terrae et maris anhelitu, quae cum altius elevatae fuerint, aut solis calore resolutae, aut vi ventorum compressae stillantur in terris."
33. Ray, *Wisdom of God*, p. 82.

gave his gibe here is an indication that what we have been considering as two separate cycles, an atmospheric and a subterranean, were in fact one cycle to the earlier investigator—a mystery whereby the noxious sea was purged and made to bestow life-giving waters to an otherwise barren world. The secular theories emerging at the end of the seventeenth century no longer retained any sense of the great wonder of the confluence of the heavenly and the earthly realms that the circulation of the waters foreshadowed. Fortunately for us, a few poets kept this mystery alive.

❦[III]❦

THE TYPOLOGY OF THE
WATERS OF LIFE

When Adam and Eve are expelled from the garden, they lose the tree of life and the waters of life; in the fulness of time, at the very end of the narrative of cosmic history, the tree and waters of life are restored to a redeemed mankind. These two images thus help generate expectations about the beginning and end of biblical narrative—the paradise mankind loses but will eventually regain. Because of its association with grace and baptism, the imagery of the waters of life is consequently quite prominent in Scripture, though it is not often accorded its due by modern readers. This imagery was understood by Renaissance readers to constitute a pattern describing an essential Christian tenet, the renewal or regeneration of the believer made possible by Christ's intervention in time. As a system, these signs are not reducible to any fixed content, but rather must be seen in relation to other signifiers and signifieds: put another way, the theological usage governs the illustrative or symbolic usage of these signs. Water, for instance, is not simply manifested as the dew of grace—just as the sun does not only signify the light of reason (the sun/Son pun), but also at times signifies the blazing heat of fallen nature in distinction to the comforting shade of the garden.[1] Because meaning in any sign system is produced by the relationships among its constituent elements (even the signified is, after all, a mental image—not an objective reality—and so the relational values determine "meaning"), various signs drawn from the storehouse of biblical water imagery must be seen as part of the entire system and in terms of the reading practices that govern that

1. Stanley Stewart, *The Enclosed Garden: The Tradition and the Image in Seventeenth-Century Poetry*, pp. 60–96, discusses how the blazing sun can become a symbol of the fall, thereby making the shade (made possible by the cross) a gift of God.

system—in the case of the waters of life, biblical typology. In addition to the dew of grace, this system of signs also includes the primitive waters of the creation, the destructive waters of the flood, and the dissolution of the universe at the end of time. Because these very different manifestations of biblical "waters" were related in the minds of seventeenth-century Christians, we must recover the entire system of signification in order to locate markers of difference.

The crux of the typology of the waters of life is Christ's statement that "Except a man be born of water and of the Spirit, he cannot enter into the kingdom of God" (John 3:5). While the subtleties of this verse enabled it to serve many masters, it has certain elements upon which most commentators and theologians could agree. First of all, the source of this regenerative water is Christ, who proclaims himself to be the fountain of living waters (John 4:14). Second, and most important for this study, the immersion in baptismal waters—a ritual annihilation of the old self and a consequent rebirth in the waters of life—only begins the process of regeneration that would be eventually completed by means of the waters issuing from the throne of God in the New Jerusalem (*born . . . of the Spirit* was interpreted by some as referring to the regeneration at the end of time). Baptism thus only represented the *adoption* of the Christian into the mystical union of Christ with each believer; because of human weakness, or what was commonly known as the doctrine of imperfect sanctification, each believer continually fell into sin and required infusions of the waters of life. It is useful to recall that regeneration in the Pauline paradigm for salvation (as it was interpreted by the reformers) was an involved process that began with God's act of forgiveness, the imputation of his righteousness.[2] In the Trentine formulations, the will of the believer could cooperate in "imparting" righteousness, but the reformers held that this quality could not be created, only bestowed by a merciful God who chose to *elect* some for salvation. An infusion of irresistible, "prevenient" grace then made the heart recep-

2. See A. Mitchell Hunter, *The Teaching of John Calvin: A Modern Interpretation*, pp. 113–16; William H. Halewood, *The Poetry of Grace: Reformation Themes and Structures in English Seventeenth-Century Poetry*, pp. 74–75; Barbara K. Lewalski, *Protestant Poetics and the Seventeenth-Century Religious Lyric*, pp. 13–27; and Dewey D. Wallace, Jr., *Puritans and Predestination: Grace in English Protestant Theology, 1525–1695*.

tive to the blessings of salvation; as a result, one heard a *calling*. The next step, *justification*, was an immediate experience of faith and an assurance of the forgiveness of one's sins. *Adoption* properly came after receiving the sacrament of baptism, and the image of God in the believer was gradually restored by infusions of grace (confirmed through the sacrament of communion), a process called *sanctification* that continued often throughout the lifetime of the believer. The final stage was the perfect restoration of the image of God in the fulness of time, *glorification*. As a metaphor for the descent of grace and the consequent ascent of the soul to God, the circulation of the waters of life thus play a central role in the Christian hope.

As a method of decoding, or more properly as a set of reading practices, typology determined largely the way many seventeenth-century readers perceived the organizing structures (both narrative and metaphoric) of the Bible.[3] Thus we must begin by briefly examining typology as a formal method of decoding a text. We shall see that, as it became increasingly recognized as the fundamental symbolic mode of the Bible, the reformers began to use biblical typology in a more complex way than simply matching Old Testament types with New Testament antitypes. The Bible was seen as telling one essential story, Christ's; but through his story, the history of the creation, fall, redemption, and glorification of both mankind and the universe was told typologically. It is necessary to recognize, therefore, in addition to the familiar *Christological* types, *sacramental* types—through which the individual's salvation history is told in imitation of Christ—and *eschatological*

3. The *locus classicus* on typology in the context of English Protestantism is Lewalski's *Protestant Poetics*. The work of Jean Daniélou remains helpful on patristic typology, especially *The Bible and the Liturgy* and *From Shadows to Reality: Studies in the Biblical Typology of the Fathers*. On the literary application of typology, see William G. Madsen, *From Shadowy Types to Truth: Studies in Milton's Symbolism*; Murray Roston, *Biblical Drama in England from the Middle Ages to the Present Day*; Earl Miner, ed., *Literary Uses of Typology from the Late Middle Ages to the Present*; Paul J. Korshin, *Typologies in England, 1650–1820*; Ira Clark, *Christ Revealed: The History of the Neotypological Lyric in the English Renaissance*; Mason I. Lowance, Jr., *The Language of Canaan*; and Joseph A. Galdon, *Typology and Seventeenth-Century Literature*. General studies on typology include Erich Auerbach, "Figura," in *Scenes from the Drama of European Literature*; Victor Harris, "Allegory to Analogy in the Interpretation of Scriptures During the Middle Ages and the Renaissance"; and John R. Mulder, *The Temple of the Mind*, pp. 130–50. For a general bibliography on typology, see Sacvan Bercovitch, ed., *Typology and Early American Literature*, pp. 245–337.

types—through which the ultimate glorification of Christ, the believer, and the universe is foreshadowed and fulfilled. The implications of this complex view of typology are especially significant for students of the devotional poetry of the early seventeenth century, since so much of this literature was influenced by and dependent on the way the Bible was read and understood.

To recover the full range of significance, we must examine the major Old Testament types of the waters of life: the fountain of the garden of Eden and its connection with the primitive waters of the deep, the flood and the destructive potential of the deep, the crossing of the Red Sea and the sustenance of the chosen people by Horeb's waters, and lastly the *fons signatus* of the garden of the Canticles. All these prefigurations of the waters of life were fulfilled in the antitype, Christ, who became the source of regeneration at the crucifixion when his side was pierced.

I intend to show that Renaissance commentators—in part based on long-standing traditions of the Greek and Latin Fathers—discerned a complex typological relationship among these biblical events. (Since my concern is primarily with the more accessible Renaissance texts, I shall refer to patristic traditions mainly in the notes.) The next task will be to examine this Christological fulfillment and the way the individual could now reenact this mystery through sacramental recapitulation. Then the eschatological fulfillment of these types in the crystal fountain of the New Jerusalem will be discussed. Finally, I shall argue that biblical typology essentially reflects a particular view of history in which three distinct but intersecting moments in time are linked: the salvation drama of each believer as well as the whole span of sacred history are understandable only in terms of the history and drama of Christ's life (as foreshadowed and then fulfilled in the two testaments). The wealth of commentary on these key moments in sacred history—the creation, the flood, the exodus, the crucifixion, and the apocalypse—demonstrates that Scripture was read as a unified and complex whole. Although the actual aridity of ancient Palestine may constitute a functional explanation for the prominence of this pattern of imagery, the reading practices of those trying to recover the full signification of this system of signs reveal more importantly how Christians thought analogically about the symbolic universe that gave meaning to their lives.

The Complexities of Biblical Typology

The English reformers who wrote the most widely read guides to Scripture—William Perkins, John Weemes, John White, and Henry Lukin—all accepted as axiomatic the Protestant emphasis on the literal level of the text, *scriptura sola*, by proclaiming that Scripture rightly studied provided its own key to interpretation.[4] As Perkins stated emphatically, "The supreame and absolute meane of interpretation, is the Scripture it selfe."[5] All agreed that the first step in reading was philological: "words have some determinate signification, else they were of no use, to no purpose; but as a *Trumpet giving an uncertain sound*, 1 Cor. 14.8. But for their signification, we must have recourse to Use and Custome."[6] A knowledge of Hebrew and Greek was helpful, but etymology alone was not sufficient, since meaning or "signification" was dependent in part on context—"that sense, which they have by use obtained."[7] Studying scriptural "Use and Custom" implicitly established the Bible as a unified whole that permitted, indeed required, diligent comparison of text with text to recover meaning. The reformers were also guided by the collective wisdom of their best theologians. Since God had to accommodate things divine to human understanding, the Bible contained infinitely subtle points that could easily be misunderstood. Readers were urged furthermore to be guided in their interpretations by those principles of faith commonly agreed upon in the tradition of the *analogia fidei* (derived from Rom. 12:6).[8]

To accomplish their basic goals of using Scripture as its own best

4. For a fuller explanation of the reading practices of seventeenth-century Protestants, see Donald R. Dickson, "The Complexities of Biblical Typology in the Seventeenth Century."

5. William Perkins, *The Arte of Prophecying*, in *The Works of that famous and worthie Minister of Christ*, 2:651.

6. Henry Lukin, *An Introduction to the Holy Scriptures*, p. 34.

7. Lukin, *An Introduction*, p. 34.

8. Perkins, *Arte of Prophecying*, 2:651–52, wrote: "The *analogie* of faith, is a certaine *abridgement* or *summe* of the Scriptures, collected out of most manifest & familiar places. The parts thereof are two. The first concerneth faith, which is handled in the Apostles' Creede. The second concerneth charity or love, which is explicated in the tenne Commandements." See also John White, *A Way to the Tree of Life: Discovered in Sundry Directions for the Profitable Reading of the Scriptures*, pp. 166–67, and Lukin, *An Introduction*, p. 33.

key, Perkins, White, Lukin, and others offered a method of reading that began with philological comparisons and advanced to comparisons of one text with another.[9] Perhaps the most scholarly and systematic methodology can be found in Weemes's *Christian Synagogue*. He stated that the first task was *dittologia*, or marginal line reading of the Mazora Bible for use in glossing one line with another. The second task was *sigmatologia*, or the right pointing of the text (that is, the vowel points and accents of the Hebrew text). Once these philological tasks were settled, the third step was *analogia*, or the collation of one text with another.[10] All four authors affirmed that collation was the key to perceiving the unity of the whole. As William Perkins explained, "The collation or comparing of places together, is that, whereby places are set like parallels one beside another, that the meaning of them may more evidently appeare."[11]

The practice of reading Scripture by collating text with text had both historical and biblical precedent, as the reformers well knew. The Hebrews had from an early time divided the Pentateuch into fifty-four weekly lessons, called *parashah*. When Antiochus Epiphanes came to power in the second century B.C., he forbade the reading of the Mosaic law, so the Jews then chose their readings from those parts of the Prophets "most answerable" to the forbidden parts of the Law, as Weemes explained it.[12] Once this tradition was established, each reading from the Prophets, or *haphtarah*, was still read with its *parashah* even after the tyranny of Antiochus was ended. Thus, the Law had been collated with the Prophets in Old Testament times. When the Apostles used the same method of collating text with text "to let us see the harmony and consent that is betwixt the Old and New Testament,"[13] they were following the historical precedents of their forefathers. Furthermore, the authors of the New Testament recognized and noted certain events from the Old Testament—such as the flood, the exodus, the exile, and the return—as foreshadowings of events that would be reiterated and consummated in Christ and his church (see, for example, 1

9. White, *A Way to the Tree of Life*, pp. 160–69; Perkins, *Arte of Prophecying*, 2:650–54; and Lukin, *An Introduction*, pp. 32–37.

10. John Weemes, *The Christian Synagogue*, pp. 42–84.

11. Perkins, *Arte of Prophecying*, 2:652.

12. Weemes, *Christian Synagogue*, pp. 58–59.

13. Weemes, *Christian Synagogue*, p. 60.

Cor. 10:1–5). So the practice of collating texts to recover the meaning of the whole had solid scriptural authority, and it became a common practice among the apostolic Fathers.

While apostolic teaching simply showed that types had been fulfilled in Christ, the early Fathers of the church incorporated typology into a more complex exegetical method—based also on the Pauline distinction between "letter" and "spirit," law and grace—and began to apply types to eschatology (Irenaeus and Origen) and to the interior life of the Christian (Clement and Ambrose).[14] Their fourfold exegesis, though, tended to devalue the historical or literal level of the text, for if "the letter killeth but the spirit giveth life" (2 Cor. 3:6), then the letter of the text was obviously in an inferior position.

Thomas Aquinas provided the theory of signs underlying the medieval hermeneutic developed by Augustine and Hugh of St. Victor that emphasized the spiritual sense of the text. He posited that the words of Scripture, the *sensus litteralis*, mean one thing only; *verba* (words) always signify *res* (things). The *sensus spiritualis*, however, derives not from the words but from the relationship of one referent (*res¹*) with other referents (*res²*).[15] In practice, the Old Testament was treated as a book of hidden mysteries that had to be unveiled; taken to the extreme, an exegete such as Philo could find symbolic meaning in every detail however small it might have been. According to H. A. Wolfson, Philo "compares the 'mere letters of Scriptures' to 'shadows (σκιας) of bodies' and 'the meanings which are apparent to investigation beneath them' to 'things which truly exist.'"[16] Philo thus encouraged the reader to discover the hidden, allegorical meaning of the text, which corresponded to the incorporeal mind of the Logos. The literal level of the text thereby came to exist only as a signifier of one of the threefold spiritual levels. Though this method of exegesis had been widely accepted for over a thousand years, the Protestant reformers were

14. For a brief account of the history of patristic typology, see Daniélou, *From Shadows to Reality*.

15. St. Thomas Aquinas, *Summa Theologiae*, 1:37, 39. See James Samuel Preus, *From Shadow to Promise: Old Testament Interpretation from Augustine to the Young Luther*, pp. 50–51; and Lewalski, *Protestant Poetics*, pp. 114–16, for an account of medieval sign theory. For a precis of current theories, see Terence Hawkes, *Structuralism and Semiotics* (Berkeley and Los Angeles: University of California Press, 1977).

16. Harry A. Wolfson, *The Philosophy of the Church Fathers*, p. 31.

troubled that such allegorical interpretations frequently bore little relationship to the literal text, the revealed Word.. Luther, especially, maintained that no allegory was valid unless the same truth was expressly stated elsewhere in Scripture.

Where medieval exegetes had ignored *verba* and even *res*[1] for *res*[2] (the hidden thing signified in the text), Protestants insisted that any figurative meaning was a dimension of the literal text—not a distinct *sensus spiritualis*. Though all authority was said to rest in a literal interpretation of the text, obviously for certain passages the literal meaning had to be figurative also—as when Christ proclaims he is the true vine (John 15:1). Yet the reformers would not accept that any text could have more than one meaning. Though the literal level of the text often pointed beyond itself to a symbolic meaning, the key to interpretation still resided in and was controlled by the literal meaning. As John Weemes wrote:

> Yet it will not hence follow, that the words of Scripture have *two senses*, or give an uncertain sound, (to allude to that, 1 *Cor.* 4.8.) The words have one determinate signification, but the things themselves, which the words do *properly* and *literally* signifie, do import yet something else.[17]

Because Lukin saw this "something else" as the type or the antitype, the relationship of one referent to another could be controlled; "signification" or meaning thus emerged from the literal, historical level of the text. As Weemes instructed his many readers, the sense of Scripture is simple (that is, literal) or compound: "A compound sense, is that whereof there are two parts, literall and figurative, to make up one sense, which is fulfilled two manner of wayes, *Historicê* and *Propheticê* in the type, and literally in the thing signified."[18] Typology thus became a way to recover the symbolic dimension of the Bible, and it was particularly acceptable to the reformers because it could be rigorously, even scrupulously, applied—unlike the arbitrary allegorizing of the Fathers. Not only was typology divinely sanctioned (even Christ himself practices it; for example, Luke 4:21), it also was closely connected with the literal text of the revealed Word. Such an approach made a closed system of Scripture, which thus could offer its own principle of verification. Typology, as it was elaborated in sermons and tracts,

17. Lukin, *An Introduction*, p. 124.
18. Weemes, *Christian Synagogue*, p. 230. See also White, *A Way to the Tree of Life*, p. 167.

established a spiritual relation between two historically real events, such as the flood and baptism. The mistake of the Gothic monkish allegorists, in the view of the reformers, had been to remove the sign from its historical context in the literal narrative of Scripture, which had led to unlimited semiosis: any sign could have any number of referents, unless there was a way to predict or control the process of signification. The historicity of types gave an evidential value to Protestant hermeneutics that allegory did not have. That the type foreshadowed the antitype, which in turn illuminated the meaning of the type, in no way impinged on the absolute historicity of each as events recorded in the Bible. Thus, typology came to occupy an important place in the hermeneutics of Luther and an even more central one for Calvin and Erasmus.[19]

Those few who dealt systematically with the thorny problems of the complex language of the Bible—under the influence of Augustine and Aquinas—argued that typology was mainly concerned with things (that is, events) rather than with signs. Even so, they acknowledged that God resorted to metaphor, which advances understanding by denoting a concept using a concrete referent, in order to accommodate divine things to human abilities.[20] They agreed further that metaphors ought to be interpreted by considering the literal level before the spiritual,[21] thereby subjecting metaphor to the same rigid controls to which typology was subject. But, though the typologists usually tried to deal with types and antitypes as things or events, their explications show that the images and metaphors that render those events, as signs, were inseparable from their understanding of them. The river of living waters (Rev. 22:1), therefore, may not be an actual river as we know it here on earth; nonetheless, as a sign it existed in some relationship with all other signifiers of this thing—whether with the prototypic fountain in Eden, with any of its many Old Testament types (for example, Ezek. 47:1), or with its New Testament antitypes (for

19. On Calvin, see Lewalski, *Protestant Poetics*, pp. 118–19; on Erasmus, see David Quint, *Origin and Originality in Renaissance Literature: Versions of the Source*, pp. 17–21.

20. Weemes, *Christian Synagogue*, explained: "God hath so tempered the Scriptures, that hee hath not onely expressed his will in words, but also in matter, in types and figures. There is an Allegory in words, and an Allegorie in matter; in words, Metaphors; in matter, Types; in Figures, the Antecedent signifies the thing consequent; & the literall sense is fulfilled before the mysticall sense" (pp. 232–33).

21. Weemes, *Christian Synagogue*, wrote: "The nature of a Metaphor, is to proceed from sensible things to spirituall, and not contrarily" (p. 244).

example, John 4:14). Through an understanding of the complexities of the language of Scripture and of the relation of the Old
Testament as foreshadowing promises to be fulfilled in the New,
the Bible became a highly complex text that required collation of
both signifier and signified with other signs to recover its full
meaning.

Typology became so important to Protestant hermeneutics that
second and third generation reformers constructed fairly elaborate
rules for reading Scripture typologically; there existed, in other
words, what critics would now designate as a reading code. Understanding the complexities of this code is obviously important for
students of the devotional literature of the age since its poets frequently depended on the Bible for inspiration and models. There
were three fundamental principles that all the typological handbooks and guides seemed to agree upon. The first—and perhaps
the most important for legitimizing typology as a mode of analysis—is that both types and antitypes involve historically real persons or events.[22] The second is that the type foreshadowed or
prophesied some event that would occur in the New Testament—
that is, the imperfect order of the law prepared for the more perfect
order of grace. As one typologist wrote, God in the nonage of the
church "appointed diverse types and ceremonies, as *rudiments* and
introductions [Gal. 4:3], fitted to the grosse and weake sences of
that Church, which was to be brought on by little and little,
through such shadows and figures, to the true Image and thing
signified."[23] The last major principle is theologically the most significant, for it aligns seventeenth-century hermeneutics with St.
Paul's understanding of the relationship of the testaments. The
antitype represents a fulfillment of the type, or, as Auerbach terms
it in his well-known essay, the *forma perfectior*.[24] The source for
most of the systematic typological studies published in England

22. Benjamin Keach, *Tropologia: A Key to Open Scripture Metaphors,* I, sig. A3ᵛ,
wrote: "Types are only Historical, as such; and the Truth of Fact agreeing in the
Antitype makes them up." Auerbach, "Figura," pp. 49–60, discusses this at length.

23. Thomas Taylor, *Christ Revealed; or, The Old Testament explained,* pp. 2–3. The
usual metaphor was shadow before the light, and the type was often called *umbra* or
imago. William Guild, *Moses Unvailed; or, those figures which served unto the patterne and
shaddow of heavenly things,* sig. A3rᵛ, stated: "As in the Creation darknes went before
the light, or as the dawning precedes the brightnesse of the day . . . Even so . . .
darke shaddowes were the fore-runners of that bright substance, obscure types were
harbingers to that glorious Anti-type the Messiah, who was coming after."

24. Auerbach, "Figura."

during the Renaissance was the *Philologia sacra* of Salomon Glass (Jena, 1623–1626). Popular works, such as William Guild's *Moses Unvailed* (1620), Thomas Taylor's *Christ Revealed; or, The Old Testament explained* (1635), Samuel Mather's *The Figures or Types of the Old Testament* (1683), and Thomas Worden's *The Types unveiled* (1664), presented general readers with detailed lists of types. Benjamin Keach, whose monumental *Tropologia: A Key to Open Scripture Metaphors* (1682) became the English sourcebook for typology, simply translated large portions of the *Philologia sacra*.[25]

The one significant matter that the typologists apparently did not agree upon was how to distinguish *kinds* of types. At issue was whether types were strictly Christological and strictly limited to those few mentioned explicitly, or whether typology was more encompassing. Only a few interpreters insisted that every type had been identified as such in the Bible.[26] Keach was perhaps more representative in distinguishing between "innate" types (those that Scripture specifically designates) and "inferred" (those identified by other interpreters). In addition, he also differentiated, somewhat idiosyncratically, between "prophetical" types and "historical" types, the former involving the actions, dreams, and visions of the prophets and the latter everything else in the Old Testament that adumbrates the New.[27]

25. *Tropologia* contains three parts: Part I, entitled "Sacred Philology," was taken largely from Liber V of Glass ("Rhetorica sacra"); Parts II and III, entitled "Practical Improvement of . . . Metaphors, Allegories, and express Similitudes," listed numerous examples of the figurative language of the Bible. The last parts were published separately as *Troposchemalogia: Tropes and Figures* (London, 1682), which was further identified on the title page as "Philologia Sacra, the Second Part . . . together with a treatise of Types." This little treatise was a direct translation of part of Glass's Liber II. The second edition of *Tropologia* (London, 1779) gathers all these parts together and continuously paginates them (though "Philologia sacra" is inserted after Part I).

26. Though Clark, pp. 12–17, cites William Whitaker, *Disputatio de Sacra Scriptura contra huius temporis Papistas*, among others to show that some did limit types to those specifically mentioned in the Bible, many of the popularizers of typology published thick guides that listed non-scripturally sanctioned types. Samuel Lee's *Orbis miraculum; or, The Temple of Solomon*, a work Clark cites as favoring scripturally sanctioned types, was in fact less literal minded than Clark indicates. While Lee argued that types can only be deduced by Scripture, he did not insist that the antitype specify its type unequivocally. The injunction Lee offered was to ascribe to nothing "but to such as Holy Scripture doth either directly, or by strong and clear consequence hand forth to us" (p. 170). As long as an argument for a particular typological relationship is grounded in the text itself, Lee allowed the interpreter certain liberties. Indeed, it is useful to recall that the *Orbis miraculum* devoted over three hundred folio pages to explicating the typology of Solomon's temple.

27. Keach, *Troposchemalogia*, 2:28–32.

Keach's distinctions for the kinds of types have little or no theological backing and represent the only real break he made with his
major source, Glass. The *Philologia sacra* mentioned several other
ways of categorizing types (Keach simply neglected to translate
them). Glass began his section on the division of types by offering
the definition of types made by Junilius, author of an early introduction to the exegesis of Scripture (c. 550), which distinguished
types according to time: *"quod sit praesentium aut praeteritarum aut
futurarum rerum ignotarum, per opera, secundum id, quod opera sunt,
manifestatio."*[28] To this division according to past, present, and future, he added his own that distinguished among types as literal
things, types as acts, and types as sacraments (in the original Christian sense of the word that rendered the Greek, μυστήριον any
ritual observance or spiritually symbolic act). The first simply
matches literal, historical things that bear an obvious similarity:
"Typum historiae vocant, qui simpliciter ex re ista desumitur" (they
refer to the *type of the literal thing,* as simply that which is chosen or
determined from the thing itself)—as Jonah was three days in the
belly of the whale, so Christ was three days in the tomb. The
second involves acts that are similar to Christ's: *"Typum facti* ap-
pellant, cum factum unius est typus facti ab alio gesti vel gerendi"
(they call it a *type of a deed,* when the act of the one is a type of the
thing done by another, either already accomplished or to be
done)—as Samson crushed his enemies by his death, so too did
Christ. The third is the most significant since it opens typology in
general up to a variety of figurative significations: *"Typum Sacramenti* vocant, quando sub sensilibus res occultae, mysticae, & futur-
ae, tanquam sub typis & figuris proponuntur" (they call it a *type of
the sacrament,* when under sensible things, hidden, mystical, and
future things are set forth as under types and figures)—as baptism
is a type of the submersion of the old Adam and the emersion of the
new.

That Keach omitted these two different systems of classification
in favor of another indicates that no single terminology was widely
adopted; however, the efforts to distinguish among kinds of types
ought to indicate that the exegetes perceived types in a rather com-

28. Salomon Glass, *Philologiae Sacrae . . . libri quinque,* 1:450–53. Junilius, *De
partibus Divinae Legis libri II,* was evidently well regarded by the reformers. Glass
quoted him, and Matthias Flacius Illyricus reproduced the entire second book of *De
partibus Divinae Legis* in the section on typology in his own *Clavis Scripturae Sacrae;
seu de sermone sacrarum literarum.*

plex way. The reductive paradigm of promise and fulfillment (that is, regarding all types as simple Christological ones) that some scholars have used to describe them does not permit us to see the subtleties of these texts. In practice, the popular typological guides like Guild's or Taylor's accepted many types that did not involve Christ as antitype, such as the ark as a type of Ecclesia, the crossing of the Red Sea as a type of baptism, and so forth.[29] Though no broadly used terminology from this time survives, devising one helps us to understand and discuss the complex way typology—as a symbolic mode—was used by seventeenth-century devotional poets.

In practice, few typologists confined their lists of types strictly to Christological ones, since typology as a symbolic mode seemed to unify Scripture as a whole. Sacramental (in its old sense of *mysterious*) participation in Christ's life, the story of which is told through types, is obviously at the very heart of Christian hope. Though Protestants rejected the Roman Catholic belief in the efficacy of works, they certainly believed in the transcendent powers of sacramental grace. Salvation, for Luther and the reformers, was already won by Christ; it had only to be accepted in an act of faith (*sola fides*) or trust in the operation of God's free and unearned grace. The consequence of God's forgiveness, once the believer had made the act of faith, was *sanctification*, the inner regeneration effected by the Holy Spirit.[30] Particularly in the Anglican church, the two biblically sanctioned sacraments were accepted as "certain sure witnesses and effectual signs of grace and God's goodwill towards us, by the which He doth work invisibly in us."[31] By the action of grace, the individual Christian could become Christ-like and hence could recapitulate Christological types. Thus, while grace could not in any sense be "merited," its actions were certainly as important for Protestants as it had been for Catholics.

Even though Glass's distinction between *typus facti* and *typus sacramenti* seems not to have been widely adopted, he has given us a useful term with which to distinguish between Christological types

29. Lukin, *An Introduction*, p. 114, defined types broadly as "such things as were in the Old Testament intended by the Holy Ghost to signifie, and prefigure Jesus Christ, or something belonging to his Spiritual Kingdom: and that which answers thereto, we commonly call the *Antitype*."

30. Horton Davies, *Worship and Theology in England from Cranmer to Hooker, 1534–1603*, pp. 17–25.

31. Edgar C. S. Gibson, *The Thirty-Nine Articles of the Church of England*, p. 585.

and those in which the individual's sacramental participation in Christ's sacrifice is adumbrated. These can be properly called *sacramental* types, a term that enjoyed some currency in the seventeenth century. The theologian Thomas Jackson spoke of communion wine as the complement of Christ's blood, calling it the "Sacramental Type sealed to every one in particular."[32] Most English typologists of the seventeenth century were clearly aware of the concept, for they wrote at great length of the "application" of the one typological sense of Scripture "to our instruction, faith, and manners." In *The Arte of Prophecying*, for example, Perkins suggested that two kinds of application be made after Scripture was expounded: mental application to advance or refute doctrine and practical application to reform one's life.[33] Similarly, in his exposition on one of the innate types sanctioned by Scripture, the rock of Horeb that follows the Israelites to sustain them in the desert, Thomas Taylor implicitly emphasized the significance of the type in both Christological and sacramental terms: "So the waters of grace streaming from the Rocke Jesus Christ, follow the beleeving Israel of God through the wildernesse of the world to the heavenly Canaan. . . . Where God begins with a man in sound and saving grace here, it will carry him into the land of promise. True grace must end in glory."[34] Taylor devoted about ten pages to explicating the rock as a type of Christ and about five pages to "applications" to help his readers avoid "Hardnesse of heart, which keepes the soule dry and barren" lest "all the waters of this spiritual rock are lost upon it."[35] In both meditations and sermons, Protestants insisted on a similar "application of the self" to the texts being meditated upon.[36] Particularly for types of the biblically sanctioned sacraments, the typologists underscored the importance of the indi-

32. Thomas Jackson, *Blasphemous Positions of Jesuites and other later Romanists, concerning the Authority of their Church*, in *The Works . . . of Thomas Jackson, D.D.*, 1:395. Cited by C. W. Dugmore, *Eucharistic Doctrine in England from Hooker to Waterland*, p. 52.

33. Weemes, *Christian Synagogue*, p. 234, used the notion of typological application to explain how the "Papists" had gone astray with their fourfold interpretation, since the allegorical, tropological, and anagogical "are not properly divers senses but divers applications of one sense to our instruction, faith, and manners." Perkins, *Works*, 2:668–69.

34. Taylor, *Christ Revealed*, p. 295.

35. Taylor, *Christ Revealed*, p. 301.

36. Barbara K. Lewalski, *Donne's "Anniversaries" and the Poetry of Praise*, pp. 73–107, discusses the similarities between Protestant sermons and meditations.

vidual's mysterious participation in the fulfillment, typologically, of promises made possible through Christ.[37] In addition to the traditional Christological types and the sacramental types explained above, one other kind of type was implicitly recognized by seventeenth-century typologists. Their handbooks make frequent reference to what can be called the typology of the *eschaton* to describe the ultimate perfection of the events prefigured by both Christological and sacramental types, which would occur in the fulness of time. If the type was but a shadow compared to the antitype, that light is weak compared to the blaze of glory with which the truth shall be illumined in the kingdom of glory:

> Even now, in this marvellous light of the Gospell, we have our divine ceremonies and sacraments, see him afarre off, know but in part, darkly as in a glasse, and receive our best contentment by the acts of faith, while the Word and Spirit make us know the things freely given us of God in Christ Jesus. But time shall bee when (to say nothing of the estate of the Church after the ruine of Antichrist, and calling of the Jewes) we shall in heaven see him whom we beleeved, face to face, clearly, perfectly, immediately, without Sacraments or Types, in the fullest vision, nearest union, and absolutest fruition.[38]

Eschatological typology describes the ultimate fulfillment of God's promise in the New Jerusalem—to which even New Testament antitypes were merely shadows. This eschatological perfection would also be a recapitulation of Christ's perfection: "Christ's glorious transfiguration, was a forerunner of that glory that wee shall have in heaven: *wee shall be made conformable to his glorious body, 1 Joh. 3.2.*"[39] Milton, in a well-known passage in *De Doctrina Christiana*, described the "incomplete glorification" that believers attain in this life and the "complete glorification" that would be attained in eternity. And Isaac Ambrose in his sermons on regeneration and the last things, *Prima & Ultima* (1640), wrote:

37. Taylor devoted considerable attention toward explaining how Jewish ritual prefigured the New Testament sacraments, which themselves have become the "witnesse and signe" of the new covenant (pp. 203–5). See also Davies, *Worship and Theology, 1534–1603*, pp. 32–34, 62–64.

38. William Jemmat, "Epistle Dedicatory" to Taylor's *Christ Revealed*, sig, A2ᵛ. See also Guild, *Moses Unvailed*, p. 76, and Lukin, *An Introduction*, p. 117.

39. John Weemes, *The Portraiture of the Image of God in Man in His Three Estates, of Creation. Restauration. Glorification*, pp. 38–39.

everie part and power of body and soule must have its part of sanctification, though no part his full perfection, before the dissolution of
our earthly tabernacles: Hence (say Divines) there is a regeneration, or
sanctification (it is all one) *inchoata* and *consummata*; *inchoata*, begun in
this life, *consummata*, perfected in that other.[40]

Though other scholars describe the "application" of types differ-
ently—notably Lewalski, who prefers to describe them as "correla-
tive" or recapitulative types—the terms *Christological, sacramental,*
and *eschatological* correspond better with Glass's division of types
(according to past, present, and future time) and to the complexities of the actual typological commentary, especially its eschatology.[41] These terms also correspond to Luther's schema for the
multiple exegesis of texts, which he based on the three advents of
Christ—in the flesh, in the soul, and eschatologically.[42] We can
easily make these distinctions consonant with Auerbach's terminology: if the type is the *forma inferior* and the antitype is the *forma
perfectior,* in the *eschaton* the believers can look forward to the *forma
perfectissima.*

The seventeenth-century practice of relying on three kinds of
types in sermons and the like does bear some similarity to the
medieval fourfold exegesis that discovered four distinct senses hidden in a text. Dante, for example, in his well-known letter to Can
Grande della Scala explained that Psalm 114:1–2 described the de-
parture of the children of Israel from Egypt (the literal sense), the
redemption wrought by Christ (the allegorical sense), the conversion of the soul from grief (the moral sense), and the deliverance of
the faithful to the New Jerusalem (the anagogical sense).[43] While
the reformers would have accepted Dante's explication of the text,
they would have done so only because their commentary on the
typology of the exodus could be confirmed by other textual evidence from the Bible. In theory, the reformers continued to reject
the notion that Scripture has more than one sense. Generally they
argued that the allegorical, tropological, and anagogical "are not

40. John Milton, *Christian Doctrine,* 6:502, 614. Isaac Ambrose, *Prima & ultima:
The First & Last Thinges; or, Regeneration and Meditation Sermons,* pp. 10–11.
41. See Barbara K. Lewalski, "*Samson Agonistes* and the 'Tragedy' of the Apocalypse." Daniélou, *The Bible and the Liturgy,* pp. 5–6, and *Shadows,* p. 277, also
distinguishes among Christological, sacramental, and eschatological types to explain
the traditions of the liturgy (though he does not use them systematically).
42. See Preus, *From Shadow to Promise,* pp. 192–99.
43. Charles S. Singleton, *Dante's "Commedia": Elements of Structure,* pp. 84–90.

properly divers senses but divers applications of one sense."[44] By insisting that any additional level of meaning must be recovered as a dimension of the literal level of the text, the reformers were trying to avoid the mistakes of medieval exegetes, who had, they believed, erred in removing the sign from its literal, historical context. Once the text was freed from the interpretive constraints of its context, there seemed to be no way of governing how the texts could signify, and they attributed the excesses of patristic allegory to just such privatistic readings. In practice, however, the typologists of the seventeenth century were as capable of producing readings as idiosyncratic as their patristic forebears (as we shall see below). The complexities of the three kinds of types recognized implicitly by Protestant commentators ought to be a reminder of the continuity between medieval and Renaissance, even between Roman and reformed, spiritual practices. While the terms *Christological, sacramental,* and *eschatological* do not exactly correspond to the terminology of fourfold allegory and while the reformers' methodology was more firmly grounded in the literal text itself, the similarities reveal the common difficulties of recovering the riches of an intricate, demanding text.

Typology links three distinct but intersecting moments of time in the history and drama of Christ that foreshadows the typological drama of the believer (synchronically) and of the whole span of sacred history (diachronically), each of which is preparing for and moving toward one end. Put another way, there is one Christian faith—Christ mysteriously dead and risen—but this mystery is manifested in different ways: it is prefigured in the Old Testament and realized historically in the New; it is reenacted mysteriously through the sacraments; and it will be consummated eschatologically in the fulness of time. Typology links these decisive moments in Christological, personal, and sacred history together, revealing how one essential salvation drama is being played through the archetypal patterns of the Christian *mythos.* Readers of the Bible in the seventeenth century recovered these multiple levels of signification by collating text with text, image with image. To respect the complexity of the figuralism in Protestant devotional poetry, we must therefore recognize the complex typlogical wit of devotional poets such as Herbert, Vaughan, and Traherne.

44. Weemes, *Christian Synagogue,* p. 234.

The Types of the Waters of Life

The Fountain of Eden and Other Baptismal Types

The New Testament itself specifically indicates three important types of the baptismal waters of life: the flood (1 Peter 3:20–21), the crossing of the Red Sea (1 Cor. 10:1–3), and the rock of Horeb (1 Cor. 10:4). These three clearly designated types were linked by early patristic sources with two others, the primitive waters of Genesis and the *fons signatus* of the Canticles, to demonstrate that baptism stood in line with the great works of creation and redemption in the Old Testament.[45] Tertullian's *De baptismo* was the first major catechetical work to show how various Old Testament types were fulfilled in the sacrament. He identified the first type of baptism as the creation of the universe from the waters of the deep—an act that baptismal regeneration parallels and fulfills. The dove hovering over the waters at the creation and at Christ's own baptism emphasized the obvious symmetry of type and antitype. And so the creation was usually designated by the Fathers as the prototype of baptism. Ambrose in his *De mysteriis* recognized the creation, the flood, and the Red Sea crossing as the main prefigurations of baptism, and they became a standard series for later commentators.[46]

Since the Bible spoke with an authoritative voice on matters of cosmology as well as theology, the thought that the waters of life have their prototypic source in the primitive waters of the abyss became the subject of endless elaboration in the commentaries, in literature, and in the visual arts. The opening verses emphatically establish the image of the waters of life as a compelling phenomenon: "In the beginning God created the heaven and the earth. And the earth was without form, and void; and darkness was upon the face of the deep. And the Spirit of God moved upon the face of the waters." As the early history of man and the foundation for understanding the whole future course of time, Genesis was by far the most heavily annotated book of Scripture.[47] Nearly all the Genesis

45. For a full account of the typology of baptism see Per Ivar Lundberg, *La Typologie baptismale dans l'ancienne Église*, and Daniélou, *The Bible and the Liturgy*.

46. Tertullian, *De baptismo* in *Patrologia Latina,* ed. J. P. Migne, 221 vols. (Paris, 1844–1864), I, col. 1202; Ambrose, *De mysteriis*, in *Patrologia Latina*, 16, cols. 392–93.

47. On the importance of the Genesis commentaries in the Renaissance, see Arnold L. Williams, *The Common Expositor: An Account of the Commentaries on Genesis, 1527–1633*.

commentators were at great pains to elucidate how the universe was created out of these mysterious waters. Poets as diverse as Dante and Milton were fascinated by the connections between the unfathomable abyss and the fountain of Eden, which sustained the garden and formed the headwaters for the four rivers and hence the entire earth.[48] Iconographers had also made the fountain in the garden a popular figure, usually depicting it as an octagonal baptistery to emphasize it as a prefiguration of baptism.

The fountain of Eden became the symbolic representation for the prototype of the waters of baptism in part because the Vulgate reads *"fons"* at Genesis 2:6, where the King James version has "mist."

> But there went up a mist from the earth, and watered the whole face of the ground. . . . And the LORD GOD planted a garden eastward in Eden; and there he put the man whom he had formed. . . . And a river went out of Eden to water the garden; and from thence it was parted, and became into four heads. (Gen. 2:6–10)

The early Fathers—Augustine, for example, in his *De Genesi ad litteram*—interpreted the *fons* of Genesis 2:6 as the connection with the waters of the abyss, which still lurked beneath the earth.[49] Furthermore, because a verse in Ecclesiastes (1:7) taught that all the waters of the earth endlessly circulated from fountain, to river, and to the deep, where they were purged of salinity and percolated up as fresh water springs, the Fathers traced the sustenance of all terrestrial life to this fountain (and in fact sometimes identified the fountain as the river Jordan). The great Jesuit exegete, Benedict Pererius, was still very much indebted to the Fathers for his understanding of the connection between the river that waters the garden (Gen. 2:10) with the abyss. For the waters of the deep, he explained,

> ascendens autem de abysso, quae est matrix omnium aquarum, in illam quasi magni corporis terrae mammam, id est, Paradisi fontem,

48. See, e.g., *John Milton: Complete Poetry and Major Prose,* ed. Merritt Y. Hughes, *Paradise Lost,* 4:223–46, where the ambiguous description of the central fountain and the four rivers reveals his deep respect for the difficult biblical account of how Eden had been situated and watered. See Paul A. Underwood, "The Fountain of Life in Manuscripts of the Gospels," on the iconography of the fountain of life.

49. *Patrologia Latina,* 34, col. 329–30. The fountain in Eden, as the source of the four rivers, was a favorite subject for Tertullian, Isidore, Bede, Rabanus Maurus, Peter Comestor, and others. For a good survey, see Joseph E. Duncan, *Milton's Earthly Paradise: A Historical Study of Eden,* pp. 38–88.

quodammodo lacteam assumit dulcedinem, & irrigat universae terrae
superficiem . . .

(ascending yet from the abyss, which is the source of all waters, into
that [fountain], as if into the breast of the great body of the earth, that
is the fountain of Paradise, which in a certain way receives the milky
sweetness and waters the surface of the entire earth.)[50]

The Protestant editors Junius and Tremellius emended *fons* to read
vapor ullus at Genesis 2:6, for textual reasons, but created a new
problem. How were the four rivers formed if not by the waters of
the deep as Ecclesiastes taught? David Pareus, the noted Protestant
theologian at Heidelberg, argued that Augustine had no authority
for assuming that the central fountain formed the headwaters of the
river, since Septuagint and Hebrew versions favored *mist*; but he
himself was unable to solve the conundrum of the origins of the
waters.[51] Though the connection between the primitive waters of
the creation and the life-sustaining waters of the fountain of Eden
was a subject that was more to be marveled at than made an article
of faith, it was still quite a significant matter because of its importance in articulating metaphorically the agency of baptismal regeneration. Even the relatively late *Annotations* of the Westminster
Assembly (1648) recognized implicitly the importance of this passage, for they explained that this mist

> went up, and came down in a dew whereby the earth was softened,
> and disposed to let out the seminal vertue, whereby God hath endowed
> it, for putting forth plants, fruits; and whereby those that were already
> brought forth were cherished: and if they were not produced and
> perfected in an instant, (which God might easily do) they might have a
> further degree of proceeding to perfection, by means of this mist.[52]

Whether the prototype of baptism was associated specifically
with the fountain of Eden that nourished the garden or more generally with the primitive waters of the deep, there can be little doubt

50. Benedict Pererius, *Commentariorum et disputationum in Genesim tomi quatuor*, p.
146. Pererius' source for this quotation is Rupertus of Deutz, though he cited the
hexameral writings of Basil and Ambrose most often. In the mid-seventeenth century, the idea that paradise had been located in the Holy Land was developed by
certain writers; therefore, speculation that the river that flows through Eden in
Genesis 2:10 was the Jordan became common; see Duncan, *Milton's Earthly Paradise*,
pp. 211–12.

51. David Pareus, *In Genesin Mosis commentarius*, cols. 324–31.

52. Westminster Assembly, *Annotations upon All the Books of the Old and New
Testament*, I, sig. A4ʳ.

that baptismal regeneration was conceivable precisely because the creator once had fashioned the universe from these same waters, as Tertullian had first observed. "Primus liquor quod viveret edidit ne mirum sit, in Baptismo, si aquae animare, noverunt" (This liquid brought forth that which had life, lest it be a marvel that, in Baptism, the waters knew how to give life.)[53] Most hexameralists agreed that God created the waters of the deep *ex nihilo* as the *prima materia* of the universe.[54] This view was emphasized in the early centuries of Christianity to challenge the prevailing Greek view that matter was somehow outside the godhead and therefore eternal. Augustine, in one of the perennially cited commentaries, claimed that the actual material formation of the universe was effected by the *rationes seminales*, infused by the Holy Spirit within the formlessness that is represented by the waters of the deep (alluded to, for example, in the passage from the Westminster *Annotations* cited above). Augustine called this *confusa et informis materia* by its Greek name, chaos. Because he did so, learned men would inevitably equate it with the chaos of Hesiod and Ovid to show the harmony of views on the creation.[55] Chaos was likened to water because of its formlessness and fluidity, in which all the qualities of things combined and recombined purposelessly. Many commentators had noted that the Vulgate translated the Hebrew *rachaph*, a primitive root meaning "to brood," as *incubabat* or *fovebat* (where the AV has "*moved* upon the face of the deep") to emphasize the power of the Holy Spirit in nurturing this seed or egg.[56] From this watery chaos, as from the baptismal font, all life was generated.

After the waters of the deep were created as the source of life, God separated these waters into two parts (Gen. 1:6–8), some below the firmament and some above the firmament. Throughout the Old Testament the Hebrews were dependent on God for life-

---

53. Tertullian, *De baptismo*, in *Patrologia Latina*, I, col. 1202.

54. Gervase Babington, *Certaine Plaine, briefe and comfortable Notes upon every Chapter of Genesis*, p. 9, wrote: "God made first of nothing a matter, a first matter whereof he made all other things."

55. Augustine, *De Genesi contra Manichaeos*, in *Patrologia Latina*, 34, col. 178. The seeming consonance of Greek and Christian cosmology became a common feature of later commentaries. Bartholomaeus Anglicus, *On the Properties of Things*, 1:442, said: "To the makinge of this worlde the vertu of God made primordial mater, in the whiche, as it were in massy thinge, the foure elementis vertualliche and nought distinguid in tale and noumbre as beth now, but he were imeddelid. And that massa and lompe Plato clepith *yle in Thymeo*."

56. See, e.g., Sir Walter Raleigh, *The History of the World*, p. 6.

giving water: either on the rain and dew that fell from the upper waters or on the springs that rose from the fountains of the deep. They conceived of the earth as a small, flat disc supported by an encircling ocean, which flowed out of the waters of the abyss beneath it.[57] The disc of the earth was thought to be encircled and penetrated by the *Tehom*, the waters of the deep beneath the earth (for example, see Exod. 20:4; Deut. 4:18; Ps. 24:2). All the waters below the firmament had their origin in the subterranean freshwater streams of the *Tehom* (Eccles. 1:7). In Hebrew myth, the *Tehom* was apparently a single body with three divisions—the upper *Tehom* above the firmament, the lower (the abyss), and the encircling ocean.[58] A perfect confluence of the upper, lower, and terrestrial waters existed before the fall. Because of mankind's transgressions, life-sustaining water would become problematic: either there would not be enough or there would be too much, as at the great flood. Against this background we can then appreciate the significance of the Hebrews' metaphors praising Yahweh the sustainer, "The dew unto Israel" (Hos. 14:5), and their fear that he might "shut up the heaven, that there be no rain, and that the land yield not her fruit" (Deut. 11:17). Jacob's blessing on his twelve sons thus quite naturally includes the "blessings of heaven above, and blessings of the deep that lieth under" (Gen. 49:25).

The fountain of Eden, therefore, represented the temporal source of life, not only because it was the source of the four great rivers, but most importantly because it was connected with the waters of the deep and hence with the creation. Furthermore, its privileged position at the very beginning of the biblical narrative created certain expectations for readers who collated text with text to recover levels of signification that would otherwise be unapparent. Thus, when God proclaims that he will be a fountain of living waters to his people, a promise frequently made through the prophets in the Old Testament, we can expect that the image of the fountain in Eden would be recalled along with other types of the regenerative waters of life.

The second major type of baptismal regeneration, one specifi-

57. Renaissance commentators believed that the abyss was located within great caverns of the spherical earth. Pererius, *In Genesim*, p. 477, wrote: "Ego crediderim, vocabulo Abyssi [Gen. 7:11] hoc loco significari subterraneas cavernas, praecipue amplissimas & profundissimas."
58. Arent Jan Wensinck, *The Ocean in the Literature of the Western Semites*, pp. 15–39.

cally indicated in the New Testament, is the flood, "when once the longsuffering of God waited in the days of Noah, while the ark was a preparing, wherein few, that is, eight souls were saved by water. The like figure [αντιτυπον in the original] whereunto even baptism doth also now save us by the resurrection of Jesus Christ" (1 Peter 3:20–21). As a type of baptism, the flood provided the complementary image that was crucial to the later development of baptismal theology that is not clearly present in the waters of the creation. For these verses differentiate between baptism as merely a washing away of sin from baptism as a participation in the death and resurrection of Christ. The new life of the Christian is defined thereby in contrast with what it is not—universal death. As we shall see below, the theology of baptism has long emphasized new life through death and regeneration in full accordance with the potent symbolism of the flood, when the earth was returned figuratively to its primitive, chaotic state. Out of this annihilation comes a new creation, and the faithful remnant are saved through the ark of the church, built by one man. Though God established a new covenant (Gen. 9:1–19), through which he promised never to destroy the earth by water again, the fear of the waters of the abyss was difficult to assuage. The Midrash relates that God began the construction of the earth by laying at its center the foundation stone of the Temple, the *Eben Shetiyah*, upon which was engraved the ineffable name of God. It was on this foundation stone that the ark of the covenant was to stand. Digging the foundation for the Temple, David uncovered the *Eben Shetiyah*. When he picked it up, the waters of the abyss threatened to flood the earth again. So Ahithophel quickly inscribed the name of God on the shard and threw it into the abyss to force the waters to subside.[59] Thus, in Jewish myth even the great temple was uneasily founded upon the waters of the deep. Similarly, in a mid-seventeenth-century sermon, Robert Gell found the flood an apt prefiguration of the destruction and re-creation at the apocalypse:

> There was a flood prepared in the dayes of *Noah* to take all those away who were *eating and drinking, marrying, and giving in marriage.*
> And there is a like flood of Calamities, a new deluge, an overflowing scourge prepared in the days of the coming of the Son of Man to take the like offenders away.[60]

59. Louis Ginzberg, *The Legends of the Jews*, 1:12, 352; 4:96.
60. Robert Gell, *Noah's Flood Returning*, p. 10.

As Gell noted, the imagery used in the second Petrine epistle, where the "dissolution" of the elements is foretold (3:10–13), pointed to a watery re-creation at the end of time; the lake of burning fire in Revelation 19:20 and 20:10 also seemed to support this view.

The full significance of the flood as a type of baptism was developed at length by popular typologists in the Renaissance. Both Noah and Christ, Thomas Taylor observed, built arks: "But *Noah* of a materiall; Christ of a spirituall, the Church. *Noah* to save sinners from the deluge of water temporall: Christ to save sinners from the deluge of Gods wrath eternall." As there was only one door in the ark, so there was but one door to the church, Christ (John 10:7–9). Both Noah and Christ were the head of a new race, born out of the mystery of the water and wood (that is, the ark and the cross). The eight people saved in the ark foreshadow the eternal eighth day. Taylor also noted that the flood and baptism both will be eschatologically fulfilled in the holy mountain of the New Jerusalem: "When the flood of waters bated, the Arke rested on a mountain of Ararat, *Gen. 8.4.* So when the waters of affliction are dried up, the Church hath her rest in the holy mountain of God, *Ps. 15.*[61] As God made a covenant with Noah and his posterity and confirmed it with the sign of the rainbow (Gen. 9:11–13), "*So in Christ with the Church hath the* LORD *made a new Covenant of mercy, and ratified it with Sacraments, Mat. 3.17.*"[62] And, at both the creation and Christ's baptism, a dove was sent out over the waters. These correspondences between type and antitype had, of course, been well developed by the Fathers. Tertullian's *De baptismo*, in fact, brought nearly all of them together in a single catechetical text.

The next major type concerns the drama of the Exodus, which is usually identifiable by any one of its three major events: the miraculous crossing of the Red Sea, the crossing of the desert where the Israelites are sustained by the waters of the rock of Horeb, and the crossing of the Jordan into the promised land. For the Fathers of the early church, the Jordan was considered the entryway to the underworld, as Homer's Oceanus had been, and so Christ's later descent into the Jordan at his baptism had been victory over death and the devil.[63] Indeed, in the older T-in-O maps (with Europe, Asia, and

61. Taylor, *Christ Revealed*, pp. 11, 17.

62. Guild, *Moses Unvailed*, p. 14.

63. John Freccero, "The River of Death: Inferno II, 108," pp. 25–42, has an excellent discussion of this issue.

Africa arranged in a T-shape) the Jordan was situated at the exact center of the world (we should also recall that the sacred spring of Siloam flows near the Temple). But because the Red Sea crossing and the rock of Horeb are specifically identified in the first epistle to the Corinthians (10:1–5) as types of baptism, Renaissance commentators dealt with them as types more readily and more often.[64] These types add to the associative dimension of an emerging pattern of water imagery by replacing the fear of annihilation by water with the promise of redemption through the waters of life. The prophets hereafter began to announce a new exodus at the end of time, especially in Isaiah; appropriately enough, Christ's passion and resurrection took place during Passover, the commemoration of the deliverance, just as baptism was ordinarily administered only at Easter in the early centuries of the church.

The Westminster *Annotations* noted the fitness of the typological relationship between the Red Sea crossing and baptism in the "red sea" of Christ's blood for the following reasons: first, baptism by water is a means of safety for the Christian as it was for the Israelites; second, "their going in the chanel, (the waters on each hand) was as a being in a grave, and we are said to be *buried with Christ* by Baptisme, Rom. 6.4."; and third, coming out of the waters to the shore was a resurrection after burial for the catechumens and for the Israelites.[65]

The rock of Horeb as a type continues the drama of the deliverance from the desert. Moses is said to have struck the rock two different times (Exod. 17:6 and Num. 20:1–13) to provide life-sustaining water for the chosen people. The waters from the rock are related to the manna, a type of Christ's body, and together they foreshadow the "feast" to be provided at the last supper, on the cross, and elsewhere. An elaborate series of correspondences was offered by the typologists to emphasize the importance of this event.[66] The firmness and stability of the rock typify Christ's strength. It appeared dry and barren, as Christ outwardly appeared unlikely to afford the waters of grace. A most suggestive feature was that the rock had to be struck to release the water, showing the

64. Because the Jordan, like the Thames, is a tidal river and flows back upon itself, it was often regarded as a type of the Logos—divine wisdom that flows from the godhead to mankind and back again. See Quint, *Origin and Originality*, pp. 133–66.

65. Westminster *Annotations*, I, sig. P4ᵛ.

66. See Guild, *Moses Unvailed*, pp. 77–79; and Taylor, *Christ Revealed*, pp. 288–302.

believer that regeneration was made possible only by the atonement: "That as all the spiritual benefit . . . comes home to them through this spiritual Rock of Jesus Christ: so the original cause of it was from Gods striking of him with the stroke of his wrath for sin, *Isa. 53 10.*"[67] The typologists also emphasized the dramatic contrast between the weariness and discomfort of Israel wandering in the desert and "the waters of regeneration and comfort, [which] coole and refresh the dry and thirsty soule."[68]

The last major type, the *fons signatus* (Song 4:12), completes the series of prefigurations of the waters of life in the Old Testament. This type restores the life-bestowing fountain to a garden setting and thus links the Edenic prototype with its eschatological antitype, the pastoral New Jerusalem. The Song of Solomon was read by the Fathers as the epithalamion of the wedding feast of Christ and his church, which looks ahead to its antitypical fulfillment through the sacraments and ultimately to its eschatological fulfillment in the New Jerusalem—where the tree of life and the crystal fountain will constitute the final feast. Tertullian had placed special emphasis on the nuptial aspects of baptism: "When the soul comes to the faith, recreated of water and the Holy Spirit by its special birth, it is received by the Holy Spirit. The flesh accompanies the soul in this wedding with the Spirit."[69] Ephesians 5:25–26 also serves as the warrant for the relationship between baptismal initiation and spiritual marriage: "Husbands, love your wives, even as Christ also loved the church, and gave himself for it; That he might sanctify and cleanse it with the washing of water by the word." Protestants, on the other hand, were beginning to understand the marriage as "the pilgrimage of all elect Christian souls from tentative beginnings to an assured condition of hope and expectation of glory."[70] Protestants did see the bride, still waiting for the groom at the end of the Song, as a figure for the reformed churches awaiting the consummation of the spiritual marriage in the New Jerusalem, but primarily they emphasized the relationship between Christ and each believer. Since Christ had "unsealed" the fountain

67. Thomas Worden, *The Types unveiled, or, the Gospel pick't out of the Legal Ceremonies*, p. 56.

68. Taylor, *Christ Revealed*, p. 292.

69. Tertullian, *De anima*, in *Patrologia Latina*, 2, col. 720, quoted in Daniélou, *The Bible and the Liturgy*, p. 192. See also pp. 191–207 for a summary of the patristic commentary on the Song. See also Stewart, *The Enclosed Garden*, pp. 31–59.

70. Lewalski, *Protestant Poetics*, pp. 62–63.

on the cross when his side was pierced, the *fons signatus* became an important type of the church and the believer. The Westminster *Annotations*, in discussing the confusion in the Vulgate over the terms *spring, garden,* and *spouse* in verse 4:12 ("A garden inclosed is my sister, my spouse; a spring shut up, a fountain sealed"), finally concluded that the difference between these particular signs is unimportant precisely because they are so interrelated typologically:

> It is no great matter which, whilst all are but one and the same Type of her [the Christian church and the believer], who is not indeed the well of life, but hath the well of life springing and flowing in her, and is full of living waters, Joh. 4.14.[71]

The garden with its sealed fountain was, thus, another confirmation that God would provide the waters of life necessary for spiritual regeneration, when the drama being developed through these major types would be fulfilled in its antitype, Christ, who would make possible a sacramental recapitulation for the believers.[72]

The Fountain of Living Waters as the Source of Sacramental Grace

Having seen how central, both metaphorically and theologically, the typology of the waters of life is to the Old Testament, we turn now to its antitypical fulfillment in the New Testament. Christ provided the key to the interpretation of these types at Jacob's well, a deep spring fed by both surface waters and underground streams, where he announced to the Samaritan woman that he was the true fountain of life: "But whosoever drinketh of the water that I shall give him shall never thirst; but the water that I shall give him shall be in him a well of water springing up into everlasting life" (John 4:14). Christ's promise here was proleptic, looking forward as it did to the crucifixion when the water and blood would flow from his side.

71. Westminster *Annotations*, I, sig. 8G2ʳ.

72. Other types of the waters of life were recognized, but they were less prominent than the major types discussed above. These lesser types include the bitter waters of Marah that are sweetened when Moses casts a tree into them (Exod. 15:23–25; see Guild, *Moses Unvailed,* p. 50); the brazen laver of the temple (Exod. 30:18–21; see Guild, pp. 114–15, and Worden, *The Types unveiled,* pp. 210–14); the grapes of Eshcol that were a foretaste of the promised land (Num. 13:23–24; see Worden, pp.77–79); and the crossing of the Jordan into the promised land (Jos. 3:13–17; see Guild, p. 148, and Worden, pp. 67–68, 311–22).

For Jesus to have chosen this moment, just after Passover, to give the first clue toward unraveling the many Old Testament prophecies about living water (for example, Isa. 41:17–18) is quite important for understanding the full significance of the waters of life. As a celebration of the deliverance, Passover commemorates among other things the Red Sea crossing and the rock of Horeb. To readers sensitive to the nuances of typology (as the Fathers and Renaissance Protestants certainly were), John 4:14 implicitly established a crucial typological lineage for its discussion of the waters of life and the sacraments. That is, by seeing the living waters of the sacraments in the context of earlier types, one would recover a level of meaning that related individual salvation to the larger drama of the history of the chosen people: the creation, the destruction of the flood, and the deliverance from Egypt were reenacted in the spiritual regeneration of baptism. The true meaning of the rock of Horeb was only recoverable when a text like John 4:14 or John 7:38, its companion verse, was collated with it. One commentator wrote:

> As from that Rock issued waters to wash and cleanse themselves and their garments: so from this Rock streame waters of ablution or washing; which serve to wash away both the guilt of sinne, and stain of sinne. For the former; the precious blood of Christ streaming out of his side is the onely mundifying water in the world, to wash the soule from the guilt of sinne, and to scowre away all the execration of sinne from the sight of God, *I. Joh. 1.7. the blood of Jesus Christ cleanseth us from all sinne.* For the latter; from the same side of Christ our Rock issueth water as well as blood, even the waters of regeneration, called (*Tit. 3.5*) *the washing of the new birth*, by the Spirit of grace and holinesse, which daily cleanse the staine and filthinesse of sin. Of these waters reade, *Joh. 7.38.*[73]

As the water from the rock of Horeb washed and cleansed, so the water and blood from the true rock washes and cleanses the stain of sin.

The promise represented by the fountain of Eden, the rock of Horeb, the *fons signatus*, and others was then typologically fulfilled when the rock was split open and the fountain unsealed at the crucifixion. Only John, the gospelist most interested in interpreting the powerful symbolism Christ adopted from the Old Testament (particularly that of the sacraments), recorded the phenomenon of the water and blood flowing from Christ's side in his account of the

73. Taylor, *Christ Revealed*, p. 291.

passion (19:34). John also recalled this event in his first epistle: "This is he that came by water and blood" (1 John 5:6). Tertullian had linked these Johannine passages with the prophecy in Luke in which Christ says, "I have a baptism to be baptized with" (12:50), for the incarnate Christ came:

> ut aqua tingueretur, sanguine glorificaretur, proinde nos faceret aqua vocatos (*Joan.* XIX), sanguine electos. Hos duos baptismos de vulnere perfossi lateris emisit, quia qui in sanguinem eius crederent, aqua laverentur: qui aqua lavissent, etiam sanguinem potarent.

> (that he might be baptized by the water, glorified by the blood—just so he made us called by the water (John 19), chosen by the blood. He sent forth these two baptisms from the wound of his pierced side, because they who believed in his blood, would be bathed by the water: they who had bathed in the water, also would drink the blood.)[74]

In the Renaissance, commentators believed Christ's heart to be the physical source of this vivification. John Trapp wrote that the water and blood flowed as a result of

> The *pericardium* being pierced, which nature hath filled with water to cool the heat of the heart. Hereto S. *John* alludes, when he saith, that *Christ came by water and bloud*, to teach us, that he justifieth none by his merit, but whom he sanctifieth by his Spirit. *Possumus etiam asseverare ex latere Christi fluxisse nostra sacramenta*, saith *Calvin*, We may safely say that our Sacraments issued out of Christs side.[75]

This piercing of the side was also important for the typologists because it satisfied a key metaphoric dimension of the Old Testament types: the waters of life could flow freely from the fountain as a result of his sacrifice. It had been a commonplace of medieval iconography, as is well known, to show Ecclesia, the bride of Christ, emerging from Christ's wound, just as Eve had been formed from the first Adam's side.[76]

The meditation on living water at Jacob's well was supported by another, made this time at the Temple during the Feast of the Tabernacles, at which a daily libation ceremony was performed. This second passage (John 7:38–39) more strongly—though just as

---

74. Tertullian, *De baptismo*, in *Patrologia Latina*, I, col. 1217.

75. John Trapp, *Commentary or Exposition upon the four Evangelists and the Acts of the Apostles*, 3:135–36.

76. This concept continued to be recognized as the implicit origin of the sacraments. See, e.g., George Hutcheson, *An Exposition of the Gospell of Jesus Christ according to John*, p. 387.

mysteriously—insisted that Christological typology must be recapitulated by the individual through sacramental typology. The
feast of the tabernacles, in part, commemorates the waters from the
rock of Horeb. On each day a full golden pitcher was carried from
the pool of Siloam into the Temple, except on the last day, which
ritually signaled the entrance into Palestine, where the Israelites
found springs and watercourses to sustain them. It is once again
significant typologically that Christ chose this particular time to
announce that he was the true fountain of life: "If any man thirst, let
him come unto me, and drink. He that believeth on me, as the
scripture hath said, out of his belly shall flow rivers of living water." To which John himself commented: "(But this spake he of the
Spirit, which they that believe on him should receive: for the Holy
Ghost was not yet given; because that Jesus was not yet glorified)"
(John 7:37–39). John's addendum suggests that the true baptism
could not take place until the crucifixion; it also calls attention to
the promise that living water will flow from the belly of the believers just as it will flow from Christ's. This is precisely the same
claim made at Jacob's well—"the water that I shall give him shall be
in him a well of water springing up into everlasting life" (John
4:14)—and it implies that through grace, the Christian could reenact the salvation pattern established by Christ; believers would
somehow have fountains of grace springing from within in imitation of Christ.

Many expositions of John 7:38 were offered. Augustin Marlorat,
a leading Continental theologian, following a line first taken by
Calvin, asserted, "The bellye of the inwarde man, is the conscience
of the heart, And by floodes, hee meaneth the manifolde Graces of
the Spyrite, which are necessary to the spirituall life of the Soule."
And while he agreed that the "Metaphor in shewe seemeth harde,"
he concluded, "notwithstanding the scence and meaning, is plaine
inough, that the beleeving shall never want any spirituall goodnesse."[77] Another expositor, using an analogy taken from Galenic
medical theory, explained that just as the heart produces "spirits" to
sustain the body, the soul must be sustained with an infusion of
grace:

> As a spring sends forth streames to water the ground about it, and as
> the heart of man sendeth forth life and refreshment to every faculty
> and member . . . So graces of the Spirit in beleevers will flow forth

77. Augustin Marlorat, *A Catholike and Ecclesiasticall exposition of the holy Gospell
after S. John*, p. 270.

into their behavior and carriage, to make their heart strong, to make their tongue to drop what is savoury, to make their feet like hindes feet, &c. and to refresh and gain ground upon others.[78]

Despite differences over the exact interpretation of this difficult passage, most commentators agreed that grace somehow would generate rivers of living water within the individual through the sacrament. The eclectic Westminster *Annotations*, for example, explained that John 4:14 was to be regarded as the antitype to the *fons signatus* of the Canticles, which is fulfilled through the church that "hath the well of life springing and flowing in her."[79]

The language of the baptismal rites has traditionally emphasized the divergent symbolism associated with the various types of the waters of life. Baptismal traditions stem from two scriptural sources. St. John declared that man was "born again" through baptism (3:3–5), so the font could be considered a mystical womb. St. Paul, though, wrote that "we are buried with him by baptism into death" (Rom. 6:4–5); the font could thus be seen as a mystical tomb. In the Pauline tradition, Christ was thought to have recapitulated symbolically Old Testament types by stepping into the Jordan at his baptism to fight with Satan, an act he completed when he descended into hell to redeem the patriarchs. This drama reenacted part of the creation story found outside of Genesis, the battle with the monster of the deep.[80] The rites of baptism were considered a successful reenactment of Adam's temptation because Christ had now beaten Satan in the waters of the Jordan.[81]

The Pauline baptismal tradition emphasizing ritual death gradually gave way to the Johannine view that baptism was a regeneration in the mystical womb of the church. This doctrinal shift, which emerged as the Fathers discovered the typological parallels

78. Hutcheson, *An Exposition of the Gospell*, p. 144.

79. Westminster *Annotations*, I, sig. 8G2ʳ.

80. Evidence of other creation myths in Scripture can be found in Ps. 74:13, 89:10, and 104:5–9; Prov. 8:29; and Isa. 27:1. For an account of the probable source of these cosmographic fragments, see *The Babylonian Genesis*, trans. and ed. Alexander Heidel.

81. Daniélou, *The Bible and the Liturgy*, p. 41, cites a passage from the *Mystagogic Catecheses* of Cyril of Jerusalem, who had explained to the newly baptized that the efficacy of the rites derived from Christ's victory over the dragon: "The dragon Behemoth, according to Job, was in the waters, and was taking the Jordan into his gullet. But, as the heads of the dragon had to be crushed, Jesus, having descended into the waters, chained fast the strong one, so that we might gain the power to tread on scorpions and serpents. Life came so that henceforth a curb might be put on death."

between Christ and the church, is reflected by a change in decorative motifs of baptisteries.[82] Cross-like fonts were replaced with the familiar octagonal ones, suggesting the eternal eighth day, the *ogdoad*. The inscription on the frieze above the entryway to the octagonal baptistery at the papal see, St. John Lateran (built in the fourth century), for example, reads: "Gens sacranda polis hic semine nascitur almo, Quam fecundatis Spiritus" (a race of people to be consecrated, is born here by this nourishing seed, which the Holy Spirit brings forth from the waters of fecundity). Similarly, many baptisteries used a paradise motif, with Christ as the shepherd with his flock in a garden setting, to emphasize birth into a new life.[83]

The ritual of the Anglican church, through its explicit typological references, preserves this dual lineage of baptism. Though it emphasizes the Johannine tradition that baptismal waters are the living waters of the Holy Spirit, baptismal regeneration was also seen as the death of the old Adam (and the natural tendency toward sin) and the consequent new birth into righteousness. The ritual asserts, furthermore, that each particular baptism is the fulfillment of the Old Testament types considered above:

> Almighty and everlasting God, which of thy great mercy didst save Noah and his family in the ark from perishing by water, and also didst safely lead the children of Israel thy people through the Red Sea, figuring thereby thy holy Baptism, and by the baptism of thy well-beloved Son Jesus Christ, didst sanctify the flood Jordan and all other waters to the mystical washing away of sin: We beseech thee.[84]

The waters that created and destroyed the world, that defeated the Egyptians and sustained the Israelites, have now been sanctified by Christ, the second Adam (1 Cor. 15:45–47). The typological relation, whereby the catechumen recapitulates sacramentally this act and so becomes the second Adam, is emphasized in a prayer near the end of the ceremony: "O merciful God, grant that the old Adam in these children may be so buried, that the new man may be raised up in them."[85] The intricate relationships preserved in the

---

82. Walter M. Bedard, *The Symbolism of the Baptismal Font in Early Christian Thought*, pp. 2–47.

83. Daniélou, *The Bible and the Liturgy*, pp. 35–53, discusses the changes in the baptismal rites themselves during this period.

84. *The Book of Common Prayer, 1559: The Elizabethan Prayer Book*, ed. John E. Booty, pp. 271–72.

85. *Book of Common Prayer*, p. 274.

Anglican baptismal ritual were thus understood as a sacramental recapitulation of Christological types.[86]

Baptism as annihilation and regeneration in the waters of life was not in itself inconceivable; after all, the world had been created and annihilated in these waters. Yet how rivers of living water or a well of water springing up into everlasting life could be generated within the believer as a consequence of regeneration, as both John 7:38 and 4:14 indicated, was comprehensible only when it was made clear that the source of the water was not in the believer but was, rather, in God the fountainhead from whom and to whom all grace eternally proceeded. The individual's imitation of Christ as "fountain" was comprehensible only when the notion of the circularity of waters—already implicit in the Renaissance concept of the fountain and the abyss mutually sustaining one another—was recognized as a feature of the typology of the waters of life. The living water Christ bestows to the believer will become a fountain of water that will eventually, like all water, return to its source.

Using precisely this metaphor to explain John 4:14, Daniel Dyke stated,

> Now this water it descends from heaven, and thither therefore it will returne againe. As the water in the Rocke followed the Israelites into the Land of *Canaan*, so this water that comes from Christ, figured by that Rocke, *I Cor. 10* followes us to the heavenly *Cannan*, during our peregrination here in this world."[87]

Similarly, George Hutcheson reasoned that, after the apocalypse, the "well of water" (John 4:14) would become an ocean when the final confluence of upper and lower waters takes place. After judgment,

> wherein all the banks of incapacity, sin, distance, ignorance, mortality, &c. being broken down, and the windowes of heaven being

---

86. Jackson, *A Treatise of the Consecration of the Son of God, to his Everlasting Priesthood,* in *The Works,* 2:1091, observed similarly how the uncreated world was like the sinner before baptism: "As was the condition of this visible World or formless Earth, before the Creation of light, or the division betwixt it and darkness, such altogether was the condition or state of the intellectuall World before it was new made or redeemed by the Son of God. The corrupted Masse of Mankind was overspread with darkness, and covered with the Mantle of Death. . . ."

87. Daniel Dyke, *The Second and Last Part of the Works . . . viz. Sixe Evangelical Histories,* pp. 284–85. For a full account of the patristic commentary on John 7:38, see Hugo Rahner, "Flumina de ventre Christi: Die patristische Auslegung von Joh 7, 37. 38."

opened, this stream and well becometh an Ocean, and grace, smothered here under corruption and infirmity, gets leave to expatiate it selfe in glory; for, *It shall be a well of water springing up into everlasting life.*[88]

Implicit in both these passages from seventeenth-century biblical commentaries—and similar passages in the poetry, devotional prose, sermons, and the like—is an understanding that the regenerative waters of life will ultimately return to their source, Christ. Just as all the streams and rivers emptied into the great abyss of waters, that same abyss is mysteriously the source of all fresh water springs and fountains (Eccles. 1:7). The notion of circularity, in other words, permitted a way of understanding and furthermore of articulating metaphorically the sacramental recapitulation of the typology of the waters of life; hence, it is the key to understanding many of the devotional lyrics to be examined in the following chapters.

Seventeenth-century readers, in short, regarded various Old Testament types—particularly, the Edenic fountain, the rock of Horeb, and the *fons signatus*—simultaneously as historic events, as figures of Christ, and most significantly as figures of the phenomenon of grace that could be reduplicated endlessly for each individual. Once the typological imitation of Christ is explained in this way, it is easy to locate and interpret the origins of much of the metaphoric language of seventeenth-century devotional poetry. As Christ, for example, was the true rock split open, so too must the hard rock of the believer's heart be split open so that living water can flow from it.[89] Readers familiar with the emblematic title page of *Silex Scintillans* will recognize the significance of this metaphor as the proper introduction for Vaughan's lyrics. Similarly, we find numerous references to the spiritual aridity or thirst that can only

88. Hutcheson, *An Exposition of the Gospell*, p. 53.

89. For example, Taylor, *Christ Revealed*, p. 291, pointed out that the antitype to the rock of Horeb was the living water that would flow from the heart. To prevent damning up the waters of the true rock, Taylor advised his readers to avoid "Hardnesse of heart, which keeps the soule dry and barren; and abiding in the naturall hardnesse of a rock, all the waters of this spirituall rock [Christ] are lost upon it" (p. 301). Similarly, Obadiah Sedgwick, *The Fountain opened: and the waters of life flowing forth, for the refreshing of thirsty sinners*, devoted 524 pages to explicating three verses from Isaiah (55:1–3), which began: "Ho, every one that thirsteth, come ye to the waters. . . ." The epigraph on the title page (John 7:37) indicates that Sedgwick recognized explicitly the typological relationship involved. Nearly 80 pages dealt with spiritual thirst and with water metaphors.

be slaked by the fountain of living waters that must flow from within. Or, we read of the spiritual garden that is made to flower with the dew of grace that falls to succor it. These last two metaphors are obviously of major importance in *The Temple*.

Moreover, as with all linguistic structures, the terms of the metaphor of the fountain of life are subject to further selection and combination. Since no fixed connection between signifier and signified exists, the terms of the metaphor can be transformed in artful ways (signifiers, in other words, can combine with other signifieds to become signifiers for still other signifieds).[90] Such a phenomenon is observable in part with the transformations of the notion of the abyss (which existed in the Old Testament as a profoundly ambiguous agent of destruction and of fructification): once Christ "sanctifies" the abyss through the atonement, the believer can desire to be annihilated in its depths to return to the source of all waters in a great circulation. For instance, a John Hall emblem depicts the emanation and return of divine love (Figure 4). The heart of the speaker wings upward to Christ; the Spouse (the speaker as bride waiting for the bridegroom to return, Song 8:14) sits in a position of repose while divine Cupid sends shafts of love to impell the heart onward.[91] The third stanza announces the lover's aim of transcending the limitations of the body:

Swell heart into a world and keep
That humid sea:
Become, my bosome, one great deep
That it may lodge in Thee;
That glorious sun with his Celestiall heat
will warm't, and mak't evaporate.

(ll. 13–18)

The difficulty of these lines can be resolved when we recognize that the "humid sea" and the "great deep" are metaphoric equivalents. The lover imagines his heart, as a token of his love for Christ, expanding to the size of the earth itself. The ocean of this world-sized heart or bosom (which has expanded to contain the enormous

90. On the relationship of selection and metaphor with combination and metonomy, see Roman Jakobson, "Closing Statement: Linguistics and Poetics," in *Style in Language*, ed. Thomas A. Sebeok (Cambridge: MIT Press, 1960), pp. 350–77; on semiosis, see Roland Barthes, *Elements of Semiology*, trans. Annette Lavers and Colin Smith (Boston: Beacon, 1970).

91. John Hall, *Emblems with Elegant Figures, 1658*, pp. 52–55.

Figure 4. The Emanation and Return of Love (from John Hall, *Emblems with Elegant Figures, 1658,* ed. John Horden [Menston, Yorkshire: Scolar Press, 1970], p. 52).

heart) is now capable of merging with Christ, the "Spring-head of life," who will heat the waters of the lover and allow them to rise and flow into the abyss itself. In the following stanzas, the lover finds himself "Intomb'd" and "annihilated" in this abyss:

> Spring-head of life, how am I now
> > Intomb'd in Thee?
> How do I since th'art pleas'd to flow,
> > Hate a dualitie?
> How I am annihilated? yet by this
> Acknowledge my subsistence is
> Still may I rise; still further clime
> > Till that I lie
> (Having out-run-short-winded time)
> > Swath'd in Eternitie:

So may my youth spend and renue, so night
Never alternate with my light.

(ll. 19–30)

Hall's emblem depends as much on a belief in the circularity of the
waters as it does on the spiritual marriage of Christ with the Christian. From the heart of the bride flows the waters of life (as a gift of
grace from Christ), which will flow back into their source, the
abyss of the godhead. The notion of annihilation in this abyss, also
a potent theme in Traherne's Dobell Folio *Poems*, requires that we
examine Renaissance views on the heavenly source of the waters of
life, the crystal fountain.

The Crystal Fountain as Eschatological Antitype

While the New Testament teaches that the kingdom of God is
truly a present spiritual reality for the faithful (sealed by the sacraments), the primary hope is for a future kingdom to be enjoyed in
the fulness of time. The vision of that kingdom, foreshadowed in
the prophecies of Isaiah and Ezekiel, is given its fullest expression in
the apocalypse of St. John. As the copestone to Scripture, Revelation is the primary document on the future course of sacred history.
It describes the seventh day of the cosmic week heralding the eternal eighth day, the *ogdoad* or day of rest foreshadowed in Genesis.[92]
In the midst of many striking, indeed horrific, details, the image of
the lamb at the throne bestowing the crystal bright waters of life on
the faithful is a comforting one. The uncertainty and struggle characteristic of the earthly pilgrimage will for all time be over; time
itself will be at an end. The waters of life, which can both annihilate
and regenerate, will finally be transformed into the pacific river of
the water of life in the New Jerusalem. Those who in their lifetime
have received grace intermittently will at last enjoy the waters of
life directly and for all eternity. The crystal fountain is thus the
eschatological or eternal antitype to the temporal waters of life
outlined above.

It is significant to note that the new garden or paradise for the
faithful descends to a world that has been regenerated or re-created:

92. The *ogdoad* is the sacred number eight, borrowed from the pagan cult of Helios
the sun god; the eighth day was the day of the sun, just as for Christians the eighth is
the day of the Son, whose resurrection on the eighth day foreshadowed mankind's.
For a contemporary discussion, see Giacopo Brocardo, *The Revelation of S. John
reveled*, trans. James Sanford, fol. 158ʳ. For patristic sources, see Daniélou, *The Bible
and the Liturgy*, pp. 262–86.

"And I saw a new heaven and a new earth: for the first heaven and the first earth were passed away; and there was no more sea" (Rev. 21:1). The expositors knew that the heavens and earth must be returned to a state not unlike that of the watery chaos as a precondition of their deliverance from bondage. In the second Petrine epistle, they could read the prophecy that "the heavens being on fire shall be dissolved, and the elements shall melt with fervent heat" (2 Pet. 3:12). In the apocalyptic vision of Isaiah, it is also written that, at the end of the world, the land will be reduced to primordial chaos. The language of Isaiah 24:18–19, especially, recalls the description of the flood: "And it shall come to pass, that the windows from on high are open, and the foundations of the earth do shake. The earth is utterly broken down, the earth is clean dissolved, the earth is moved exceedingly." Because of the *dissolution* here and in 2 Peter, some commentators believed that the creation was certainly the type of this re-creation.[93] In the so-called Apocalypse of Noah in the apocryphal Book of Enoch and in Second Baruch, the eschatology of the flood is also quite prominent: at the end of time a catastrophe, from which only a faithful remnant will be saved, will annihilate the world.

There was also much debate over the fact that "there was no more sea"—a prospect that troubled precisely because of the manifold significance of the waters discussed above. Many of the Fathers in fact believed that the sea would be altered to a more "glorious estate," just as the earth would be. In his authoritative *Ecclesiastica Interpretatio* (1627), John Mayer, however, offered the view that came to be most widely accepted among Protestants. He argued that only the upper waters, the *coelum chrystallinum*, would remain in the New Jerusalem. He interpreted the "sea of glass" as the "perspective glass" that would make all things clear for the faithful: "for this may well be called a sea, seeing at the creation waters were placed there as well as below, so that as ours is the earthly sea, so that is the Lords heavenly."[94] Mayer took solace in

---

93. See, e.g., John Lightfoot, *A few, and new, observations upon the Booke of Genesis*, pp. 1–2, who stated: "the Resurrection is taught by the Creation, and the end of the world from the beginning for God that made that to be, that never was, can much more make that to be, that hath been before." Bartholomaeus Anglicus, *On the Properties of Things*, 1:443, argued (following Augustine) that the re-creation would involve a return to the primal state of the universe: "the first matiere of the whiche the worlde is kyndeliche imaad is ingenerable and incorruptible; and of that matiere al material things bigynneth and turneth agen into that matiere as into the modir."

94. John Mayer, *Ecclesiastica Interpretatio: or, the expositions upon . . . the seven*

the destruction of the lower waters, the domain of the great beast, since the sea represented for him "that bottomless pit boiling with fire and brimstone."[95]

Mayer's fear of the Satanic associations of the abyss—despite the reassuring image of the crystal fountain itself—should sharpen our sense of the importance of this debate over the exact condition of the "sea" in the New Jerusalem for seventeenth-century minds. The sea, as the underworld abode of the monster of the deep, is absent from the redeemed universe. Throughout history, as it was recorded in Scripture, the waters of the abyss have been capable of destruction as well as creation. In the Old Testament the direct control of the sea is usually attributed to God (especially at the exodus, Isa. 51:9; see also Ps. 65:7, 77:16, 89:9). For this reason, Jesus' ability to calm the storm and walk on water is theologically important, and the ultimate redemption of the chosen people will occur only when the monster inhabiting the waters of the deep is slain. In Revelation we are reminded that, until the final conflict is over, water still flows through the serpent's mouth (12:15).

For many, the opposition of death and life, the destruction and creation contained implicitly in the radical potential of the waters, signified the human dilemma; both poles of this opposition in fact are necessary to fix the precise drama of Christian choice. During the earthly pilgrimage, these waters can be used to describe a variety of experiences: the soft, comforting dew of grace; the raging floods of affliction; the harshness of spiritual thirst; annihilation in the waters of the deep; and so forth. William Cowper found the "sea of glass mingled with fire" of Revelation 15:2 just such a paradigm of the human condition:

> Such then is the estate of the world, that nothing is in it without a mixture. In heaven *there is a pure River of the Water of Life*: In Hell, *there is wine of wrath without mixture, in the cup of Gods indignation*, is it powred forth: But in the earth, *there is a Sea mingled with fire*: there is joy in Heaven without sorrow; there is griefe in Hell without comfort; in this life no state without mixture.[96]

Epistles called Catholike, and the Revelation, p. 303. Another major expositor who believed "the sea . . . shall be renued as well as all other elements, and be set free from bondage by the restitution of man" was Augustin Marlorat, *A Catholike exposition upon the Revelation of Saint John*, fol. 284[r].

95. Mayer, *Ecclesiastica Interpretatio*, p. 523.

96. William Cowper, *Patmos, A Commentary upon Revelation*, in *The Workes*, p. 1088.

That mankind received grace intermittently in this life and was subject to spiritual vicissitude only served to intensify the longing to emerge from the eschatological palingenesis and to be at last able to enjoy the unceasing flow of the waters of life in the New Jerusalem.

The importance of the sea that is to be somehow transformed is underscored by the eschatological visions of the Old Testament, all of which feature the river of life, the "apocalyptic or idealized image," to use Northrop Frye's term, and its "demonic counterpart," the wasteland of drought or the Dead Sea.[97] The paradisal vision is always of a desert made fruitful, a garden oasis: "and thou shalt be like a watered garden, and like a spring of water, whose waters fail not" (Isa. 58:11).[98] In Ezekiel, the river of life springs from the threshold of the Temple and flows east, with trees lining its banks; it even regenerates the stagnant Dead Sea (Ezek. 47:8). In Jeremiah, the oracle foretells an Israel "without form, and void" (4:23) that Yahweh will make "as a watered garden" (31:12) because he is "the fountain of living waters" (17:13). These eschatological visions, which seemed to influence the author of Revelation, clearly are indebted to the accounts of paradise in Genesis, thus establishing a typological relationship between Eden and the New Jerusalem. In Deutero-Isaiah (especially in 51:9–11), the prophet established a correspondence between the creation conflict with the monster of the deep, the deliverance from Egypt, and the future deliverance to Zion.[99] The culmination of this hope was the final taming of the waters of the deep. In the Midrash, the Hebrews' respect for the power of the abyss is still preserved; the Leviathan of legend was thought to be the substance of a Messianic banquet, the last feast necessary to satisfy bodily needs.[100]

The difference between Old and New Testament eschatology is that Christ's defeat of the dragon in his descent into hell, foreshadowed by his stepping into the waters of the Jordan, has made possible the relocation of the holy to its ultimate state. The fountain of life flows not from the abyss as in Jewish writings, but rather from its perfect source—the throne of God, because of Christ's intercession. The consummate image of this transformation is the vision of the New Jerusalem in Revelation:

97. Northrop Frye, *The Great Code: The Bible and Literature*, pp. 145–46.
98. See also Isa. 35:6–7, 41:17–20, 43:20, 44:3–4, 51:3, and 55:1–11.
99. George W. H. Lampe and Kenneth J. Woollcombe, *Essays on Typology*, p. 26.
100. Ginzberg, *Legends of the Jews*, 1:28 and 5:43–44.

And he shewed me a pure river of water of life, clear as crystal, proceeding out of the throne of God and of the Lamb. In the midst of the street of it, and on either side of the river, was there the tree of life, which bare twelve manner of fruits, and yielded her fruit every month: and the leaves of the tree were for the healing of the nations. (Rev. 22:1–2)

The paschal lamb standing by the origin of all life, the throne of God, recalls the blood and water that flowed from the wound in Christ's side. Most expositors interpreted the crystal fountain as the perfected source of fructification, the fulfillment of all the covenants made throughout time. William Fulke, the meteorologist and biblical scholar, contrasted the crystal fountain as antitype to the fountain in Eden and the river in Ezekiel, its types:

> But this river flowing out not of the earth, nor out of the temple of Jerusalem, but oute of the throne of God almightie and of his Christ, doth minister the joyes of eternall life most aboundantly to the Citizens of the new Jerusalem. They therefore need never feare death, which drincke dayly of the river of the water of life. Neither can sorrowe or anye griefe happen to those, which drawe water oute of the moste pure founteynes of this river, which are more clearer then any crystall. For the purenesse, and clearenesse of this water is opposed to those troublesome rivers and muddie waters, of whiche wretched men doe quenche there thirst, and afterwarde are subjected to sundrie calamities and diseases.[101]

As John Bale pointed out, "The nature of this water is none other but evermore to clense, evermore to revive & evermore to make whole & perfight"; it is also the fulfillment of the promise made in Ezekiel: "I wyl poure cleare water upon you (sayeth the lorde in Ezechyell) and ye shall be cleane from all fylthynesse."[102] But the passages the commentators associated most often with the vision of the crystal fountain were the words of Jesus himself in the Gospel of John.[103] Marlorat glossed "I will give unto him that is athirst of the fountain of the water of life freely" (Rev. 21:6) by referring primarily to John 7:38: "For he that receiveth the holy Ghost by

101. William Fulke, *Praelections upon the Sacred and holy Revelation of S. John*, fol. 145ᵛ.

102. John Bale, *The Ymage of Bothe Churches after the . . . Revelacioun of Saincte John the Evangelyst*, sig. I.i.4ᵛ–5ʳ.

103. Hugh Broughton, *A Revelation of the holy Apocalyps* in *The Works of the Great Albionean Divine . . . Hugh Broughton*, p. 520, glossed Rev. 22:1 with passages from the Song of Songs, with Ezekiel (47:1), with 1 John (5:6–8 is the most relevant passage but Broughton's text reads 1 John 4), and with John 7:38.

faith, hath a vain that gusheth out of sinfulnesse into rightuousnes, out of damnation into salvation, out of death into life, & out of the earth into heaven. Certain it is therefore that this water is the holy Ghost."[104] Benjamin Keach saw the crystal fountain as the antitype to the rock of Horeb: "That celestial Stream, Spring, and River of Comfort, *viz.* the Spirit, proceeds from the Throne of God, and the Lamb: From this Rock, saith a worthy Writer, the clear and crystalline Streams of living Water bubble forth."[105] The crystal fountain, thus, is the fulfillment of earlier promises that will, in Pareus's words, "vivifie the Elect."[106]

Perhaps the most helpful gloss on the crystal fountain comes from Revelation itself: "It is done. I am Alpha and Omega, the beginning and the end. I will give unto him that is athirst of the fountain of the water of life freely" (21:6). The narrative structure of the Bible is thus given closure with the restoration of mankind to the paradise that was lost. The fountain in the garden of Eden—the point of entry for the subterranean waters that arise to fecundate paradise and, through the four rivers, the entire earth in an endless circulation—is fulfilled by its antitype.[107] Though the fountain in Eden was in an earthly paradise, it pales in comparison to the celestial paradise and the crystal fountain:

> But that River was not cleare as Chrystall, but drawing filth along with it, neither was it of *living water*, but corruptible, neither did it proceed out of the *throne of God and the Lambe*, but out of *Eden*. . . . Therefore the elegancy of the *Earthly Paradise* is nothing to the pleasantnesse of this Coelestiall Citie.[108]

Giacopo Brocardo developed the correspondence between paradisal type and antitype even more cogently by connecting it with the regeneration that would take place at the apocalypse involving

---

104. Marlorat, *Revelation*, fols. 287ᵛ–288ʳ.

105. Keach, *Tropologia*, 2:171. Elsewhere (2:173) he connected other Old Testament passages, including the fountains of Gen. 7:11, with the crystal fountain.

106. David Pareus, *A Commentary upon the Divine Revelation*, p. 575.

107. Josue de La Place, *De primo typo, videlicet creatione mundi*, in *Opuscula nonnulla*, p. 90, connected the river in Eden not only with Rev. 22:1, but also with other Old Testament types and New Testament antitypes: "Qui fluvius, quatenus est in Ecclesia, etiam agente in terris, describitur plenius Ezech. 47. Est autem Spiritus sanctus Joh. 7.38. Esai. 44.3 &c., fluvius justitiae & pacis Esai. 48.18. & 66.12 & voluptatis Ps. 36.9." See also Bale, *Ymage*, sig. I.i.5ʳ⁻ᵛ, for a similar treatment.

108. Pareus, *Revelation*, p. 574.

the believers themselves. In language that strongly recalls the pre-creation chaos of Genesis, he explained that mankind would be re-created so that they might enjoy what Adam lost in Eden:

> [When] Adam & Eve left of[f] to be [in] heaven, they becam *void & empty* erth & the heart of men which came after was *darkened*. At length those heavens whych then were when the Worlde was over-flowne wyth Water, ceased to be, as Peter sayth. But God again calleth man backe unto hym, and unto heavenly Thyngs through a *new regeneration* which is *perfected by fayth*. Hee bryngeth man through the 7. seasons or times, and through the 7. Workinges of his holy Spyrite: hee bryngeth him through the thre states of Circum[ci]sion of the Baptisme of water and of the baptisme of the spirit that he may be called back to the same things that in the beginning were set oute to Adame.[109]

As a result of this regeneration, the faithful will be able to drink the waters of life and eat of the fruit of the tree of life for eternity.

Thus, the vision of the pastoral New Jerusalem describes the feast that sacramentally and eschatologically recapitulates and consummates Christ's sacrifice. By ingesting the fruit of the tree and imbibing the waters of life, the faithful will be glorified as Christ. As one commentator wrote:

> when one is come to Christ, and hath drunk of these waters, he is now like *a tree planted by the rivers of waters. I am the Vine, ye are the branches: He that abideth in me, and I in him, the same bringeth forth much fruit*, John 15.5. In *Rev.* 22.1. *There is a river of water of life*; and in *verse* 2. *on either side the river there was the tree of life.* . . . Jesus Christ is a living root, and a fruitful root, and every one who is come to him, and partakes of him, is a living Christian, and a fruitful Christian: he hath a fruitful heart, and a fruitful life.[110]

Mystically, the faithful will become Christ-like as branches of the tree of life and fountains of living water springing up into life everlasting.

Time, Eternity, and the Circulation of the Waters

That such a pattern—whereby certain signs are arranged systematically according to an understanding of typology as Christologi-

---

109. Brocardo, *Revelation*, fol. 156r-v (italics added).
110. Sedgwick, *The Fountain opened*, p. 72.

cal, sacramental, and eschatological—was discernible to Renaissance commentators seems likely, given the evidence. The concept underlying this system of signs is theologically simple: through faith and the gift of grace, the elect could for a time be restored to the condition of the perfect man, Christ (that is, they could become Christ-like or Christian). Because of imperfect sanctification, however, they would always fall into sin again, so regeneration was a continuous process. Metaphor was necessary in describing this mysterious participation in Christ because such a transformation was beyond human understanding. A systematic usage of the metaphor of the recirculation of the waters of life thus emerged in the writings of theologians and poets, a usage founded on the essential narrative and imagistic structure of the Bible.

Though mainly evidence from Renaissance Protestant sources has been adduced, most of the basic typological correspondences can be found in the Greek and Latin Fathers who were still widely read by the reformers. One particular source, Nicholas of Lyra's *Biblia sacra cum glossa ordinaria et postilla*, made detailed typological lore available to Protestants. (Since Nicholas had often attacked those who multiplied the mystical senses of Scripture needlessly and concentrated on the literal sense, it is sometimes quipped, "If Lyra had not lyred, Luther would not have danced.") Donne, in fact, gave Lincoln's Inn a six-volume presentation set of the Vulgate with the *Glossa ordinaria*.[111] Many of the annotations of the great Protestant Bibles, such as the Geneva (1560), the Bishops' (1568), and the Junius-Tremellius (1569–1579), derived from medieval compilations like it. As the later chapters will demonstrate, Herbert, Vaughan, and Traherne, the major English devotional poets of the seventeenth century, were amplifying a pattern of associations that celebrated the individual's participation in this Christian mystery, a pattern that had been recognized by Christian writers since its beginnings.

Though articulated most fully by poets and scholars, the typology of the waters of life would have been familiar to the Anglican audience of Herbert, Vaughan, and Traherne through a more direct source—Scripture itself. For this reason, it is unnecessary to assume that these poets directly influenced each other—though many

111. See A. G. Dickens, *The English Reformation* (London: Batsford, 1964), p. 65; R. C. Bald, *John Donne: A Life* (New York and Oxford: Oxford University Press, 1970), p. 382.

critics have discerned a "school of Herbert" in the seventeenth century. As Anglican divines, Herbert and Traherne would have read to the congregation the whole Psalter through every month, the New Testament three times a year, and the Old Testament once a year in its entirety. Such continual rereading would have emphasized the recurrence of certain patterns. One set of daily readings, made uniform by the *Book of Common Prayer*, emphasizes the typology of the waters of life and helps create the essential biblical narrative structure of paradise lost and regained. On Septuagesima Sunday, the lessons for Matins are Genesis 1:1–2:4 and Revelation 21:1–9; for Evensong they are Genesis 2:4 and Revelation 21:9–22:6; and the Introit for the service is the twenty-third Psalm (BCP version): "The Lord is my shepherd: therefore can I lack nothing. He shall feed me in a green pasture: and lead me forth beside the waters of comfort." This conjunction of passages that so obviously emphasizes the beginning and the end of time (and features as two of its major images the waters of the creation and the crystal fountain) is not without special significance.

Because only the ordinary of the Mass was unchanging in its form and the proper could be altered for special emphasis, the medieval Church had developed the notion of the liturgical year in order to shape perceptions of time to lead the faithful to eternity. Perhaps the most important celebration in the liturgical year is the Easter cycle. To give proper devotional significance to the triduum of Holy Week, a Lenten fast was included; gradually preparations for Lent were extended to Septuagesima Sunday. From Septuagesima on, purple vestments were worn until Holy Week, and the word "Alleluia" was not used until Easter, when the promise of new life through resurrection in Christ is delivered. The full Easter cycle begins on Septuagesima, reaches its climax on Easter, and ends on the octave of Pentecost. This liturgical season, as Jacobus de Voragine explained in his widely read *Golden Legend*, represents in the life of the believer the period of the fall:

> The whole of this fugitive life is divided into four periods: the period of erring, or wandering from the way; the period of renewal, or returning to the right way; the period of reconciliation; and the period of pilgrimage. The period of erring began with Adam and lasted until Moses, for it was Adam who first turned from God's way. And this period is represented, in the Church, by the part of the year which runs from Septuagesima to Easter. During this part of the year the

Book of Genesis is recited, this being the Book which contains the
account of the sin of our first parents.[112]

In the Middle Ages, the Mass, as O. B. Hardison has shown, was
understood to dramatize the atonement as an *agon* or conflict between Christ and Satan that ended in the triumph of the resurrection.[113] The basic symbolism of this liturgical season in both the
Roman and Anglican communion centered on the alienation of
sinners from God, who in Voragine's words were "wandering
from the way" and hence needed deliverance. As the celebration of
this deliverance from death into eternal life, Easter was regarded as
the most fitting occasion for baptism, which ritually reenacted the
death and rebirth of the catechumen. In fact, the church only permitted baptism during two seasons of the year, Easter and Pentecost. The typological implications of the catechumen's sacramental recapitulation was made especially clear in the liturgy. Even the
number seventy associated with Septuagesima was typologically
important, according to Jerome, since it signified the seventy-year
period of the Babylonian captivity that necessitated the deliverance
of the chosen people.[114] Septuagesima was also associated with the
seven days of the creation, as the readings from Genesis indicated.

The imagery of the waters of life played a prominent role in the
liturgy. The readings, prayers, and sermons all taught the catechumens that they were spiritually dead and had to be reborn in Christ
through the waters in the font on Holy Saturday. Baptism was thus
seen as a miracle of deliverance, and throughout this season the
typology of the exodus, particularly the crossing of the Red Sea as a
type of baptism, was prominent. Following long-standing tradition, the Collect for Easter Even in the *Book of Common Prayer*
reminded auditors that "we are baptized into the death of Christ,"
and the readings for the service reminded the congregation of the
typology of baptism (1 Peter 3:17 and Matt. 25:57). The sorrowful
tone of the Lenten season gave way to joy on Easter at the miraculous salvation wrought by Christ when the entire drama was
made available to the catechumens: "Clothed in white garments,
radiant with newness of spirit, they are visible analogues to the
invisible mystery of the Resurrection."[115] On Septuagesima, the

112. Jacobus de Voragine, *The Golden Legend*, p. 1.
113. O. B. Hardison, Jr., *Christian Rite and Christian Drama in the Middle Ages*, pp.
80–138. This account of the Lenten *agon* is based largely on Hardison's work.
114. Hardison, *Christian Rite*, p. 87.
115. Hardison, *Christian Rite*, p. 95.

readings from Genesis and Revelation that reminded the congregation of the paradise mankind lost but would regain were then given
emotional closure on Easter, when the high drama of the Mass was
revealed to those who had been reborn through the waters into the
mystical body of the faithful.

The typological implications of the liturgical year remind us
also that the Bible changed the perceptions of time and eternity in a
subtle, but powerful way. Indeed, the footing upon which typology rests—and the best supporting evidence for the threefold typology being argued for here—is the Renaissance understanding of
time as sacred history. As is evident from the discussion above,
typology presupposes a teleological view of history and a providential ordering of events that progresses linearly to that end.
This biblical view of time differs substantially from the classical
notion of cyclical time. Plato held that time was a reflection of the
eternal order of Ideas; the cyclical movement of the heavens was "a
movable image of Eternity."[116] Readers will also recall Virgil's
depiction of the great wheel of history in book six of the *Aeneid*.
But from the earliest period—especially with Origen and Irenaeus
in the third century—Christian theologians have understood time
as an inexorable progression to the second coming. Time became a
manifestation of sacred history as every event worked toward the
end foretold in Revelation. This view of history was given powerful expression in Augustine's *Civitas Dei*, in which the origins of
the city of man were traced from Adam's fall (the first city was
physically "built" by Cain) to its ultimate collapse at the apocalypse. Augustine also traced the foundation of the city of God,
especially the Old Testament's preparation for Christ, and looked
forward rapturously to its perfection in the New Jerusalem. At the
same time, in the early centuries of Christianity, St. Paul's notion
of typology was being developed to show the continuity of the Old
and New Testaments in order to demonstrate the providential ordering of all time since the creation. Typology was used to establish
relationships between the crucial events of sacred history that bore
the certain imprint of God's ordering of time. Typology, as
Daniélou has pointed out, always has been an interpretation of the

116. Plato, *Timaeus*, 37d–e, pp. 75–77. For an excellent survey of the Christian view of history, see C. A. Patrides, *The Grand Design of God: The Literary Form of the Christian View of History*, and Achsah Guibbory, *The Map of Time: Seventeenth-Century English Literature and Ideas of Pattern in History*.

history recounted in Scripture and not simply a mode of exegesis.[117]

A typological view of historical time joins the Judaeo-Christian linear concept of history with the classical idea of the cycle of creation and destruction. Time could be both cyclical and linear when the salvation history of the individual was viewed as a recapitulation of a timeless typological paradigm. Or, put another way, the typological reading of the Bible makes time and history simultaneously diachronic and synchronic. This mystery is rendered precisely in the drama played out in the Christian liturgical year as well, where in a ritual cycle Christ's advent, trial in the desert, passion, and resurrection are endlessly celebrated. Indeed, one of Crashaw's magi hails the Christ-child himself at the Epiphany as the "All-circling point. All centring sphear. / The world's one, round, Æternall year."[118] In the cycle of the medieval mystery plays, in which the grand drama of sacred history is played fully in the span of a single day, we can also perceive how typological recapitulation both compresses and expands time.[119]

That Herbert, Vaughan, and Traherne should be so concerned with time and eternity is not surprising. At no other period in England's history was the interest in the second advent of Christ so great as it was in the second, third, and fourth decades of the seventeenth century—a time of economic depression, political upheaval and the threatened extinction of Protestantism.[120] The book of Revelation was, after Genesis, the most popular book of the time, if we can judge its popularity from the number of commentaries devoted to explicating it. The Dutch theologian Hugo Grotius reported that over eighty different works on the second coming had appeared in England by 1649.[121] Even James I tried his hand at illuminating a portion of it in *Ane fruitfull Meditatioun con-*

117. Jean Daniélou, "La typologie d'Isaac dans le Christianisme Primitif," p. 369, wrote: "La typologie n'est donc pas d'abord une exégèse des *livres* de l'Ancien Testament: elle est une interprétation de l'histoire même que ces livres racontent. Elle établit des liaisons entre les événements de ces deux histoires. C'est dire également qu'elle ne porte que sur les événements où cette action divine se manifeste."

118. Richard Crashaw, *The Poems, English, Latin and Greek*, p. 255.

119. See Verdel A. Kolve, *The Play Called "Corpus Christi"* (Stanford: Stanford University Press, 1966).

120. See H. R. Trevor-Roper, *Religion, the Reformation and Social Change, and Other Essays* (London, Melbourne, and Toronto: Macmillan, 1967), pp. 47–89.

121. Bryan W. Ball, *A Great Expectation: Eschatological Thought in English Protestantism to 1660*, p. 33n.

tening ane plane and facill expositioun of the 7, 8, 9, and 10 versis of the 20 chap. of the Revelatioun.[122] The second coming, of course, plays a momentous role in the overall scheme of Christian theology, and so some interest in latter day events is to be expected. But popular writers and theologians seemed convinced that worldwide cataclysm was impending: all manner of portents proclaimed it and biblical chronologists speculated widely on its precise date.[123] Given the existing conditions in the church and in the world, people had no trouble believing that the consummation of sacred history was at hand.

Since the shrill clarion of the apocalypse was also thought to signal the end of time, the notion of waters returning to their source—to the abyss of the godhead who is paradoxically the fountain of life as well—was a prominent metaphor to describe the reintegration of time with eternity, and it was employed by writers of all sorts. One of the most graceful formulations begins the hexameron of the cosmographer John Swan:

> *Time*, by whose revolutions we measure hours, dayes, weeks, moneths and years, is nothing else but (as it were) a certain space borrowed or set apart from *eternitie*; which shall at the last return to eternitie again: like the rivers, which have their first course from the seas; and by running on, there they arrive, and have their last: for before *Time* began, there was *Eternitie*, namely GOD; which was, which is, and which shall be for ever: without beginning or end, and yet the beginning and end of all things.[124]

Similarly, Thomas Jackson, citing a host of ancient authorities to prove that the idea of the circle of perfection was ubiquitous, explained:

> His Eternity then, is the inexhaustible fountain or infinite Ocean, from which time or duration successive (in what finite substances soever they be seated) with all their several Branches or Appurtenances, do perpetually flow; and unto Eternity, they have if not the same proportion, yet the same references, the same dependances on it, which finite and created magnitudes have to Divine Immensity.[125]

122. James's *Ane fruitfull Meditatioun* was first published in Edinburgh in 1588, and another edition was brought out in London for his courtiers in 1603.

123. Ball, *A Great Expectation*, pp. 89–125. Some of the many dates advanced for the end of time were: 1649, 1650, 1655, 1666, 1670, 1686, 1688, 1695, and 1700.

124. John Swan, *Speculum Mundi, or, a Glasse representing the Face of the World. . . . Whereunto is joyned an Hexameron*, p. 39.

125. Jackson, *A Treatise of the Divine Essence and Attributes*, in *The Works*, 2:29. The

In some of the most quoted couplets from *Cooper's Hill,* John Denham pays tribute to the river Thames using the same conceit:

> *Thames,* the most lov'd of all the Oceans sons,
> By his old Sire to his embraces runs,
> Hasting to pay his tribute to the Sea,
> Like mortal life to meet Eternity.[126]

So common a formulation is this that when Vaughan, in "The Water-fall," has his speaker begin his meditation with the observation, "With what deep murmurs through times silent stealth," the biblical echoes of the river of time (and of the emanation and return of the waters of life) take on an evidential value that will resonate throughout the poem.

The typology of the waters of life, therefore, rendered a rather complex series of associations. As a code, typology directed the seventeenth-century reader to certain relationships between events (and of course to the linguistic structures that articulate them). Three related patterns constitute this typological structure involving the waters of life: Christological, sacramental, and eschatological types; these three were founded on an understanding of the three advents of Christ, in the flesh, in the soul, and in the *eschaton.* As Luther explained, "Just as the law was a figure and preparation of the people for receiving Christ, so our doing what is in us (*factio quantum in nobis est*) disposes us to grace. And the whole time of grace is preparation for future glory and the second advent."[127]

In the seventeenth century, the Bible was read as a single, unifying narrative structure that linked these distinct but intersecting moments of time: literally, Scripture told the parallel histories of the creation, destruction, redemption, and future glorification of both mankind and the universe. Symbolically, through Christological typology, the Old Testament foreshadows the story of the perfect man who will effect this salvation. Because of Christ's intervention in time, both mankind and the universe can be regenerated—mankind will be redeemed by reenacting the pattern of the perfect man and the fallen world will be restored as the seat of the New Jerusalem. The ultimate circulation of the waters of life de-

---

plenitude of grace was frequently likened to the circularity of waters in occasional meditation. See, e.g., Thomas Taylor, *Meditations from the Creatures,* pp. 100–101.

126. Brendan O Hehir, *Expans'd Hieroglyphicks: A Critical Edition of Sir John Denham's "Cooper's Hill,"* p. 149, ll. 161–64.

127. Quoted by Preus, *From Shadow to Promise,* p. 194.

scribes this complex metaphoric and narrative relationship perfectly: just as the waters flow from the abyss of the godhead first to create, then to destroy, and finally to regenerate the universe (annihilating time in eternity), so do they regenerate and will some day perfect mankind. For Christ, through his sacrifice, has himself restored the waters to mankind and the universe by opening the fountain of life on the cross. It is precisely this central Christian mystery that Herbert, Vaughan, and Traherne celebrate in their poetry.

HERBERT AND THE
WATERS FROM THE HEART

Why, Caesar is their onely King, not I:
He clave the stonie rock, when they were drie;
But surely not their hearts, as I well trie:
            Was ever grief like mine?

This reproach, intended for all those passing before the cross (or
contemplating it in retrospect), relies in part on a significant network of typologically related images that helps to articulate the
major conflict in *The Temple*: the speaker's long struggle to surrender fully to God.[1] Though much attention has been given to
Herbert's indebtedness to the Bible, few critics have acknowledged
the systematic usage made of the waters of life that flow from the
stony heart—which, as we have seen, was considered by seventeenth-century readers as one of the most important biblical tropes.[2]

1. "The Sacrifice," ll. 121–24. All quotations are taken from *The Works of George
Herbert*, ed. F. E. Hutchinson, and will be cited internally.

2. Many have written on the heart of stone as a metaphor in *The Temple*—
notably, Chana Bloch, *Spelling the Word: George Herbert and the Bible*—though no
one has pursued the imagery of the waters of life in connection with the heart of
stone. In the current debate over the works of George Herbert, two critical positions
can be discerned. On the one hand stand those who champion the originality of the
poem and writer, such as William Empson, *Seven Types of Ambiguity*; Stanley Fish,
Self-Consuming Artifacts: The Experience of Seventeenth-Century Literature; and Helen
Vendler, *The Poetry of George Herbert*. On the other are historical critics who champion the cultural heritage that, in effect, determines the individual, such as Rosemund Tuve, *A Reading of George Herbert*; Joseph H. Summers, *George Herbert: His
Religion and Art*; and Barbara K. Lewalski, *Protestant Poetics and the Seventeenth-
Century Religious Lyric*. Barbara Leah Harman, *Costly Monuments: Representations of
the Self in George Herbert's Poetry*, pp. 1–38, has recently argued that we ought to
study the dialectical relationship between the two. This study will explore the
relationship between tradition and the individual talent in regard to one of the most
significant and consistently formulated patterns of imagery in *The Temple*, the
waters of life.

As a devotional poet attempting to chronicle the journey toward God, Herbert was necessarily concerned with the inner workings of grace for the regeneration and sanctification of the sinner; hence, the speaker's desire that the waters of life flow from his stony heart remains one of his greatest hopes. Though Herbert was familiar with the traditional types and figures used to depict grace, as evidenced by the reference to the rock of Horeb in the lines quoted above, he did not employ them as simple coded phrases. Rather, following common Renaissance literary practices, he creatively imitated the traditional figures for his own purposes.

One of his most creative strategies is counterpoint, through the implicit narratives contained in the three kinds of types, to present the complex relationship of the believers with Christ. By establishing the perfect pattern of the spiritual life with well-known Christological types, he had a ready fund of potent metaphors with which to narrate the speaker's recapitulation of this salvation drama. Because the speaker is not always successful, the sacramental types are usually employed to magnify his despair over the gulf that separates him from God, though on occasion these types express his elation over the experience of grace. At the same time, Herbert exploited the eschatological dimension of typology to represent the speaker's hopes for a future consummation and hence to provide closure for the narrative of his movement toward God that loosely structures *The Temple*. The interplay between narrative levels and the kinds of types involving the waters of life thus offers an illuminating way to study the speaker's salvation drama.

In *A Priest to the Temple*, Herbert offered a partial clue to his use of metaphor when he stated, "People by what they understand, are best led to what they understand not" (p. 228). Since the water imagery of the Bible both influenced and was influenced by the common understanding of hydrologic phenomena, the water-cycle was a powerful tool for use in depicting the descent and reascent of grace for the learned and laity alike. The complex typology of the waters of life provided Herbert with a rich field of signification for the elaboration of a basic Christian paradigm: the regeneration of the sinner in imitation of Christ's own sacrifice. When viewed as a whole, the imagery involving the waters of life forms one of the most important metaphoric substructures for *The Temple*. As Mary Ellen Rickey once observed, Herbert's poetry is multileveled, or "laminar."[3] That is, one of Herbert's basic strategies in *The Temple*

3. Mary Ellen Rickey, *Utmost Art: Complexity in the Verse of George Herbert*, pp.

was to counterpoint different metaphoric subtexts to create a complex but unified narrative. This he accomplished by exploiting the resources of Christological, sacramental, and eschatological typology. Recognizing that Herbert has counterpointed the three kinds of types in his elaboration of the metaphoric waters of life provides readers with a vocabulary and conceptual framework with which to appreciate the artistry of Herbert's complex typological wit.

Typological Strategies in *The Temple*

In his extended "character" of the country parson, *A Priest to the Temple*, Herbert established a method for meditating on Scripture, a work he called "the chief and top of [the Parson's] knowledge . . . the book of books, the storehouse and magazene of life and comfort" (p. 228). This method seems substantially indebted to the one favored by the popular guides written by Weemes, Perkins, and Lukin. Herbert's methodology shows us that he approached the Bible as a literary text that must be studied carefully to recover its full meaning.[4] To glean all that he can from the Bible, Herbert urged the parson, first of all, to cultivate a devout life so that he can understand Scripture in the same spirit in which it was written; second, to pray for guidance and inspiration before reading; third, to undertake "a diligent Collation of Scripture with Scripture"; and, fourth, to read biblical commentaries and the writings of the Fathers as aids for studying the text (pp. 228–29). The first two steps emphasize the importance of what the reformers called the Analogy of Faith: to interpret Scripture accurately requires that one be imbued with the spirit, which will then guide the reader in understanding the text. The third step patently encourages typological interpretation, the collation of text with text: "For all Truth being consonant to it self, and all being penn'd by one and the self-same Spirit, it cannot be, but that an industrious, and judi-

---

60–61. More recently, Sidney Gottlieb, "How Shall We Read Herbert?: A Look at 'Prayer' (I)," has written on Herbert's use of the art of juxtaposition and sequencing.

4. Herbert's interest in traditional typology was first documented by Tuve; many critics, however, now place his poetry in the forefront of the Protestant poetics that emerged in the early seventeenth century. See especially Lewalski, *Protestant Poetics*, pp. 283–316; Richard Strier, *Love Known: Theology and Experience in George Herbert's Poetry*; Ira Clark, *Christ Revealed: The History of the Neotypological Lyric in the English Renaissance*; and William J. Scheick, "Typology and Allegory: A Comparative Study of George Herbert and Edward Taylor."

cious comparing of place with place must be a singular help for the right understanding of the Scriptures" (p. 229). The fourth advises the reader to confirm personal meditations by studying the writings of others. Such commentaries, as we have seen, generally treated Scripture as a richly poetic text and focused at length on its typological symbolism.

In addition to these explicit instructions from "The Parson's Knowledg," Herbert provides further evidence that he approached the Bible as a work requiring a complex reading act in his sonnet "The H. Scriptures (II)." In the octave, the speaker exclaims (both in wonder and despair) that he wishes he knew all the possible combinations of verses and what they would teach him.

> Oh that I knew how all thy lights combine,
>   And the configurations of their glorie!
>   Seeing not onely how each verse doth shine,
> But all the constellations of the storie.
> This verse marks that, and both do make a motion
>   Unto a third, that ten leaves off doth lie:
>   Then as dispersed herbs do watch a potion,
> These three make up some Christians destinie.
>
> (ll. 1–8)

Though these lines seem to present a clear task for the reader—discerning the subtle connections between various texts to discover "some Christians destinie"—the relationship between reader and text is not so simple. The sestet provides a *volta* or turn in the argument that suggests Herbert understood typology in the same complex way that the commentators did.

> Such are thy secrets, which my life makes good,
>   And comments on thee: for in ev'ry thing
>   Thy words do finde me out, & parallels bring,
> And in another make me understood.
>   Starres are poore books, & oftentimes do misse:
>   This book of starres lights to eternall blisse.
>
> (ll. 9–14)

The sestet asserts that Scripture has an enabling power in the lives of the believers by articulating their stories, by enabling representation. It has become a critical commonplace to hold that "For Herbert, the understanding of Scripture is inextricably bound up with self-understanding."[5] Put another way, learning to read the Bible

5. The quotation is from Chana Bloch, "Spelling the Word: Herbert's Reading of

typologically—learning, that is, that it tells not merely the story of
the Christ's coming but of the salvation of the chosen people—
allows the speaker to know his own story in its truest sense: it
"make[s] me understood." Or, as Herbert wrote in "Discipline,"

> Not a word or look
> I affect to own,
>   But by book,
> And thy book alone.
>   (ll. 9–12)

The typological drama that Herbert perceived in Scripture, in its
truest sense, permits self-representation.

While what I have termed sacramental typology provides, in
Barbara Harman's words, "an already written text," the speaker
can only "rewrite" this text by reexperiencing it for himself.[6] She
may overstate her case when she cites the lines from the dedicatory
poem,

> Lord, my first fruits present themselves to thee;
> Yet not mine neither: for from thee they came,

and the injunction from "Jordan (II)" to copy the "sweetnesse read-
ie penn'd" to suggest that the "speaker who sings best is clearly one
who claims no ownership" for his poems.[7] Though he learns that
his most genuine experiences are common to all believers, this does
not mean that these experiences are any less his own. The fact that a
type (originally an experience or event) had a prior existence in Old
Testament history in no way detracts from the historicity of either
the antitype or, more to the point, the individual's recapitulation of
it. The crucial lesson that the speaker seems to discover in *The
Temple* is that his personal history has permanence and value precisely because it recapitulates a timely and timeless pattern established in Scripture. What he may lose in surrendering his rights to
invent an individual story (which is ultimately fragmentary and
ephemeral when told apart from Christ's), he gains in permanent
identity as one among the faithful through reenacting certain ty-

---

the Bible," in Claude J. Summers and Ted-Larry Pebworth, eds., *"Too Rich to
Clothe the Sunne": Essays on George Herbert,* p. 16.

6. Harman, *Costly Monuments,* p. 128, observed that the tension in the poetry is
created precisely because the speaker's surrendering his own personal story is fright-
ening, for "it is not easy for speakers to accept the idea that embodiment is both an
obstruction and an illusion."

7. Harman, *Costly Monuments,* p. 63. See also pp. 43–51.

pological experiences.[8] Representation, Herbert implies, is most complete when the speaker aligns his story with the "already written text."

In his last message to Nicholas Ferrar, Herbert wrote that his poems represent "*a picture of the many spiritual Conflicts that have past betwixt God and my Soul, before I could subject mine to the will of* Jesus my Master: *in whose service I have now found perfect freedom.*"[9] Herbert's readers are increasingly becoming aware of how apt these familiar lines really are. Though we can easily point to moments when he feels the "sugred strange delight, / Passing all cordials made by any art, / Bedew, embalme, and overrunne my heart," equally as often he is plagued by "many a bitter storm" ("The Glance," ll. 5–7, 9). Such inconstancy, though characteristic of most Christian experiences, was accorded a special prominence in reformed theology. The Roman Catholic belief in achieving salvation through works offered a steadily attainable path to God, made possible by the gift of grace that the church itself bestowed in the sacraments. With its emphasis on justification by faith, the reformed churches presented a more tortuous, solitary path. Furthermore, the doctrine of imperfect sanctification, as formulated in Article XV of the Anglican Church, held that only Christ was perfectly sanctified.[10] To be reborn does not mean that believers are free from sin, nor that joy will be everlasting on earth; Herbert's speaker will always draw toward Canaan, only to be "Brought back to the Red sea, the sea of shame" ("The Bunch of Grapes," l. 7). To be aware of one's unworthiness, aware of the hardness of one's heart, however, is at least a sign that regeneration might occur, for the unregenerate are incapable of even discerning their true spiritual condition; even the slightest twinge of conscience is, after all, the product of prevenient grace.[11]

8. One familiar example of the "application" of the type is "The Bunch of Grapes," in which the speaker finds himself replaying the drama of the exodus typologically. When the significant events of his own history are seen rightly, they are understood in terms of such experiences. His "murmerings" (l. 18) against God are the complaints of the Israelites in the wilderness; he must likewise contend with the torments of the desert, the "sand and serpents" (l. 17). But above all he can enjoy at times the sacramental wine of the new covenant, crushed from the grapes by the wine-press of the passion, which fulfills the promise figured by Noah's vine in Genesis 9.

9. Izaak Walton, *The Lives of John Donne, Sir Henry Wotton, Richard Hooker, George Herbert, and Robert Sanderson,* p. 314.

10. Strier, *Love Known,* p. 16.

11. Diana Benet, *Secretary of Praise: The Poetic Vocation of George Herbert,* pp. 195–96, also makes this point.

In *The Temple* the speaker will at times feel tremendous elation at successfully recapitulating typological experiences, but at other times he will despair at the gulf that separates him from God. Such a rhythm of contrition and praise, John Booty observed, also characterizes the *Book of Common Prayer*.[12] Believers are forever wavering between assurance and fear and thus need to be continually regenerated: "Except thou make us dayly, we shall spurn / Our own salvation" ("Giddinesse," ll. 27–28). The comforting waters of life that signify God's prevenient grace are therefore a constituent feature of much devotional literature, as is the case in "H. Baptisme (I)."

> So when I view my sinnes, mine eyes remove
> More backward still, and to that water flie,
> Which is above the heav'ns, whose spring and vent
> Is in my deare Redeemers pierced side.
>
> (ll. 3–6)

A great deal of the drama in Herbert's devotional lyrics can best be articulated by examining the interplay or dialectic between Christological, sacramental, and eschatological types. In "The Bunch of Grapes," the joy the speaker has experienced in the past, "the taste / Of mine inheritance," has left him. Though the Christian does have the sacramental type in the form of communion wine—in contrast to the Israelites who had only the promise of the grapes of Eshcol—the wine is still only a tantalizing foretaste of the perfect joy to be experienced in the New Jerusalem, where the type will be consummated. While the distinction between the old and new dispensation helps to shape the poem, we need to recognize that the speaker remains in a position similar to that of the Israelites marveling at the giant cluster of grapes. In fact, his despair is all the more bitter for having been vouchsafed a taste of this joy. The eschatological dimension of this poem, which alone is capable of providing the closure the speaker implicitly demands, is usually overlooked.[13] Only the taste of this consummate joy will bring an end to his ceaseless pilgrimage between "Canaan" and "the sea of shame." The complementary, the satisfying, images are always awaiting the speaker in the new world to come. The interplay

12. John E. Booty, "George Herbert: *The Temple* and *The Book of Common Prayer*."

13. Tuve's analysis of "The Bunch of Grapes," *A Reading of George Herbert*, pp. 112–23, is predicated on typology. For a more recent one, see Strier, *Love Known*, pp. 154–59.

between successive levels of typology in "The Bunch of Grapes" points to what one critic has aptly called "the inaccessibility of closure" in *The Temple*.[14] The goal of this chapter is to study the imagery of the waters of life, images that are restlessly referring to a consummation, a closure, in the fulness of time.

Writing the Tale Already Told

The opening sequence of poems in The Church, which culminates in the two baptismal poems, implicitly evokes the imagery of the waters of life as a subtext against which to mark the spiritual aridity of its speaker. As the titles of these thirteen poems suggest, Herbert focuses our attention on the central drama of the Christian life and the church year, the events leading to Holy Week, a time in which the catechumen is traditionally prepared for baptism.[15] Beginning with perhaps the most prominent image in *The Temple*, the stony heart that must be regenerated through the waters of life, "The Altar" introduces us to a speaker being initiated into the mysteries of the faith. As Herbert's critics of late have noted, the speaker is presented as a resistant self, who often claims what he in fact should be relinquishing. In Stanley Fish's terms, he is struggling to *let go*.[16] This dynamic is at work throughout the opening

14. Harman, *Costly Monuments*, p. 147. On the other hand, Louis L. Martz, "The Action of the Self: Devotional Poetry in the Seventeenth Century," in *Metaphysical Poetry*, ed. Malcolm Bradbury and David Palmer, pp. 101–21, argues that "What we have in his poetry . . . is the *memory* of states of restlessness now securely overcome and retrospectively viewed as dangers overpassed" (p. 108). As I shall try to show, especially in "Love (III)," the speaker as Christian Everyman is still restless and insecure as his story draws to a close.

15. The liturgical nature of this sequence has been discussed by Louis L. Martz, *The Poetry of Meditation: A Study in English Religious Literature of the Seventeenth Century*, pp. 288–95; Fredson Bowers, "Herbert's Sequential Imagery: 'The Temper,'" 202–13; Florence Sandler, "'Solomon vbique regnet': Herbert's Use of the Images of the New Covenant," pp. 147–58, and reprinted in *Essential Articles for the Study of George Herbert's Poetry*, ed. John R. Roberts, pp. 258–67; Ilona Bell, "'Setting Foot into Divinity': George Herbert and the English Reformation"; and Susanne Woods, "The 'Unhewn Stones' of Herbert's Verse."

16. Fish, *Self-Consuming Artifacts*, pp. 156–223, has termed this struggle a "poetics of tension" between the egocentric vision and the enabling vision of the divine; Harman, *Costly Monuments*, pp. 41–63, has focused on the speaker's desire to create "fictions of coherence," which constitute the self on its own terms rather than according to God's.

sequence, as a parallel is established between baptismal regeneration or re-creation and poetic creation. The evidence comes both from within "The Altar"—the obsession with physical form that points toward an outmoded covenant based on works rather than faith—and perhaps most convincingly from that poem's contextual position in relation to the other liturgical poems. This sequence dramatizes the paradoxical situation in which the poet-speaker finds himself: his desire to tell his idiosyncratic personal "story" undermines his efforts to submit to God's *writing*; hence he must learn to relinquish some of his claims before he can be initiated into the church through baptism. As it is put in "The Thanksgiving," the speaker struggles to submit to the self-denying fact that "the tale is told" (l. 8). "The Altar" thus serves as the fitting introduction to the far more sophisticated mode of discourse evident in The Church (and to this study), for it demonstrates how deeply rooted are the spiritual conflicts facing his readers in order to prepare them for the total submission to God's agency that is necessary before immersion in the waters of life.

By its very title, Herbert's volume of poetry places the notion of temple-building as a metaphor in the foreground, recalling St. Paul's admonition to the Corinthians, "Know ye not that ye are the temple of God, and that the Spirit of God dwelleth in you" (1 Cor. 3:16). Since the first poem so clearly annouces its understanding of the relationship between the Old Testament altar of unhewn stones and the altar of the new covenant in the heart, most readers have assumed that the speaker has already accomplished the task of preparing a foundation fit for the Holy Spirit (based on the guidance offered by the moral precepts of "The Church-porch").[17] Herbert, though, took pains in the opening sequence to show the impossibility of completing such a task. By maintaining a critical distance from his speaker, he reaffirmed a cardinal principle of the reformers. One can never merit salvation through adherence to the law, whether it be the old or the new; only through faith alone and the

17. Many critics see Herbert's dedication of himself on the altar of his poetry as the appropriate, worthy, and efficacious act that best introduces *The Temple*. See Summers, *Herbert: His Religion and Art*, pp. 140–43; Thomas B. Stroup, "'A Reasonable, Holy, and Living Sacrifice': Herbert's 'The Altar'"; Booty, "Herbert: *The Temple and The Book of Common Prayer*"; Martin Elsky, "George Herbert's Pattern Poems and the Materiality of Language: A New Approach to Renaissance Hieroglyphics"; Gene Edward Veith, Jr., *Reformation Spirituality: The Religion of George Herbert*, pp. 55–56; and Bart Westerweel, *Patterns and Patterning: A Study of Four Poems by George Herbert*, pp. 53–139.

unmerited gift of grace could one be saved. Indeed, for Calvin the sin of sins is the pride of self-hood that inspires the believer with the desire to become like God. The speaker's very effort to construct an altar, upon which to make his contrite offering, thus appears to undermine his very intentions.

                    "The Altar"
    A broken A L T A R, Lord, thy servant reares,
    Made of a heart, and cemented with teares:
        Whose parts are as thy hand did frame;
        No workmans tool hath touch'd the same.
            A H E A R T alone
              Is such a stone,
              As nothing but
              Thy pow'r doth cut.
            Wherefore each part
              Of my hard heart
            Meets in this frame,
            To praise thy Name:
        That, if I chance to hold my peace,
        These stones to praise thee may not cease.
    O let thy blessed S A C R I F I C E be mine,
    And sanctifie this A L T A R to be thine.

What has most struck readers through the centuries is the poem's hieroglyphic arrangement. Though many scholars have assumed that this poem represents Herbert's profound submission to God, it may be true that the very perfection of its poetic form compromises the act of submission. In the opening line, the speaker calls special attention to the "broken ALTAR" of his heart that he is "rearing" before the reader's very eyes. The creative act of writing—hewing and arranging the altar stones—in some sense has appropriated the task reserved for God. The verbs that dominate the second line reinforce his claims for agency; this altar has been "made" and "cemented" by the speaker's own efforts, using the broken pieces of his contrite heart. Most readers have thought that the opening lines focus on "the brokenness of the altar and the devotion involved in rearing it."[18] But two difficulties arise that may require us to reconsider the accepted reading: is the pride of craftsmanship at odds with the act of contrition he is making, and, more to the point, is human contrition in any way sufficient? The reformers adamantly viewed all human merit—even contrition—as irrelevant

18. Strier, *Love Known*, p. 192.

for salvation. Herbert had himself affirmed as much in his *Briefe Notes on Valdesso's "Considerations,"* when he urged that "man presume not to merit, that is, to oblige God, or justify himselfe before God, by any acts or exercises of Religion" (p. 312). For as Donne observed in one of the Holy Sonnets about the paradoxical nature of grace as a gift,

> Yet grace, if thou repent, thou canst not lacke:
> But who shall give thee that grace to beginne?[19]

If repentance itself is the result of an unmerited gift of grace, then only by faith alone was the believer saved.

Time and again in *The Temple*, we witness the speaker struggling against his own rationalism, the consciousness of which creates the illusion of a self apart from God. For the poet, whose stock in trade is the language and sense of narrative that makes consciousness possible, abandoning the autonomy of the self is particularly difficult. He wants a personal account of the self, and silence, as an alternative, is untenable. The speaker must eventually reconcile himself to the fact that true representation is possible only when he surrenders his idiosyncratic, independent story for the collective one that represents the real truth of his life, which is, in Harman's words, "a prior account, already written and in place, an account toward which one might turn if one were not occupied with inventing alternatives."[20] This "prior account" I take to be the salvation drama being told typologically in Scripture. While "The Altar" is not solely about the problems of *writing*, the poem's form calls attention to this problem, which Herbert addresses more directly in later poems in the opening sequence.

The speaker's ability to *write*, to re-create a lasting, viable account of the self, is precisely what the form of this poem calls to our attention. The word "frame" in line 3 that describes Christ's role in creating the heart—"Whose parts are as thy hand did frame"—is significant in establishing precedent for the poet as maker, who in a similar act creates "this frame, / To praise thy name" (ll. 11–12). By creating this altar-shaped poem, the speaker thus patterns himself after Christ as priest (sacrificer) and poet ("maker" as its Greek root suggests). Even the typography of the poem, with its capitalization of ALTAR (l. 1), HEART (l. 5), SACRIFICE (l. 15), and ALTAR (l. 15), also reinforces the identification of the poet with

19. *The Complete Poetry of John Donne*, p. 339, ll. 9–10.
20. Harman, *Costly Monuments*, p. 176.

the priest who bears the special responsibility of offering a fitting sacrifice, the metaphoric "base" of which is the claim, "That if I chance to hold my peace, / These stones to praise thee may not cease" (ll. 13–14).

Lewalski has suggested that Herbert is paraphrasing Psalm 51, a prayer recognized as a paradigm for repentance that contains the idea that the psalmist's praise is dependent on God ("O Lord, open thou my lips, and my mouth shall show forth thy praise. . . . The sacrifice acceptable to God is a broken spirit; a broken and contrite heart, O God thou wilt not despise" 51:15, 17).[21] These lines more directly echo Christ's rebuke of the Pharisees who had objected to the disciples' praises of joy when he entered Jerusalem: "if these [the disciples] should hold their peace, the stones would immediately cry out" (Luke 19:40). Christ here emphasizes that the Pharisees only have the power to silence the disciples, while God has the power even to make stones speak. In the logic of the poem, the speaker hopes that the altar of praise, fashioned out of the pieces of his stony heart and cemented with his own tears, has been framed into these speaking stones. But the speaker's declaration that the artifact, which represents or incorporates his contrite heart, will praise God even if he should hold his peace forever, once again, draws attention to his part in offering a fit sacrifice. His implicit claim for merit thus works against the typological "lesson" about the temple of the heart under the new dispensation. The last lines of the poem plead for some assurance that God's hand is enabling him, but the opening stanza of the following poem seems to indicate that this assurance has not been forthcoming.

Such a gesture toward participation in his own salvation through the artistry of his sacrificial offering serves as a proper introduction to *The Temple*, for the speaker characteristically struggles to preserve his own identity by overvaluing his efforts and necessarily undervaluing Christ's. He seeks to create what Harman, after Hannah Arendt, calls "the space of appearance," a personal story that will preserve and articulate the self:

> The knowledge Herbert's speakers alternately reject and embrace is, then, not only sacramental knowledge, it is also knowledge about their own dissolution, knowledge about death. . . . [T]hey want a body that endures, that is coherent, meaningful, distinguishable from others, safe from change. In the absence of access to such a body the retrospective speaker even produces its illusion—a coherent account

21. Lewalski, *Protestant Poetics*, p. 302.

whose boundaries are fortified against dangerous knowledge, and within whose walls the self appears both to have substance and to be safe. The desire to conserve experience *as story* repeats, in other words, the desire to conserve the body, for both reflect the belief that having presence means being coherently manifest, means having material form . . . means making the self substantial and discrete, guaranteeing in some way its ongoing life.[22]

The solidity of the poem's hieroglyph thus not only signifies the substantiality of the speaker's contrition and lays claim for his own merit, but also asserts his individual identity in a subtle way. It is precisely because he cannot relinquish his control over his fate by submitting to God's writing that he creates a role for himself, even the limited one of gathering together the broken pieces of his heart, in recapitulating Christ's sacrifice.

"The Altar" is a difficult poem that introduces us to a speaker seemingly aware of his inadequacies, but a speaker still reluctant to surrender to God. It is difficult perhaps for a modern reader to regard this heartfelt gesture, uttered in appropriately biblical language, as anything but humble and self-effacing. Hearing the poem, indeed, is quite a different experience from our observing it creating its own shape as we read; the heightened exhortatory couplets with which the poem closes seem straight from the heart. This gesture, however, is put into its proper context theologically and emotionally in the following poem, "The Sacrifice," by the absolute disparity between human efforts and divine. In actuality, "The Altar" presents a stony heart that still must be transformed, and so there is a certain fitness ironically to the "brokenness" of the altar the speaker rears. What is absent though is the recognition that Christ is truly the "servant" who has reared the altar, made of his heart and "cemented" with his blood, upon which the believers can worship; only Christ can truly be said to *write* his epistle on the heart in order to sanctify it (as the final couplet reminds us). It is precisely this understanding toward which the poems that follow move. Perhaps the most helpful gloss for "The Altar" is from Jeremiah: "But this is the covenant which I will make with the house of Israel after those days, says the LORD: I will put my law within them, and I will write it upon their hearts" (31:33). Until the speaker surrenders his desire to represent the self through his own enabling act—here, to create his own sacrifice and his own offertory poem—he has misconstrued God's *writing*. Indeed, the phys-

22. Harman, *Costly Monuments*, pp. 111–12.

icality of the classical altar the speaker erects (which suspiciously resembles the pronominal "I") can be taken as a measure, finally, of his having missed the point about the new dispensation that replaces the physical with the spiritual.[23] In his desire to replicate the sacramental drama, he has undervalued the sacrifice of Christ. Thus, at the metaphoric level, the ironic interplay between the self-created (and hence undermined) sacramental or recapitulative typology and its Christological antitype has created a space for the poem.

The bitter irony of the next poem, "The Sacrifice," makes the insufficiencies of the sacrificial altar the speaker has constructed especially clear. For the speaker is assuredly brought under the sweeping charge leveled by Christ on the cross in the opening stanza:

> OH all ye, who passe by, whose eyes and minde
> To worldly things are sharp, but to me blinde;
> To me, who took eyes that I might you finde:
> > Was ever grief like mine?

The effect produced by the rhetorical question, posed sixty-one times by the refrain in each stanza, is to undermine totally any hope that the speaker or reader might harbor about the sufficiency of human merit, human contrition, or human sacrifice.[24] The crucified Christ in Herbert's poem says nothing, but waits patiently to see "If stonie hearts will melt with gentle love" (l. 90). Such melting, of course, will not happen, for this "stonie rock" is lifeless and dry.

> Why, Caesar is their onely King, not I:
> He clave the stonie rock, when they were drie;
> But surely not their hearts, as I well trie:
> > Was ever grief like mine?

23. In his perceptive analysis of this poem, Fish has focused on its typographical prominence—Herbert "chose to throw the fact of authorship and of 'wit' or 'invention' in the reader's face" (Self-Consuming Artifacts, p. 207)—in order to argue that Herbert actually foregoes any claim to real authorship. My disagreement with Fish's position hinges on the belief that the classical altar Herbert evokes through the shape of the poem is the marker of a formal, physical structure outmoded by the new covenant. Also, this poem seems to be part of a sequence that challenges the reader's conception of the Christian life in order to redefine it. On the classical shape of the altar, see Rickey, Utmost Art, pp. 9–15.

24. Bell's analysis of the irony in "The Sacrifice," which undermines "the traditional participation in Christ's grief taught by Catholic meditation," would seem to support this reading ("'Setting Foot into Divinity,'" pp. 226–29).

This passage depends on the contrast between temporal and spiritual power and emphasizes that "stonie hearts" will only melt when the water from the true rock flows, making possible the palingenesis of baptism. These images establish further continuity with "The Altar," with temple-building, and with the central metaphor for ascent and regeneration in *The Temple*—the waters of life that flow from the heart back to God as a result of the infusion of grace. Since the dozen poems that follow "The Altar" obviously depict the crucial events in the triduum of Holy Week, culminating in the baptismal ceremonies of Easter Eve, and since the imagery of the waters of life from the lifeless stone is so prominent (as discussed in Chapter 3), it is instructive to examine these poems briefly in light of the Lenten *agon*.

If the titles of these poems and some of the key images are meant to evoke the typological drama of the exodus—as critics have noted—then we need to recognize that one form of the speaker's initiation into the church involves the struggle to submit to God's agency. Submitting to the already written text—allowing Christ to inscribe his own epistle on the stony heart—makes possible the speaker's admission to the mystical body of the church. In this way artistic creation is made parallel to sacramental re-creation. Following the polemical introduction posed by "The Altar" and the response made by Christ in "The Sacrifice," the remaining poems fall into three groups. The disparity between Christ's sacrifice and the speaker's meager efforts to imitate Christ sets up the next four poems ("The Thanksgiving," "The Reprisall," "The Agonie," and "The Sinner"), in which the poet challenges the adequacy of the speaker's conception of the Christian life as a preparation for the sacramental mysteries of Holy Week.[25] These poems give further evidence of the difficulty the speaker has in relinquishing his claims for authority over his life; he still hopes to recompense God for the atonement through pious works and through the artistry of his poems. When read from this perspective, these poems establish a connection between his ability to *write* and his hope to offer praiseworthy recompense. However, in a second group on the crucifixion and resurrection ("Good Friday," "Redemption," "Sepulchre," "Easter," and "Easter-wings"), he is confronted with his utter dependence on Christ's agency. Eventually, he learns to submit by asking Christ to *write* the sanctifying word on his heart. The two

25. For a more extensive analysis of these poems, see Strier, *Love Known,* pp. 49–60.

final poems on baptism then celebrate his participation in the typological drama of the sacraments, which constitutes the true representation he has desired all along.

The definitive statement made in the final line of "The Sacrifice,"
"Never was grief like mine," only has the effect of temporarily
checking the speaker's desire to *write*. For he begins "The Thanksgiving" by asking how he can participate in Christ's passion.

> Oh King of wounds! how shall I grieve for thee,
> > Who in all grief preventest me?
> Shall I weep bloud? why, thou hast wept such store
> > That all thy body was one doore.
> Shall I be scourged, flouted, boxed, sold?
> > 'Tis but to tell the tale is told.
>
> > > (ll. 3–8)

This opening is problematic: though it alludes to the inimitable
nature of Christ's grief and acknowledges that the tale is told, that
the story has already been written, the balance of the poem shows
his continuing efforts to imitate—in order to participate in—
Christ's passion.

> But how then shall I imitate thee, and
> > Copie thy fair, though bloudie hand?
> > > (ll. 15–16)

It is only when he tries to requite the suffering involved in the
atonement, to requite Christ in kind, that he begins to understand
his own insufficiencies.

> Then for thy passion—I will do for that—
> > Alas, my God, I know not what.
> > > (ll. 49–50)

The realization that he can do nothing in recompense for the passion or the life of Christ is the theme in the following poem, "The
Reprisall" (titled "The Second Thanks-giving" in the earlier Williams MS). Only by surrendering himself to the mystery of
Christ's unmerited love and by taking comfort in the necessity of
justification by faith alone can he hope for sanctification—"in thee I
will overcome / The man [that is, himself], who once against thee
fought" (ll. 15–16). The next poem, "The Agonie," directly attacks
the human impulse toward rationalism, particularly the own desire
to understand salvation in his own terms, when the appropriate
response is simply to submit to the mysteries of the atonement.

The conjunction of sin and love, given potent expression in the transformation of blood to wine as it flows sacramentally from the pierced side along with the waters of life, recalls the many references to the waters from the true rock in "The Sacrifice" (especially lines 21–23, 89–91, 121–23, 157–59, 169–71, and 245–47). The last poem in this first group, "The Sinner," reviews the past life of the speaker and, by placing the stony heart of the sinner before us, reintroduces the central metaphor of "The Altar." Having been confronted by the unmatchable potency of Christ's sacrifice, he acknowledges that his own efforts, described metaphorically as "quarries of pil'd vanities," are totally insufficient. He is recognizing the implications of the fact that "The spirit and good extract of my heart" (l. 10)—which I shall argue below was understood as an indication of spiritual and physical health and which constituted the antidote to the desiccated, stony heart—are negligible. Here at last, in a gesture that overturns the claims made for the speaker's own *writing* in "The Altar," he calls upon Christ to restore *Christ's own* image by writing in the speaker's heart.

> Yet Lord restore thine image, heare my call:
> And though my hard heart scarce to thee can grone,
> Remember that thou once didst write in stone.
>
> (ll. 12–14)

Together, these four poems serve to redefine the Christian life—by focusing on the inadequacies of works and contrition—to emphasize total dependence on grace.

The poems on the triduum of Easter that follow this redefinition of the Christian life celebrate the culmination of the Lenten *agon*. What is of particular interest here is the prominence of the typology of the waters of life associated with the rock of Horeb. Throughout the entire opening sequence, especially in "The Altar," the speaker's desire has been to help transform his stony heart into a "living stone," just as the desert rock was made to flow with living water. "Good Friday" develops further the connection between the metaphor of the stony heart brought to life and *writing*, by emphasizing that Christ transforms the Old Testament altar stone by *writing* on it with blood and possessing it with grace.

> Since bloud is fittest, Lord, to write
> Thy sorrows in, and bloudie fight;
> My heart hath store, write there, where in
> One box doth lie both ink and sinne. . . .

Sinne being gone, oh fill the place,
And keep possession with thy grace;
Lest sinne take courage and return,
And all the writings blot or burn.
(ll. 21–24, 29–32)

Here the speaker forgoes his desire to *write* by recognizing his utter dependence on Christ's inscribing his epistle on the heart to sanctify it. True representation, in other words, is accessible only when the speaker surrenders his (hoped for) active role in constructing a personal story for a passive role in the ongoing typological drama of the sacraments. The opening line of "Easter," which bids the heart to rise, at last signals the regeneration of the heart made possible by grace. This complements the ambiguities of the preceding poem "Sepulchre," which depends on a complex typological relationship of Christ's rocky tomb and man's hard heart, both of which are transformed by the presence of the "pure rock" within (l. 10).[26] "Easter-wings" concludes this group by reminding us that sanctification is possible only "if I imp my wing on thine" (l. 19), that is, through sacramental recapitulation of Christological types.

As we have seen, the readings for the Anglican service during Lent give prominence to the recapitulative symbolism of the source of mankind's regeneration, the waters of life flowing from the rock of Horeb, reenacted traditionally on Easter Eve in the baptism of the catechumens. Having instructed his reader in one of the dark mysteries of the church in this sequence of poems, Herbert then paid tribute to the only genuine participation in Christ's passion available to mankind—through the sacramental recapitulation of baptism. Strangely, neither of these poems celebrates baptism with the sense of relief, release, and joy we might expect after the "spiritual Conflicts" of the liturgical sequence. Our attention instead shifts in "H. Baptisme (I)" away from the festivities of Easter to introduce a Christian wayfarer who understands more fully his imperfect sanctification. Like the pilgrim who fixes his eye on his goal to ward off the temptation of stopping along the way, the speaker, to avoid despair when he views his sins, similarly fixes his eye on the waters "above the heav'ns, whose spring and vent / Is in my deare Redeemers pierced side" (ll. 5–6). Here he indicates that the temporal source for regeneration is the "vent" in Christ's side that produced the sacraments, the true rock split open; further-

---

26. Benet, *Secretary of Praise*, pp. 36–39, has explained this typology fully.

more, he recognizes both that he will inevitably fall away into sin again (and thus will always need grace) and that he will only be truly sanctified in the fulness of time when he can drink of the water "above the heav'ns." Already the speaker has traveled some distance from his level of awareness in "The Altar," when he took such pleasure in having created a formal, physical structure as a demonstration of his worthiness and contrition. Throughout the opening sequence he has gradually learned about his own inadequacies and of his misconception of the Christian life; having been thus initiated into the mysteries of his faith, however, he is now prepared for his life's pilgrimage.

The Desiccated Heart and the Dissipating Soul

Even though the speaker has learned a hard lesson about human insufficiency in the opening sequence of poems, his impulse toward self-representation and his other natural weaknesses continue to work against him. Hence, he will have many "spiritual Conflicts" and will need grace continually. The rest of the poems in *The Temple* show that a greater understanding of how the typological story of Scripture intersects his own story will lead to true self-knowledge and will permit genuine self-representation. By examining the dominant image used to present the descent of grace, the waters of life, we can better understand how Herbert helped control the implicit narrative by developing a metaphor to emphasize Christ's role in "temple-building." Using images drawn from the complex typology of the waters of life from Scripture, Herbert depicted the stony heart made fleshy by an outpouring of Christ's "dew" and the "river of living water" that will flow from the regenerate heart in return (as promised in John 4:14 and 7:38).

As I have argued above, the opening sequence of poems (which culminates with the baptismal poems) as part of the celebration of Easter, only serves to introduce the Christians' dilemma: even though the believers receive grace and are sanctified (once they surrender their personal stories in favor of typological ones), they are still sinners at heart and so will fall away from grace. The "spiritual Conflicts" of *The Temple* stem from the fact that the speaker's renewal is, in a sense, only momentary. If this were not the case, it would be difficult to reconcile the range of moods and experiences in the poetry, especially after the speaker's inclusion in

the mystical body of the church at baptism. The poems immediately following the Lenten sequence, especially "Nature," establish the shortcomings of human nature and hence the inevitability
of imperfect sanctification:

> Full of rebellion, I would die,
> Or fight, or travell, or denie
> That thou hast ought to do with me.
>   O tame my heart;
>   It is thy highest art
> To captivate strong holds to thee.
>   (ll. 1–6)

Throughout the poems, the speaker discovers that his rebellious
heart is forever becoming stony and that his soul is dissipating
because of its spiritual aridity; hence, the need for the waters of life
is implicitly being evoked.

Some critics have asserted that the many references to the "infusion" of the waters of grace should be understood as "mock phys-
icality"—that is, the vehicle for the metaphor is empty or unimportant—since the poet relies instead on the experience of being loved
as the most adequate way of rendering God's relationship to the
regenerate. "The reformers insisted that grace was not a quality or
substance imparted to the soul but rather the experience of a change
in God's *attitude*. It was not to be spoken of in terms of 'infusion'
but in terms of relationship. It designated, for the reformers, not a
qualitas but a *voluntas*."[27] Though the infusion of grace to soften the
stony heart is clearly a *metaphor*, Herbert's penchant for it ought to
suggest that it served an important function in his poetry. The
mysterious operation of grace, after all, can only be understood and
articulated through such metaphors. Moreover, since Herbert's allusions to the "desiccated" heart and the "dissipating" soul (two
important corollaries to the stony heart) pointed to an actual physical condition, this metaphor is not so empty. Renaissance physicians believed that the diseased heart could not produce the vital
"spirits" necessary for spiritual health. In "Even-song," for example, the speaker proclaims that his heart is so hard that his soul has
dissipated into "bubbles, balls of winde" (l. 14). To dismiss this
way of putting the matter as mere metaphor obscures Herbert's
belief in the transformation wrought by grace: the "spirits" of the
regenerate heart may not always heal the body, but grace does in

27. Strier, *Love Known*, p. 139.

fact heal the soul. The physiological basis for the poems dealing
with the desiccated heart has received scant attention from Herbert's modern readers, despite its significance in *The Temple*. In
many poems Herbert described how sin turns the fleshy heart into a
heart of stone in order to articulate metaphorically the believer's
dependence on Christ, who, as the fountain of living waters, provides the antidote to spiritual aridity.

The lyric "Nature," placed prominently after the opening sequence, summarizes the features of the desiccated heart and the
dissipating soul. In the first and last stanzas, the speaker pleads for
God to intervene and tame his rebellious heart because he has discovered that he cannot control his defective human nature. His
heart has become so stony, so "saplesse" (l. 16), even after his
baptism and sanctification, that it is truly a sepulchre. He feels so
unworthy of the new dispensation that he wants to begin anew
with the old. The middle stanza describes the effects he fears his
stony-heartedness will have on his soul.

> If thou shalt let this venome lurk,
> And in suggestions fume and work,
> My soul will turn to bubbles straight,
> > And thence by kinde
> > Vanish into a winde,
> Making thy workmanship deceit.
> > > > > (ll. 7–12)

His rebellious nature, acting as a "venome" in his heart, will
"fume" with temptations or incitements to evil. As a result, he fears
his soul will "dissipate" or turn into a bubble and vanish like the
wind, unless Christ softens his heart again.

The notion of the soul dissipating is not simply metaphorical
hyperbole in the Renaissance. According to Galenic physiology,
when the heart (the seat of the soul) fails to produce enough purified "spirits," both body and soul are impaired. Spiritual conditions were thought to affect the health of the body, and, in turn, the
diseased heart could not produce the "spirits" necessary to govern
the understanding or the will. The notion of "spirits" as intermediary between body and soul thus forms the basis for the metaphorical "dryness" of the speaker's heart. What modern readers have
assumed to be mere metaphor was, therefore, a standard way of
understanding the correspondence between body and soul in the
Renaissance.

The notion of "spirits" as an intermediary to the soul derives in part from the Hebrew term used to denote spiritual reality, *ruach*, generally translated as *spirit* in English (in Greek πνευμα, in Latin *spiritus*), which comes from a Semitic root *ruah*, to breathe or blow.[28] The primary signification of *ruach* is "air in motion" as wind or breath. Because of the connection between breath in the body and the phenomenon of life energy, *ruach* was considered life itself, the presence of the deity in humans. In Genesis 2:7, for example, the soul is imparted to Adam by God's breath. Greek physicians—notably Galen—later developed the notion of the "spirits," a vaporous substance dispersed by the liver, heart, and brain, to account for the vital interaction of πνευμα with the body.

Until the late seventeenth century, when Harvey's theories gained widespread acceptance, the heart was likened to a furnace (instead of Harvey's fountain). Heat was vitally important to the body, and the heart, as the body's "furnace," produced it in great quantities. Harvey himself still regarded blood as "the primary seat of the soul; the element in which, as in a fountain head, the heat first and most abounds and flourishes; from whose influxive heat all the other parts of the body are cherished, and obtain their life."[29] Since the time of Galen, blood was thought to be produced in a crude form in the liver, then rarefied and aerated in the heart, where it then passed to other parts of the body as nourishment. None of the blood ever recirculated to the heart; the liver simply produced more as it was needed. Furthermore, the liver, the heart, and the brain each produced its own kind of "spirits" to enable each organ to perform the body's basic physiological processes.[30]

28. See the article on "Spirit," *New Catholic Encyclopedia,* vol. 13.

29. William Harvey, *The Works of William Harvey,* p. 377.

30. Galen was the first to describe the production of blood and "spirits." The process began with digestion (called *concoction*), which altered food into a usable form, *chyle.* From the intestines *chyle* traveled to the liver where it was changed to "venous blood" and imbued with "natural spirits." Some of this "venous blood" was used to sustain the lower body; the rest went to the right ventricle by way of the vena cava. Once in the right ventricle the "venous blood" was purified and made more spiritous by the intense, furnace-like heat of the heart. The lungs rarefied the air and the subtler part of it passed, with the now aerated blood, into the left ventricle via the pulmonary vein. Here it mixed with still more spiritous blood that had seeped through a membrane connecting the ventricles. The innate heat of the heart then completed the metamorphosis of spiritous blood into "vital spirits." The arteries distributed these "spirits" to the body along with arterial blood, though some of it was further transformed into "animal spirits" by the *rete mirabile* at the base of the brain. The most helpful accounts of Galenic physiology are as follows: Galen, *On the Usefulness of the Parts of the Body*; Rudolph E. Siegel, *Galen's System of*

These "spirits" (natural, vital, and animal) were believed to be the intermediary between body and soul, and to control both the natural, physical functions (nutrition, augmentation, etc.) and actions attributed to the soul (the ability to move, to understand, or to will). Of the three, the vital "spirits" produced in the heart were the most important:

> This spirit whilest it shineth in his brightnes and spredeth it selfe through all the Theater of the body, as the Sunne over the earth, it blesseth all partes with joy and jolitie and dies them with a Rosie colour; but on the contrary when it is retracted intercepted or extinguished, all things become horred wanne and pale and finally doe utterly perish.[31]

Like the sun, the vital "spirits" convey the innate heat of the heart to the rest of the body by means of a subtle vapor in the blood.

Crooke's description of the ill effects on the body when the "spirits" are in some way impaired underscores a Renaissance adaptation of a Galenic principle crucial to understanding Herbert's use of "spirits" in *The Temple*—the relationship of spiritual and physical health. Health, as most readers may recall, was thought to depend on the proper balance or *temperament* of the three humours produced in the liver (yellow bile, black bile, and venous blood) and the phlegm produced in the respiratory passages. The heart regulated the body by its vital heat and "radical moisture" (another term for "spirits").[32] The temperament of the humours also affected the soul, as the French encyclopedist La Primaudaye explained:

> We see also by experience, that there is great agreement between the qualities and temperature of the body, and the affections of the soule: insomuch that as the bodies of men are compounded of the qualities of heate, colde, moisture, and drienesse, so among the affections some are hote, others colde, some moist, others drye, and some mingled of these divers qualities. So that every one is most subject to those affections that come neerest to the nature, temperature, & complexion of his bodie.[33]

Physiology and Medicine; Thomas S. Hall, *Ideas of Life and Matter*; and Owsei Temkin, *Galenism: Rise and Decline of a Medical Philosophy*.

31. Helkiah Crooke, *Mikrokosmographia: A Description of the Body of Man*, p. 410.

32. Our notion of bodily "temperature" is the descendent of this Galenic principle. See W. P. D. Wightman, *Science and the Renaissance*, 1:217–19.

33. Pierre de La Primaudaye, *The Second Part of the French Academy*, pp. 230–31.

The complexion of the body thus causes a corresponding affection of the soul. For example, the affection of joy is hot and moist; sorrow, on the other hand, is cold and dry. "They that have a soft and tender heart, receive more easily the impression of joy. . . . And on the other side, they that have hard and cold hearts, receive sorrowe and griefe very soone, and retaine it long, as appeareth in melancholy and melancholike persons."[34]

Conversely, the condition of the soul can produce a corresponding ill effect on the body.

> And as the affections follow the temperature and complexion of the bodie, so they for their parts have great vertue and power over the body. Therefore we see, that joy is as it were a medicine to the body, and foode to the naturall heate and moisture, in which two qualities life chiefly consisteth, as we have already heard. For it greatly preserveth and increaseth them: forasmuch as it strengtheneth the animall and naturall vertues, stirreth up the spirits, helpeth digestion, and generally profiteth the habite and disposition of the whole body. For the heart thereby sendeth with the blood, much natural heate, and more spirits unto all parts of the body. By meanes whereof the members are watred and moistned by the humiditie contained in the fountaine of blood: whereupon it followeth, that all the parts increase in bignesse and waxe fat.[35]

Thus, joy (the affection of the morally healthy state) is an important medicine for the body. Physicians were wont to exhort the ill to be merry and to avoid sorrows, which were "cold" and "dry" and acted as consumptives because they inhibited the production of the "spirits."[36] Many works in the Renaissance, ranging from Elyot's *Castel of Helth* (1541) to Burton's *Anatomy of Melancholy* (1621), dealt with the intricate connection among spiritual, moral, and physical conditions.[37] It was thought to be as appropriate to

---

34. La Primaudaye, *The Second Part of the French Academy*, pp. 231.

35. La Primaudaye, *The Second Part of the French Academy*, pp. 231.

36. When these "spirits" are weakened, death could result. La Primaudaye, *The Second Part of the French Academy*, pp. 231, stated, "the vitall virtue and her companions being weakened, the lively colour of the face waxeth wanne and pale, and in a manner vanisheth cleane away: and so consequently the whole bodie becommeth leane and consumeth, as if it tooke no nourishment, yea death oftentimes followeth thereupon." Death, in fact, was often thought to be a "dissolution" of these spirits.

37. Sir Thomas Elyot, *The Castel of Helth*, fol. 64ᵛ, wrote that "dolour or hevynesse of mynde" was the greatest enemy to life because it exhausted the natural heat and moisture, thereby debilitating the body. To remedy the "Ingratytude" that caused melancholy, he urged the wholesome counsel of the Bible and herbs, both of

cure a malady with a regimen of prayer and contrition as with
herbs, and just as natural to expect physical distemperament from a
disaffection of the soul. Herbert devoted an entire poem, "The H.
Communion," to the parallels between physical and spiritual regeneration; it is a poem
that serves to establish and also to define the notion of the "spirits"
of the heart as a minor but significant part of *The Temple*. By
focusing on the accompanying grace, he emphasized primarily the
spiritual feasting involved in communion; however, he preserved
the full mystery of the sacrament by also noting the transformation
effected on the "spirits" of the heart as the physiological analogue
to the transformation effected by grace. In other words, the elements
that stand visibly for the invisible grace are not simply symbols
but are literally part of the transformative potency of the sacrament
itself.

> Not in rich furniture, or fine aray,
> Nor in a wedge of gold,
> Thou, who for me wast sold,
> To me dost now thy self convey;
> For so thou should'st without me still have been,
> Leaving within me sinne:
>
> But by the way of nourishment and strength
> Thou creep'st into my breast;
> Making thy way my rest,
> And thy small quantities my length;
> Which spread their forces into every part,
> Meeting sinnes force and art.
>
> Yet can these not get over to my soul,
> Leaping the wall that parts
> Our souls and fleshy hearts;
> But as th' outworks, they may controll
> My rebel-flesh, and carrying thy name,
> Affright both sinne and shame.
>
> Onely thy grace, which with these elements comes,
> Knoweth the ready way,

which have "the propertie to expelle melancolyke humours, and to comfort and
kepe lyvely the spirites, whyche have their proper habytation in the harte of man,
and moderate nourishynge of the naturall heate and humour callyd radicall, whiche
is the base or foundation, wherupon the lyfe of man standeth, and that fayling, lyfe
falleth in ruine, & the body is dissolved."

> And hath the privie key,
> Op'ning the souls most subtile rooms;
> While those to spirits refin'd, at doore attend
> Dispatches from their friend.
>
> (ll. 1–24)

Much of the poem can be understood as a metaphoric explanation
of the speaker's declaration that in the sacrament Christ nourishes
the soul by first entering into his heart. The real efficacy of the
sacrament is clearly the inward reality, the grace that accompanies
the bread and wine. Without grace the elements cannot "get over to
my soul," which Herbert described as "Leaping the wall that parts
/ Our souls and fleshy hearts." In healing and preserving the heart,
grace restores the soul to spiritual health. At the same time, however, the poet insists that the outward signs, the bread and wine,
are "to spirits refin'd"; that is, the physical elements are changed
into nutriment for the body's most subtle parts. In alluding to this
medical commonplace, Herbert emphasized that the sacrament involves a dual transformation: grace nourishes the soul directly and
the eucharistic elements nourish "spirits" that then serve as inter-
mediaries between body and soul. Herbert's "spirits" are the
friends of the soul but are nevertheless controlled by it—"at doore
attend / Dispatches from their friend." The soul, restored to health,
can use these "spirits" to conserve and control the body.[38]

If "The H. Communion" provides us with a description of the
ideal correspondence between physical and spiritual health, then
other, more recondite lines in *The Temple* can also be given sharper
focus. These allusive passages are metaphoric descriptions of decay,
yet they have as their underpinning the physiology of the "spirits"
of the heart. For example, in "The Sinner," when the speaker looks

38. A curious corroboration of the physiological workings of grace can be found
in Augustin Marlorat, *A Catholike exposition upon the Revelation of Saint John*, fol.
305ᵛ–306ʳ, who explained that the crystal fountain signifies more than baptismal
waters or grace. It is "the force of the doctrine of Chrysts spirit: according as John
speketh, John 4. v. 10, 7. v. 38. For the hearts [spirite] of all the godly be watered
with the streame of Gods word, so as they being clenzed by faith, are acceptable to
god for Jesus Christes sake." I have bracketed "spirite" because of some confusion
on the printer's part. "Spirite" appears as the catchword at the bottom of fol. 305ᵛ,
but does not in fact begin the next page ("of" is the first word on fol. 306ʳ). Whether
Marlorat intended to refer to the "spirits" of the heart that are watered with the
stream of God's word, or to refer more generally to the soul of the believer that is
infused with the spirit of Christ's grace, can not be determined; both readings would
of course be appropriate. Copies in the University of Illinois Rare Book Room, the
British Library, and the Bodleian all contain this textual irregularity.

inside his hard heart, all he finds are "quarries of pil'd vanities,"
which far outweigh the few "shreds of holinesse."

> In so much dregs the quintessence is small:
>   The spirit and good extract of my heart
>   Comes to about the many hundred part.
> Yet Lord restore thine image, heare my call:
>   And though my hard heart scarce to thee can grone,
>   Remember that thou once didst write in stone.
>
> (ll. 9–14)

As the final couplet reminds us, a portrayal of the stoniness of the
heart is the point toward which this sonnet moves; but Herbert
linked cause with effect when he wrote that the rebellious heart of
the sinner cannot effectively produce "The spirit and good extract
of my heart," which he also equated with "shreds of holinesse." As
a result, the soul dissipates metaphorically and the heart turns to
stone or dust.

"The Sinner" is typical of the manner in which Herbert used the
speaker's inability to produce "radical moisture" as a means of
amplifying the metaphor of the stony heart. In "Affliction (IV)" he
alluded to "spirits" as the *knot* that ties body to soul, just as Donne
did in "The Exstasie."[39] The speaker's thoughts wound his heart
and his soul; as a result, he has lost control. It seems likely that the
noxious vapours of the night (l. 24) that must be dispersed by the
sunlight are at least the metaphoric equivalents of the weakened
heart's "spirits."

> All my attendants are at strife,
>   Quitting their place
>   Unto my face:
> Nothing performs the task of life:
>   The elements are let loose to fight,
>   And while I live, trie out their right.
> Oh help, my God! let not their plot
>   Kill them and me,
>   And also thee,
> Who art my life: dissolve the knot,
>   As the sunne scatters by his light
>   All the rebellions of the night.
>
> (ll. 13–24)

---

39. Donne also calls the "spirits" that "subtile knot," *Complete Poetry*, p. 132, ll.
61–64.

The speaker's great fear throughout The Church poems is that his heart has become petrified and his soul arid. In "Repentance," the heart of the sinner rebuked by Christ will "Pine, and decay, / And drop away" because of the bitterness that fills it (ll. 28–29). The Williams MS original of these lines is even more explicit: the heart will

> Melt & consume
> To smoke & fume
> fretting to death our other parts.
> (ll. 28–30)

In "Church-monuments," "the blast of deaths incessant motion," which will turn the body into a heap of dust, is "Fed with the exhalation of our crimes" (ll. 1–6). Sin here produces an *exhalation* or dry wind that is linked to the dryness of the heart. In "Lent," the speaker makes an even stronger claim that temperance leads to "Quick thoughts and motions" while over-indulgence leads to "sluttish fumes, / Sowre exhalations, and dishonest rheumes" (ll. 19–24). And in "Even-song," he marvels that God still favors him when his attempts at discharging his debt end in dissipation, "bubbles, balls of winde" (ll. 9–14).

These references to the effects of the speaker's spiritual health on the production of "spirits" in the heart form a small part of the central metaphor in *The Temple*, the heart of stone. Beginning with "The Altar" and continuing throughout the volume, the speaker acknowledges that his heart has become so desiccated that it resembles the condition of mankind under the old dispensation and must be transformed by grace into a living stone, a fleshy heart. Sin turns "flesh to stone" ("The H. Communion," l. 29) and withers the heart by turning it into a "pile of dust" ("Longing," ll. 8, 41). Galenic physiology provides a concretizing analogue to the texts from Ezekiel and elsewhere that describe this spiritual phenomenon and a metaphor for elaborating its effect.

As a metaphor for spiritual decay, the desiccated heart had considerable flexibility and potency for Herbert. First, it provided him with a rich vocabulary with which to describe the erosion of the living heart, as it withers, becomes more "dry," and turns to stone. Though it is safe to assume that Herbert did not fear the actual petrification of his heart, he nonetheless made considerable use of this metaphoric condition as the *terminus ad quem* of spiritual decay. Second, it emphasized an organic, physiological connection between physical and spiritual health. The healthy soul contributes to the total health of the body by maintaining the proper balance between the heart's innate heat and its "radical moisture." Although grace did not necessarily bring complete physical regeneration—Herbert had a notably sickly constitution—he did believe in the regenerative powers of grace for the soul. Third, since the biblical promise to provide a fountain of living waters to believers established the connection between spiritual decay and aridity, Herbert could develop his metaphor as part of the biblical waters of life, especially the promise that living water will flow from the heart of the believer (John 4:14, 7:38). The notion of the regenerated "spirits" of the heart is one way this promise could be fulfilled. When we recall that the sacraments, as represented by the water and blood flowing from Christ's side, were thought actually to flow from his heart,[40] Herbert's wit seems even more remarkable: an infusion of grace—the water (or "spirits") and blood of Christ's heart—will "Bedew, embalme, and overrunne" the speaker's heart ("The Glance," l. 7) and enable it to flow with the "spirits" necessary for spiritual health. Last, the ambiguities of the notion of "spirits"—used sometimes literally, as in "The H. Communion," sometimes metaphorically—allowed Herbert the flexibility to intimate, under the guise of metaphor, that as a result of the regeneration of the soul the waters of life may flow into and out of the heart as "spirits." Thus, the "spirits" of the heart provided Herbert both with a way to describe the hidden effects of grace and with a means of deferring to the ultimate mystery involved.

Herbert did not often portray the regenerate soul; he was more apt to present moments in which the soul falters and dissipates. But in "The Sacrifice" he used the metaphor of the "melting soul" to characterize Christ's perfect spiritual health. Because of human insufficiency, Christ's soul will *melt* and *bleed* to become a "Balsome" for mankind and the universe.

> Therefore my soul melts, and my hearts deare treasure
> Drops bloud (the onely beads) my words to measure:
> *O let this cup passe, if it be thy pleasure:*
>   Was ever grief like mine?
> These drops being temper'd with a sinners tears
> A Balsome are for both the Hemispheres:

---

40. John Trapp, *Commentary or Exposition upon the four Evangelists and the Acts of the Apostles*, 3:135–36, explained that the water and blood (John 19:34) came from the *pericardium*, "which nature hath filled with water to cool the heat of the heart."

> Curing all wounds, but mine; all, but my fears:
> Was ever grief like mine?
>
> (ll. 21–28)

Christ's "melting" soul is the perfect image of sacrifice, whose soul and heart melts and bleeds to provide the waters of life. One of Christ's stated purposes in the poem is to determine "If stonie hearts will melt with gentle love" (l. 90), and the irony is that none can without the grace that his sacrifice is now providing. Thus, the speaker is always dependent on infusions of grace from above.

The Waters of Life in *The Temple*

Herbert made full use of the typology of the waters of life to describe the regeneration of the sinner through the descent of grace and the ascent of the soul to God. Using a common biblical trope, he depicted Christ as the fulfillment of the promise to provide a fountain of living waters. In the narration of the speaker's personal experience of these Christological types, Herbert exploited the nuances of his biblical sources. While the speaker longs in some poems for the healing waters that descend to embalm the heart, he also must endure the "raging waters" of affliction that plague the imperfectly sanctified. Because the speaker wavers between assurance and fear, the comforting images of hope—the dew that fructifies the soul, the balm that moistens the heart, the sun that calms the storms—point beyond themselves to a future consummation. True closure for the narrative, which he is discovering has already been created for him, is accessible only in the world to come. By examining this metaphoric structure in terms of its constituent elements—Christological, sacramental, and eschatological types of the waters of life—we can gain insight into the way Herbert's complex typological wit is employed in *The Temple*.

Herbert referred to the Christological types of the waters of life so often that his readers scarcely are aware of how frequently the poet invokes their metaphoric power. The source of the waters ultimately derives from God, "the Spring & Fountain of all Goodness" (letter to Nicholas Ferrar, p. 379).[41] Likening God's inexpressible plenitude to an endlessly flowing spring or fountain seemed an apt metaphor to render the ineffable in the Renais-

41. In "Miserie" he also designates God as "The spring, whence all things flow" (l. 60).

sance.[42] As the fulfillment of the many Old Testament promises to provide a source of living water for the believers, Christ as the antitype is sometimes represented in conjunction with such types as the fountain in Eden, the rock of Horeb, and the *fons signatus*. Since the true source of the sacraments is the wound in Christ's side, the most common manifestation of living water is the dew that falls to sustain the faithful. Grace for Herbert always drops from heaven as a gentle rain or dew, as we read in "An Offering":

> There is a balsome, or indeed a bloud,
> Dropping from heav'n, which doth cleanse and close
> All sorts of wounds; of such strange force it is.

(ll. 19–21)

The insistent refrain in "Grace" is to let grace "Drop from above," the primary image of which is the dew that makes supple the stony heart. Dew is sometimes replaced with gentle rain as the means of vivification, for dew was thought to be actually a gentle rainfall. In "The Flower," therefore, the speaker compares his "shrivel'd heart" to a flower that has since "recover'd greennesse"; now, after the long winter frost, he can "once more smell the dew and rain" that makes all things fruitful.[43] This falling dew is synonymous with Christ's blood, or, put another way, the waters of life are suffused with the blood of the atonement.[44] And so the speaker after the simple called "All-heal" that cleanses all wounds and drops from heaven as "a balsome, or indeed a bloud" ("An Offering," ll. 19–24). In "The Sacrifice" the "Balsome" that will cure all wounds is a mixture of Christ's melting soul and bleeding heart (ll. 21–28), which flows from its antitype, the true rock (ll. 121–24).

Herbert also made reference to Christ's Word as the fountain of

42. Thomas Taylor, *Meditations from the Creatures*, pp. 100–101, wrote: "The sea is like unto God, an inexhaust[ible] fountaine; for when so many flouds and rivers are run out, as so many thousand millions of creatures enjoy; it is not diminished, but remaineth in the same fulnesse: for this is the river of God that is full of waters, *Psal.* 65. So the Lord is a sea of grace; the more he giveth, himselfe hath never the lesse."

43. On the "garden" metaphor in *The Temple*, see Stanley Stewart, *The Enclosed Garden: The Tradition and the Image in Seventeenth-Century Poetry*, pp. 52–59; Lewalski, *Protestant Poetics*, pp. 307–9; and Frances M. Malpezzi, "Thy Cross, My Bower: The Greening of the Heart," in *"Too Rich to Clothe the Sunne,"* ed. Summers and Pebworth, pp. 89–100.

44. It is common in Renaissance catechisms to find the efficacy of the sacraments attributed solely to Christ's blood. E.g., William Attersoll, *The New Covenant, or, a Treatise of the Sacraments*, p. 153, argued that the outward washing of the body in baptism "*Representeth the inward cleansing of the soule by the blood of Jesus Christ.*"

living waters. In the poem "The Jews," he contrasted an Old Testament promise with its New Testament fulfillment by depicting Christ as the "sweet sap . . . purloin'd" from the Jews, who are now to be pitied for their loss.

> Poore nation, whose sweet sap and juice
> Our cyens have purloin'd, and left you drie:
> Whose streams we got by the Apostles sluce,
> And use in baptisme, while ye pine and die.
>
> (ll. 1–4)

The reference to living water and baptism is familiar enough, but the one to the "Apostles sluce," though also conventional, is not so well known. An early Christian tradition associated the four rivers of paradise and their source, Christ the fountain of living waters, with Ecclesia and the four evangelists, who revealed the plan of salvation through the sacrifice commemorated in the sacraments.[45] This medieval tradition emphasized the role of Ecclesia in dispensing the waters of life (particularly through baptism but also in the water mixed with wine in the communion rite). A Protestant, on the other hand, would regard Scripture itself, especially the four Gospels, as the "sluce" that purveys new life to the believers. Indeed, Herbert said of Scripture, "Thou art all health, health thriving till it make / A full eternitie," and he also designated it the "well" of living waters ("The H. Scriptures [I]," ll. 5–6, 9–10).

Like most Protestants of his time, Herbert was especially interested in the "application" of these Christological types. As the foregoing examples have shown, he used Christological types of the waters of life conventionally, but when depicting the way in which the typological story of Scripture became his own, he was far more creative in his imitation of the traditions. We have already followed Herbert's most creative adaptation of the metaphor of the waters of life above, through which he used Galenic physiology to present the effects of grace on the individual; the production of "spirits" in the heart becomes a sign of spiritual health (fulfilling literally and metaphorically the Johannine promise of living water flowing from the heart of the believer). Thus, the believer, through the agency of Christ, can truly become a fountain of living water in imitation of Christ. Herbert also used the sacramental participation in the waters of life to develop the notion of the circularity of water

45. The fullest account of the traditions of the rivers of paradise is Paul A. Underwood, "The Fountain of Life in MSS. of the Gospels," pp. 41–138.

as an image of union with God. The waters that descend to revivify mankind will, like all springing or living water, return to their sourcc in a grand recirculation. But the wished-for ascent is inevitably frustrated and the speaker must wait for a future consummation; this frustration prepares for the eschatological dimension of the metaphor of the waters of life treated directly in other poems.

The water of baptism and the host and wine of communion constitute the clearest sacramental participation or recapitulation of the atonement for the believer. The wine is said to make the communicant take wing and ascend toward heaven. [46]

> When I had forgot my birth,
>   And on earth
> In delights of earth was drown'd;
> God took bloud, and needs would be
>   Spilt with me,
> And so found me on the ground.
>
> Having rais'd me to look up,
>   In a cup
> Sweetly he doth meet my taste.
> But I still being low and short,
>   Farre from court,
> Wine becomes a wing at last.
>
> For with it alone I flie
>   To the skie:
> Where I wipe mine eyes, and see
> What I seek, for what I sue;
>   Him I view,
> Who hath done so much for me.
>   ("The Banquet," ll. 31–48)

Like the water with which it is mixed, the blood moistens the desiccated heart and fills the soul with "sweetness," allowing it to ascend back to God. That Christ's passion should result in such sweetness was a mystery in which Herbert delighted: "Love is that liquour sweet and most divine, / Which my God feels as bloud; but

46. Heather A. R. Asals, *Equivocal Predication: George Herbert's Way to God*, pp. 46–51, has argued that Herbert is employing the *res terrena & coelestis* trope to join the earthly and the heavenly parts of the sacrament: "Such 'Relation,' held together by 'Metonymy of the effect,' structures the poetic ellipsis of Herbert's 'The Banquet' as the speaker travels fearlessly between the *relatum* and the *correlatum* of the wine and blood" (p. 50).

I as wine" ("The Agonie," ll. 17–18). He developed this conceit of Christ as a pressed cluster of grapes here and in "The Bag," where the idea of circularity is added. As Rosemund Tuve first pointed out, in "The Bag" he probably was punning on the double meaning of *saccus* as both purse and bag for straining wine. The wound in Christ's side becomes a post-bag or mail pouch to carry requests back to God, just as it is the source of sacramental wine produced in the wine press of his passion.[47] This pun introduces the notion of human participation, albeit a passive participation, in divine circularity.

But for Herbert's speaker, this hope is usually frustrated. The distinguishing characteristic of the regenerate, according to Strier,[48] is their awareness of the obduracy of their hearts. Thus, the speaker in "Repentance," for example, who has confessed his sins, still experiences his unworthiness and insufficiencies as *wormwood* "Which thou hast pour'd into my soul" (l. 20). He experiences affliction, similar to that of Christ's agony in the garden, as the sighs and tears of a violent storm. Such metaphoric storms of contrition have the power of moving God, as we learn in "The Storm."

> If as the windes and waters here below
> Do flie and flow,
> My sighs and tears as busie were above;
> Sure they would move
> And much affect thee, as tempestuous times
> Amaze poore mortals, and object their crimes.
>
> Starres have their storms, ev'n in a high degree,
> As well as we.
> A throbbing conscience spurred by remorse
> Hath a strange force:
> It quits the earth, and mounting more and more
> Dares to assault thee, and besiege thy doore.
>
> There it stands knocking, to thy musicks wrong,
> And drowns the song.

47. Tuve, *A Reading of George Herbert*, pp. 127–30.
48. On this point Strier, *Love Known*, p. 16, cites John Downame, *The Christian Warfare against the Devill, World, and Flesh*, p. 230a: "The deare children of God do oftentimes see and feele to their great grief, their hardness of heart. Yea, in truth, this kind of hardness of heart is incident unto them alone." Unregenerate men, "though their hearts are most hard and obdurate . . . do not discerne" their condition.

> Glorie and honour are set by, till it
>   An answer get.
> Poets have wrong'd poore storms: such dayes are best;
> They purge the aire without, within the breast.
>
>   (ll. 1–18)

Metaphorically, the speaker's throbbing conscience (imaged as sighs and tears) is so great that these exhalations will ascend to the heavens. What he hopes for is some intervention by God that would end his suffering by causing a violent storm to discharge the atmosphere. Meteorologically, a sufficient quantity of vapors would condense into a thick cloud, once they had ascended into the colder middle region of the atmosphere. Some source of heat—the rays of the sun or a hot wind—was necessary to transform the cloud into a purging rain. The "answer" the speaker seeks is the agency of the sun/Son, who can assuage his sufferings.

Herbert employed a similar metaphor in "The Answer" to rebut those who chastise his impetuosity, for the speaker likens himself to a vapor that tries to ascend and fails.

> As a young exhalation, newly waking,
> Scorns his first bed of dirt, and means the sky;
> But cooling by the way, grows pursie and slow,
> And setling to a cloud, doth live and die
> In that dark state of tears: to all, that so
>   Show me, and set me, I have one reply,
>   Which they that know the rest, know more then I.
>
>   (ll. 8–14)

Those who would deter him from attempting again because he has failed in the past are answered somewhat covertly in the couplet. As a "young exhalation," he hopes he will be aided in his attempts by the sun/Son, who can elevate him heavenward. He defies those who think his attempts are futile because he knows that he can rely on the sun, even if he must suffer for a while in this "dark state of tears." One Renaissance theologian used similar images of pure and impure water to explain that Christians must often endure bitterness in this life. Just as the "sea of glass [is] mingled with fire" (Rev. 15:2) at the apocalypse, mankind is torn between heaven and hell:

> Such then is the estate of the world, that nothing is in it without a mixture. In heaven *there is a pure River of the Water of Life*: in Hell, *there is wine of wrath without mixture, in the cup of Gods indignation*, is it powred forth: But in the earth, *there is a Sea mingled with fire*: there is

joy in Heaven without sorrow; there is griefe in Hell without comfort; in this life no state without mixture.[49]

In "The Sacrifice," Christ describes this "mixed" state as "the raging waters" of his affliction (l. 95). This image recalls the ambiguity associated with water in the Old Testament, its potential to destroy (symbolized by the struggle with the monster of the deep) and to regenerate. Thus, the gentle waters of grace are frequently evoked to pacify these raging waters. Or, alternatively, Christ as a figure of the sun is called upon to calm these metaphoric storms (for example, in "The Storm" or "The Answer") and in "Affliction (IV)" where he entreats God to purge his spiritual disaffection (that is, his chaotic bodily "spirits"): "As the sunne scatters by his light / All the rebellions of the night" (ll. 23–24). Only the Son can calm such storms.

Herbert could not accept the sufficiency of human contrition, but the tears said to flow from the contrite heart, mixed with the "Balsome" of Christ's blood, could remedy affliction.[50] As Benjamin Keach asserted,

> Christ, the Sun of Righteousness, shining forth in the manifestation of the Gospel, causeth the Heart of one Man to dissolve and melt like Wax, distilling him into Tears of Repentance; others are hardned and grow obdurate as a Rock, not through the Gospel's fault, but their own obstinate and rebellious Minds.[51]

Herbert used this biblical trope in "Praise (III)" to express his desire to glorify God. He will wring sighs and groans from his heart (l. 5), knowing that all his tears are collected in a bottle in heaven, where their insufficiency is compensated for by a single drop from Christ (cf. the "glasse of blessings" in "The Pulley"):

> I have not lost one single tear:
>   But when mine eyes
> Did weep to heav'n, they found a bottle there
>   (As we have boxes for the poore)
> Readie to take them in; yet of a size
>   That would contain much more.

---

49. William Cowper, *Patmos: A Commentary upon Revelation*, in *The Workes of Mr. William Cowper late Bishop of Galloway*, p. 1088.

50. In "The Sacrifice," ll. 25–26, he wrote: "These drops being temper'd with a sinners tears / A Balsome are for both the Hemispheres."

51. Benjamin Keach, *Tropologia: A Key to Open Scripture Metaphors*, 2:219.

> But after thou hadst slipt a drop
>   From thy right eye . . .
> The glasse was full and more.
>   (ll. 25–36)

Similarly, in the lyric "Businesse," the poet knows his proper employment is to produce tears of contrition that, like rivers and springs, will return to their home.

> Rivers run, and springs each one
> Know their home, and get them gone:
> Hast thou tears, or hast thou none?
>
> If, poore soul, thou hast no tears,
> Would thou hadst no faults or fears!
> Who hath these, those ill forbears.
>   (ll. 3–8)

Perhaps the most comforting image of the waters of life mitigating the waters of affliction in *The Temple* is from "Justice (II)." Under the new dispensation, the scales of justice no longer resemble "two great pits . . . like some torturing engine"; instead they are "buckets," one drawing from the well of life and the other from the waters of affliction.

> But now that Christs pure vail presents the sight,
>   I see no fears:
>   Thy hand is white,
>   Thy scales like buckets, which attend
>   And interchangeably descend,
> Lifting to heaven from this well of tears.
>   (ll. 13–18)

Christ's white hand manipulates the scales of divine justice so that the waters of life will outweigh the waters of affliction, enabling the believer to ascend to heaven.

Images associated with the sacramental recapitulation of the waters of life have a restless quality. The story being told through these sacramental types lacks a satisfying closure in time. Though the speaker can reenact the mystery of the atonement and his regeneration, he is inevitably dissatisfied with his inconstant experience of the joy of grace and longs for a more perfect experience of it in the fulness of time. Because the metaphor of the waters of life is traditionally multileveled and can signify either in the life of Christ or that of the believer, Herbert could exploit the interplay of signifiers among its Christological, sacramental, and eschatological types to render the speaker's "repining restlesnesse." Primarily this takes the form of an intense longing for paradise, but the shifting signifiers can also be used to heighten his despair as in "The Temper (II)." We learn that although grace *raises* mankind, its absence *razes*, for the "mightie joy" of grace does not seem to last. This condition will not be stabilized until the "chair of grace"—the throne of God that dispenses grace through the crystal fountain—is revealed in the New Jerusalem.

> The grosser world stands to thy word and art;
>   But thy diviner world of grace
>   Thou suddenly dost raise and race,
> And ev'ry day a new Creatour art.
>
> O fix thy chair of grace, that all my powers
>   May also fix their reverence:
>   For when thou dost depart from hence,
> They grow unruly, and sit in thy bowers.
>   (ll. 5–12)

Because of his imperfect sanctification he needs a continual infusion of grace to keep his "powers" in "reverence" to God. And even enraptured by grace, as in "The Glance," he knows that present joy (which he feels "Bedew, embalme, and overrunne my heart") is but a foretaste of the joys of paradise (ll. 17–24). In "The Bunch of Grapes," he at first feels dispossessed because of the inconstancy of his joy. He envies the Jews who at least had had the luscious grapes of Eshcol as a foretaste of their inheritance. Eventually, he recognizes that their cluster only foreshadowed his sacramental wine; but his greatest comfort is his implicit understanding that the true inheritance of the chosen people will be given in the promised land of the new age. The interplay of signifiers for this particular type produces the tonal variations in the poem.

The image that expresses most completely the speaker's hope for consummate regeneration using the typology of the waters of life is from the lyric "The Size." Here he counsels his heart to content itself with a modest status, a "size." In contrast to the limited, fleshly pleasures of this world, true satisfaction is to be found only in the unreserved, perfect joy of the New Jerusalem, which is imaged as a confluence of the upper and the lower waters.

> Content thee, greedie heart.
> Modest and moderate joyes to those, that have

Title to more hereafter when they part,
      Are passing brave.
Let th' upper springs into the low
Descend and fall, and thou dost flow.
                                    (ll. 1–6)

This poem urges self-restraint, "modest and moderate joyes," based on the assurance that "Great joyes are all at once" (l. 19). The image of the recirculation of the waters of life, articulated most clearly in the opening stanza but also used to create closure in the last, expresses his heart-felt hope that he will be part of the regeneration at the end of time, when the universe will be dissolved and created anew. In the meantime, the speaker contents himself with a modest "size" of joy that "Doth tice us on to hopes of more, / And for the present health restore" (ll. 29–30). The final line reminds us, as do the "Affliction" poems, that grief often ends in joy: "*These seas are tears, and heav'n the haven.*"

In a few poems we find the Christological, sacramental, and eschatological types almost directly juxtaposed to render the interplay among the speaker's present fears and future hopes. In "Love unknown" a friend interprets the emblems and the apparently strange behavior of God for the naive speaker. What is most striking about the poem for its readers, especially since the emblems of the heart are so common in continental emblem books, is the incredible dullness of the speaker who seems totally unaware of their import. What does Herbert signify thereby? "Love unknown" is a crucial poem that epitomizes many of Herbert's major themes: the insufficiency of human nature, the denial of human merit, the distrust of rationalism, and mankind's total reliance on Christ for salvation. The poem turns on the shift in the meaning of "tender" in line 33 and in the final line—"from tendering sacrifices to God to being made tender by Him"—a shift that signifies an understanding that human effort is insignificant.[52] The typology of the waters of life, coupled with the metaphoric heart of stone, helps to develop this shift for us.

Characteristically, the speaker has *tendered* his own offering to God, just as he tried to do in "The Altar." But the "servant" ignores the dish of fruit, seizes his heart instead, and casts it into a baptismal font where it is bathed in the blood flowing from the rock, the Christological antitype of the waters of life.

52. Strier, *Love Known*, p. 164.

> The servant instantly
> Quitting the fruit, seiz'd on my heart alone,
> And threw it in a font, wherein did fall
> A stream of bloud, which issu'd from the side
> Of a great rock . . .
>
> (ll. 11-15)

This sacramental recapitulation of Christ's sacrifice results in the *tendering* or suppling of his heart: "there it was dipt and dy'd, / And washt, and wrung: the very wringing yet / Enforceth tears" (ll. 16-18). Inevitably, though, his sanctification is imperfect, and as he is beset with "AFFLICTION," his heart hardens. Once again, in a gesture so typical of the speaker who cannot let go, he hopes to participate actively in his own salvation and in his own terms; he wants "To fetch a sacrifice out of my fold . . . To warm his love" (ll. 30, 32). That is, he wants to determine the conditions—here, the appropriate time and by his own inititative—under which he can be saved. But his efforts to *tender* a suitable offering are met with the same response, and his hardened heart must again be made supple:

> But as my heart did tender it, the man,
> Who was to take it from me, slipt his hand,
> And threw my heart into the scalding pan . . .
>
> I found a callous matter
> Began to spread and to expatiate there:
> But with a richer drug then scalding water
> I bath'd it often, ev'n with holy bloud,
> Which at a board, while many drunk bare wine,
> A friend did steal into my cup for good,
> Ev'n taken inwardly, and most divine
> To supple hardnesses.
>
> (ll. 33-45)

Such is the condition of the believers in this world; the regeneration begun at baptism must be renewed with the grace that flows in the sacraments. More importantly, the condition of imperfect sanctification underscores the fact that regeneration will only be complete, fully consummated, when the believers are bathed in the crystal fountain in the world to come. The speaker's naïveté perfectly expresses, as does the title of the poem, the astonishment of being confronted with the selfless love of Christ, who "*did but strive to mend, what you had marr'd*" (l. 67).

Similarly, in "The Water-course," those confronted by the awful
fact of predestination must learn to trust in God's mercy. In the
garden of the world, afflictions always crowd out tender saplings;
the only remedy is the water of life. (The watercourse of the title
meant a stream or channel of water, which carried with it the
implication of flowing water eventually returning to its source in
the godhead.)

> "The Water-course"
> Thou who dost dwell and linger here below,
> Since the condition of this world is frail,
> Where of all plants afflictions soonest grow;
> If troubles overtake thee, do not wail:
>
> For who can look for lesse, that loveth $\left\{ \begin{array}{l} \text{Life?} \\ \text{Strife?} \end{array} \right.$
>
> But rather turn the pipe and waters course
> To serve thy sinnes, and furnish thee with store
> Of sov'raigne tears, springing from true remorse:
> That so in purenesse thou mayst him adore,
>
> Who gives to man, as he see fit, $\left\{ \begin{array}{l} \text{Salvation.} \\ \text{Damnation.} \end{array} \right.$
>
> (ll. 1–10)

Gene E. Veith, in his subtle analysis of this neglected poem, has
pointed out that the last line rearranges the perspective of those
who think that they are controlling the flow of grace (in l. 6, "turn
the pipe and waters course" seems to imply human sufficiency).

> God ultimately controls the flow of water—from His end, as it
> were—although from the human perspective there is the experience of
> choosing and acting to appropriate grace. The poem thus portrays
> two choices: on the human side, between life and strife, and on God's
> part, between salvation and damnation. God's choice is prior; in the
> terms of the metaphor, God must open the valve before any water can
> be conveyed. The pipes are full; from the earthly point of view, the
> "call" is extended to everyone, but only those who love "life," who
> have a prior desire for the water, will respond to the means of salva-
> tion offered by Christ.[53]

As in "Love unknown," the sacramental participation in salvation
made possible by Christ is in the foreground—in the complex
typology of water imagery, the waters represent the source of life
at the creation, sacramental grace, and the Word itself conveyed

through "the Apostles sluce" ("The Jews," l. 3). Yet in the background lies the perfect image of sustenance and hope, the crystal fountain, which resolves the tension between the two stanzas. The eschatology of the waters of life provides the only true closure for many of the poems: because of imperfect sanctification and human insufficiency, the speaker must continually be infused with grace until his consummation. The baptismal sequence of poems at the beginning of *The Temple* initiates the reader into one of the "dark and deep points of Religion" (*Priest*, p. 256): human insufficiency and its corollary, imperfect sanctification. The bulk of the poems that follow offer evidence of the speaker's struggle for self-representation and self-understanding through the struggle to submit human nature to God's will. He has discovered most fully who he is when he retells his personal story as a biblical one—that is, when he recognizes that his genuine experiences are recapitulating the typological drama of Scripture.[54] Attempts by Herbert's readers to impose some precise unifying pattern among the poems have not been universally accepted; the most convincing arrangements have come from critics who discern a number of smaller patterns or sequences.[55] As I have tried to argue, The Church section presents the rich variety of the spiritual life as the speaker journeys toward God, which Herbert termed his *"many spiritual Conflicts."* The multileveled narrative made possible by the resources of biblical typology helped Herbert to develop the disparate moments of this journey as part of a larger pattern of experiences. The typological richness of one of the dominant metaphoric structures, the waters of life, helps give it unity.

Even as the narrative draws to a close in a series of poems on the last things, the speaker still is struggling to accept the magnitude of Christ's role and the insignificance of his own. The last poem in The Church offers a form of closure to these conflicts by reenacting the dynamic at work in the first poem. Though being fed "meat" as opposed to "milk" is probably used to suggest a state of spiritual perfection or readiness (see 1 Cor. 3:1–2),[56] the word also reminds us that the speaker is looking ahead to the eschatological feast.

---

54. See Harman's argument on the Bible as countertext, *Costly Monuments*, pp. 170–96.

55. Many critics have offered explanations for Herbert's organizing strategy. See the entry "Unity of *The Temple*" in John R. Roberts, *George Herbert: An Annotated Bibliography of Modern Criticism, 1905–1974*, p. 275.

56. Westerweel, *Patterns and Patterning*, pp. 231–35.

"Love (III)" can accordingly be considered the "antitype" or complement to "The Altar," in which the problems associated with the speaker's sacramental reenactment of Christ's salvation are first broached. As the speaker approaches the table, he resists the invitation to sit and eat. He still hopes in some way to "serve" or compensate for his weaknesses, but is *commanded* to submit: "You must sit down, sayes Love, and taste my meat" (l. 17).[57]

"Love (III)" calls attention yet again to the speaker's imperfect sanctification and his continual need to be spiritually regenerated. Since the eschatological feast is the consummation of the sacrificial offering made at Calvary—"meat" stands literally for Christ's body but functions metonymically as a sign for sacramental grace —this poem dramatizes the central tension in Herbert's poetry: the speaker's reluctance to accept the absolute insignificance of his role in his own salvation. As always, his role is simply to submit to the agency of Christ's enabling grace. Herbert, as we have seen, presented this relationship most powerfully through the notion of the circulation of the waters of life flowing from Christ's heart to transform the heart of the believer, and then returning to their source. Since genuine fulfillment and coherent representation of the self are unavailable in this life, these images of regeneration point always to a future consummation, a future closure, one even beyond the dramatic moment of "Love (III)."[58] The long poem that completes the volume, "The Church Militant," also provides an important eschatological dimension to *The Temple*. "The speaker in 'The Church Militant,'" Stanley Stewart has noted, "sees the world with the vision of one in a state outside of life, a state which was achieved by the proper redemption of time in life."[59] That is, while The Church shows the salvation drama of the individual, "The Church Militant" shows that the providential pattern is replicated in the renewal of the body of the church and points toward the consummation of time and the universe eschatologically.

57. Though I do not agree fully with Fish, *The Living Temple: George Herbert and Catechizing*, pp. 131–36, that "Love (III)" concludes with the "exhaustion" of the speaker who has been "killed with kindness," I do share his view that this poem shatters his self-reliance once again. For a different reading, see Chana Bloch, "George Herbert and the Bible: A Reading of 'Love (III),'" pp. 329–40; and Benet, *Secretary of Praise*, pp. 188–90.

58. Harman, *Costly Monuments*, p. 147.

59. Stanley Stewart, "Time and *The Temple*," pp. 97–110, reprinted in Roberts, ed., *Essential Articles*.

The complex typology of the waters of life thus plays an important role in *The Temple*. These images constitute a metaphoric subtext that substantially underpins the dramatic narration of Christian regeneration in the various lyrics. It is significant that these separate images have a common biblical origin because Herbert's use of them signals the alignment of the speaker's personal story with the enduring typological one from Scripture. The interplay of narrative levels, created through the juxtaposition of the Christological, sacramental, and eschatological types of this metaphor, exemplifies brilliantly Herbert's sophisticated typological wit, through which he rendered the variety of moods characteristic of his religious experiences. It is possible that Herbert found the notion of the circularity of the waters of life in contemporary sources, but surely the subtle elaboration given in *The Temple* was the result of his own creative insights into its metaphoric possibilities. Judging by the tribute paid by one avid reader, Henry Vaughan, Herbert's seventeenth-century audience was sensitive to these nuances.

❧[V]❧

WATER OUT OF
THE FLINTY ROCK

Candidus & medicans Ignis deus est. So sings the Poet, and so must I affirme, who have been tryed by that white and refining fire, with healing under his wings.

The divine flame that sears the heart in order to refine it, as Vaughan's own testimony from *Flores Solitudinis* would seem to confirm, has been widely regarded as the most significant image from *Silex Scintillans*.[1] The title of the volume and the emblem of the flashing flint also suggest this sudden illumination.[2] However, the consequence of the spiritual regeneration that ensues—the waters of life that flow from the stony heart—is no less significant, especially when the role of the waters of life in making *Silex* a unified poetic work is examined. For Vaughan used the resources of this complex typology to help generate and unify the underlying narrative of the pilgrimage, much as Herbert did in *The Temple*.

The drama of Christ's propitiatory suffering, foreshadowed by Old Testament types and then later articulated in the New Testament in the terms established by them, provides the paradigm with which the speaker understands his own salvation—a drama of creation, fall, and regeneration that parallels the *prototypic* biblical sto-

---

1. *The Works of Henry Vaughan*, "To the Reader," *Flores Solitudinis*, p. 216.

2. In the first important critical study of Vaughan, M. M. Mahood, *Poetry and Humanism*, p. 265, emphasized the centrality of the metaphor of the *silex scintillans*, "the flint which must be struck before it can emit fire." She also noted the appropriateness of Jeremiah 23:29 as a gloss: "Is not my word like as a fire? saith the Lord; and like a hammer that breaketh the rock in pieces?" For traditional glosses on the image clusters of *Silex*, see E. C. Pettet, *Of Paradise and Light: A Study of Vaughan's "Silex Scintillans,"* pp. 24–31; and R. A. Durr, *On the Mystical Poetry of Henry Vaughan*, pp. 29–31.

ry. His attempts to recapitulate that drama typologically constitute the major action of *Silex*. Furthermore, because of his natural insufficiencies, his regeneration is inevitably incomplete; hence, the action is always pointing beyond itself to a perfect fulfillment in the new age to come. By examining the intersecting narratives (Christological, sacramental, and eschatological) in terms of the imagery involving the waters of life, we can better understand Vaughan's complex typological wit. The waters flowing from the rock are no less significant to the richness of *Silex* than the corollary metaphors of the flash of light and the garden of the soul.

Typological Strategies in *Silex Scintillans*

When *Silex Scintillans: or, Sacred Poems and Private Ejaculations* was entered in the register of the Stationers' Company on March 28, 1650, it was given only the briefest of prefatory materials: an engraved title page displaying the emblem of the "flashing flint," along with certain bibliographic information, a Latin poem explicating the emblem, and a fourteen-line dedicatory poem. In the Preface to the completed *Silex*, Vaughan acknowledged his literary indebtedness to George Herbert, but even in the earlier version he had linked his poetry to his master by using Herbert's subtitle as his own. More striking, though, is the emblem of the "flashing flint" that announces a motif familiar to readers of *The Temple*, the stony heart revivified by Christ (Figure 5). This emblem introduces to the readers of *Silex* 1650 one of Vaughan's most important biblical tropes: the rock that must be split open through affliction so that it can flow with living water, which like all flowing water will return to its source. As a metaphor for regeneration, it describes the sacramental recapitulation of Christ's act of propitiation when the true rock was split open to provide the living waters of the sacraments. In addition, this metaphor is linked in *Silex* to an eschatological fulfillment through the imagery of the upper waters in the New Jerusalem. Why Vaughan omitted this emblem in the completed edition is a significant question, but one that can be answered only after the emblem has been examined and its relationship to the structure of the completed edition of *Silex* has been considered.

The emblem shows the obdurate heart of the sinner who remains insensitive to the silent voice of God's entreaties: *"Surdus eram,*

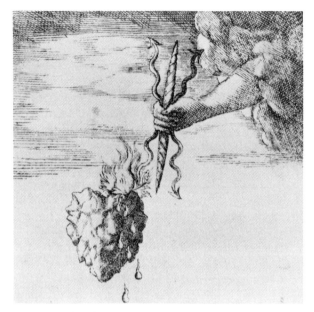

Figure 5. The Flashing Flint (from Henry Vaughan, *Silex Scintillans* [London, 1650], title page).

mutusque Silex" (I was deaf and dumb: a *Flint*), he says.[3] It is necessary that this stony heart be struck by thunderbolts from the heavens before it is once again a living heart, the heart of flesh the prophet Ezekiel speaks of (Ezek. 11:19). As Vaughan explains,

> . . . *vim*, Vi *superare paras,*
> *Accedis propior, molemque, & Saxea rumpis*
>   *Pectora, fitque* Caro, *quod fuit ante* Lapis.
> *En lacerum! Coelosque tuos ardentia tandem*
>   *Fragmenta, & liquidas ex* Adamante *genas.*

(. . . and you prepare to conquer force with *Force*, you come closer, you break through the *Rocky* barrier of my heart, and it is made *Flesh* that was before a *Stone*. Behold me torn asunder! and at last the *Fragments* burning toward your skies, and the cheeks streaming with tears out of the *Adamant*.) (ll. 8–12)

Readers of Vaughan at one time were prone to interpret this emblem as singular evidence of his own "conversion," his sudden

3. I am using the translation of Louis L. Martz, *The Paradise Within: Studies in Vaughan, Traherne, and Milton*, pp. 5–6.

illumination and turning to God. But as Jonathan Post and James Simmonds, among others, have argued, Vaughan's conversion was largely the creation of his pious readers' forcing him into the same Procrustean bed that Izaak Walton had placed Donne and Herbert.[4] The typology associated with the heart of stone, I believe, establishes a more subtle process of regeneration, based on the frequent reenactment of the pattern ordained by Christ, not the sudden and permanent transformation others have imagined.

The iconography of the emblem provides significant evidence about its appropriateness as an introduction to *Silex*. An outstretched hand can be seen emerging from a storm-darkened cloud. It strikes a heart-shaped flint, on which three contorted faces are inscribed (two in profile and one at the center). The engraving itself thus suggests that this experience is not simply the author's, but one that all must share. Scholars have identified the weapon variously as the thunderbolt of divine fire, a steel, a dart, an arrow-entwined caduceus, or the divine rod of Moses. It seems more likely—and more fitting—that the hand is holding the familiar attribute of Jupiter, the thunderbolt. In Christian symbolism, the thunderbolt traditionally signified God's sovereignty, particularly through the characteristic spindle of Fate that guided the thunderbolt.[5] Since the violent storm that purges and refines the heart is a favored metaphor in both Herbert's and Vaughan's poetry, the

4. Vaughan's dramatic conversion was accepted as a critical commonplace by scholars who tended to view *Silex* as an extraordinary achievement incommensurate with the abilities of the poet who wrote *Poems* and *Olor Iscanus*. After the work of E. L. Marilla, ed., *The Secular Poems of Henry Vaughan*, Essays and Studies on English Language and Literature, vol. 21, and James D. Simmonds, *Masques of God: Form and Theme in the Poetry of Henry Vaughan*, reshaped our understanding of the value and sophistication of Vaughan's secular poetry, critics have begun to offer more sophisticated views of Vaughan's "conversion." Jonathan F. S. Post, *Henry Vaughan: The Unfolding Vision*, pp. xv–xix, has persuasively argued that Vaughan's conversion is primarily a literary one; when he discovered a new literary master in George Herbert, his poetry accordingly changed direction.

5. See, respectively, Mahood, *Poetry and Humanism,* p. 265; Martz, *Paradise Within,* p. 5; Simmonds, *Masques of God,* p. 153; Thomas O. Calhoun, *Henry Vaughan: The Achievement of "Silex Scintillans,"* p. 137; and Cherrell Guilfoyle, "The 'Paragraph Poems' in *Silex Scintillans,*" p. 307. Guilfoyle also suggested that weapon might be the "arm of Jove, brandishing a steel from which four thunderbolts fly," though she did not discuss any of the implications of this identification. On the iconography of Jupiter, see Guy de Tervarent, *Attributs et symboles dans l'art profane, 1450–1600: Dictionnaire d'un langage perdu,* 1:194, 227. In the Bible, lightning is a sign of the wrath of God (Job 1:16) or his weapon (Ps. 18:4), and it accompanies theophanies (Exod. 19:16; Ezek. 1:13).

Jovian thunderbolt introduces the notion of metaphoric "storms" of affliction as a preface to *Silex*. Vaughan could have come across this traditional iconography in a number of Renaissance sources. Spenser, for example, mentioned Jove's "thundring dart . . . the fierce threeforked engin" in Book I of *The Faerie Queene*.[6] Because Jove was also the weather god of the ancient world (as Jupiter Tonans, god of storms), Agrippa d'Aubigné, in the canto of *Les Tragiques* titled "Vengeances," had God appear as Jupiter Tonans to destroy the world with fire and brimstone before the last judgment.[7] And in his popular emblem book *Heroicall Devises*, Paradin explained that with the Jovian thunderbolt (Figure 6),

> God our creator (as Saint Peter, James and Luke doe witnes) doth resist the proude, the high minded, lovers of themselves, and the arrogant, but giveth grace to the humble and lowlie. Wherein he seemeth to imitate the lightning, which leaveth untouched thinges that are low, and striking those that are loftie and high.[8]

Vaughan might well have had such an explication in mind when he chose the Jovian thunderbolt as part of the emblematic preface to his poems. For he knew that affliction is necessary to cause the obdurate heart to burn, bleed, and shed tears—the violent aftermath of the spiritual storm. As the motto over Paradin's emblem reminds us, God often "troubleth the earth with whirlewindes" (*Sic terras turbine perflat*).

Furthermore, Vaughan calls our attention to the explicitly typological dimension of the emblem in the moralizing verses he wrote for it:

> *Sic olim undantes* Petras, Scopulosque *vomentes*
>   *Curasti, O populi providus usque tui!*
> *Quam miranda tibi manus est! Moriendo, revixi*;
>   *Et* fractas *iam sum* ditior *inter* opes.

> (Thus once upon a time you made the *Rocks* flow and the *Crags* gush, oh ever provident of your people! How marvellous toward me is your hand! In *Dying* I have been born again; and in the midst of my *shattered means* I am now *richer*.) (ll. 13–16)

These verses point toward a typologically complex series of events and imagery that help to establish a basic metaphoric structure for

6. Edmund Spenser, *The Faerie Queene*, ed. A. C. Hamilton (London and New York: Longman, 1977), I.viii.9.

7. Agrippa d'Aubigné, *Les Tragiques*, 4:114 [Canto VI, ll. 1123–26].

8. *The Heroicall Devises of M. Claudius Paradin*, pp. 166–67.

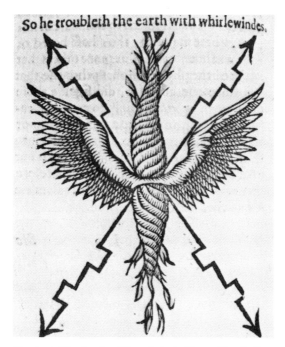

Figure 6. The Jovian Thunderbolt (from Claude Paradin, *The Heroicall Devises of M. Claudius Paradin*,
trans. P. S. [London, 1591], p. 166).

Silex Scintillans, deriving from the Bible and *The Temple*. Just as
Herbert was fascinated with the heart of stone that must be made
fleshy, as announced in his opening lyric, "The Altar," so Vaughan
announced his affiliation with Herbert and his own struggle to have
his heart of flint transformed into the New Testament temple.
Equally central for Vaughan was the imagery of the waters of life
that effect this transformation. Vaughan identified the rock of
Horeb as a figural antecedent to his flinty heart quite clearly in his
explication of the emblem. Just as God provided water to the
chosen people suffering during their wandering in the desert, so
Christ, the true rock (1 Cor. 10:4), fulfills this typological promise
through the sacramental waters of life. Vaughan's emblem, it
should be noted, advances this relationship one step further by
"application," or what can be called sacramental typology. Each
believer must recapitulate this typological drama by reenacting the
splitting of the rock, so that "out of his belly shall flow rivers of

living water" (John 7:38).[9] The tears of affliction that can be seen in the emblem offer some evidence that the speaker's spiritual regeneration is beginning. The poems in *Silex* 1650 ought to be seen as Vaughan's attempts to enact this typological drama.

In the opening poem of *Silex*, "Regeneration," Vaughan set the stage more completely. Though he did not point specifically to Easter (as Herbert did in his opening sequence), he did employ a figural time scheme to great effect in the poem. The first part of the liturgical year marks the period of mankind's wandering or erring from God; it begins in the winter and ends with the renewal of the year and of mankind at Easter. In the old calendar, the new year began near Easter—when the season was a winter-seeming spring —thus heralding a new beginning still deeply implicated in its past. Such is the spiritual condition of the speaker. As one critic has observed, this poem contains "perhaps the most astonishing celebration of the early moments of faith in all the religious poetry."[10] What too many readers of this brilliant lyric seem to overlook in their analyses of the poems that follow is that "Regeneration" is truly only a beginning, "the early moments of faith." Using a complex, but highly conventional, allegory of pilgrimage through a spiritual landscape to the garden or sacred grove, Vaughan represented the effectual calling of the sinner, which only marks the beginning of the Pauline schema for salvation.[11] Certainly no other poem from *Silex* has occasioned more scholarly commentary.[12] While it is unnecessary to rehearse all of it here, some details are

9. Matthias Flacius Illyricus, *Clavis Scripturae Sacrae; seu de sermone sacrarum literarum*, 2 vols. (Jena, 1567), I, col. 1170, explained that God can even draw water and oils from the flinty heart, citing Deut. 32:13 and 8:15: "Everywhere God produces mysteries, as in Deut. 8:15: thus he draws water from the stony flint, that is, from the hardest stone, and clearly a flinty one." (Undique Deus ei ingentia commoda protulit, sic Deut. 8. v. 15: *Eduxit tibi aquam e petra silicis*: id est, ex petra durissima, & plane silicea.)

10. Post, *Unfolding Vision*, p. 196.

11. Barbara K. Lewalski, *Protestant Poetics and the Seventeenth-Century Religious Lyric*, pp. 319–21, made the same point.

12. Some of the major discussions of the poem include Ross Garner, *Henry Vaughan: Experience and the Tradition*, pp. 47–62; Pettet, *Of Paradise and Light*, pp. 101–17; Durr, *Mystical Poetry*, pp. 79–99; Stanley Stewart, *The Enclosed Garden: The Tradition and the Image in Seventeenth-Century Poetry*, pp. 107–11; Georgia B. Christopher, "In Arcadia, Calvin . . . : A Study of Nature in Henry Vaughan," pp. 408–26; Claude J. Summers and Ted-Larry Pebworth, "Vaughan's Temple in Nature and the Context of 'Regeneration,'" pp. 351–60; Calhoun, *The Achievement of "Silex,"* pp. 141–45; and Post, *Unfolding Vision*, pp. 89–94, 196–98.

quite significant in establishing the typology of the waters of life as a central metaphor.

Of primary significance is the juxtaposition of the old law with the new dispensation, thus foregrounding typological promise and fulfillment as a central feature. The first three stanzas, Sharon Seelig has argued, show the bondage of religion to the law.[13] The scales (l. 20) measure the insufficiency of his efforts to be righteous, his "late paines" (l. 22), and hence point toward the absolute dependency of believers on the agency of another. Similarly, the reference to "*Jacobs Bed*" (l. 28) foreshadows Christ as the anointed altar for sacrifice and also its sacramental antitype.[14]

> . . . he foretold the place,
> And form to serve him in, should be true grace
> And the meek heart, not in a Mount, nor at
> *Jerusalem*, with blood of beasts, and fat.
> A heart is that dread place . . .
> ("Jacobs Pillow, and Pillar" ll. 23–27)

More significantly, as did Herbert in "The Pilgrimage," the poet discovers that the waters from the fountain collect into a "Cisterne" (l. 54), a stagnant pool, not a flowing or "living" stream (the equivalent to Herbert's "lake of brackish waters"). The reference to the cistern calls to mind Jeremiah 2:13: "they have forsaken me the fountain of living waters, and hewed them out cisterns, broken cisterns, that can hold no water." Furthermore, not all of those who are bathed in these waters are regenerated; only some of those souls in the cistern have had their flinty hearts transformed into "lively stones" (1 Peter 2:5). Either Vaughan intended to confront his readers with the awful fact of predestination and election, as some critics have argued,[15] or he was demonstrating that some are simply not prepared to accept grace. In any case, the speaker is merely an observer to this allegorical scene; he does not identify himself as one of those brought back to life. Since the distinguishing mark of the soul capable of being regenerated was a heightened awareness of its depravity, perhaps the speaker's experience of the numinous in the garden (rendered in the celebrated description in stanza six) indicates that his transformation is just beginning. It is

---

13. Sharon Cadman Seelig, *The Shadow of Eternity: Belief and Structure in Herbert, Vaughan and Traherne*, p. 77.

14. See Durr, *Mystical Poetry*, pp. 86–87.

15. Most critics read the stones and flowers as symbolic of the elect and those predestined to damnation. See, e.g., Pettet, *Of Paradise and Light*, p. 114.

entirely appropriate, then, that the speaker closes the poem with
the plea that the rushing wind of the Holy Spirit suffuse him to
allow the old man to die so that the new may be born again.

> Lord, then said I, *On me one breath,*
> *And let me dye before my death!*
>
> (ll. 81–82)

The opening lyric to *Silex*, thus, seems to show only the speaker's
calling, the first step toward his sanctification. Since "many be
called, but few chosen" (Matt: 20.16), the rest of the poems in *Silex*
narrate his pilgrimage back to the sacred garden, so that the waters
of life will revivify his heart and then flow from it back to God.

The blinding illumination of St. Paul on the road to Damascus
may have served as model for Augustine, but such a radical transformation is unusual in seventeenth-century spiritual autobiography. Izaak Walton's hagiographies of Donne and Herbert have
undoubtedly contributed to the misreading of their poetry, especially in the case of Herbert, where the Pauline-Augustinian
model became the "character-image," to use David Novarr's term,
according to which Walton framed the *Life*.[16] Herbert's own record of his "many spiritual Conflicts" is, of course, *The Temple*;
even though it was written after his own turning toward the Anglican ministry, it articulates a very uneasy walk with God—not the
quiet piety of the man Walton wished to portray to an England in
need of martyrs and saints. More typical of spiritual autobiography
as a genre is Bunyan's *Grace Abounding*, fully two-thirds of which
details Bunyan's tortuous and lengthy conversion experiences before his calling. Roger Sharrock has assured us,

> Growth in grace continued throughout the lifetime of the believer in a
> manner comparable to organic growth; it was therefore possible to
> trace its progress and to plot the symptoms of regeneration. Even
> conversion was no sudden storming of the soul by grace, but a gradual
> process marked by clearly defined stages: first came conviction of sin,
> when the Christian was convinced of his share in the general depravity
> of the human race, and sure that his own good works could avail him
> nothing; then came vocation or calling, when he had evidence of his

16. David Novarr, *The Making of Walton's "Lives,"* pp. 483–96. Novarr wrote:
"Walton not only depended, then, upon a character-image, but the image was
limited by the single-mindedness of his outlook, by his disposition toward hero
worship, by the extent and nature of his acquaintance with his subject, and by the
purpose underlying each effort" (p. 489).

election by God, and felt that an unmerited love had set him on the right hand in the awful scheme of predestination; there succeeded to this, justification, the achievement of a saving faith, and sanctification, the growth in holiness of life; finally glorification brought the pilgrim's progress to an end.[17]

If Vaughan's speaker in "Regeneration" has only been awakened to his desperate sinfulness and hence to his need for grace, then we can expect to find considerable spiritual turmoil throughout much of *Silex*. Such is the case.

"Regeneration" is truly just the beginning of the speaker's struggle to achieve salvation. Though Anglican orthodoxy held that a believer was reborn in the waters of life at baptism, it was considered impossible to maintain such a pristine state. Because of the doctrine of imperfect sanctification, Anglicans accepted the idea that believers must be continually infused with grace. Communion is thus a necessary corollary to baptism in order to repair the image of God that would inevitably decay. As is the case with *The Temple*, we find evidence throughout both books of *Silex* of a seemingly endless reenactment of the salvation drama: moments of elation and transcendence are followed by doubt and despair. Both poets seem to have taken most comfort in the affliction that led them back to God. If the life is to be presented as a pilgrimage, it must be recognized that true linear progress is in fact an illusion; only when the final regeneration takes place in the fulness of time will the ward be loosened of his bonds.

Unlike some Calvinists and certainly those extreme sectarians who believed that the elect were absolved of any moral responsibilities,[18] Vaughan believed that mankind could prepare to receive grace through devotion. Thus, his theology is somewhat different from that of his literary master, Herbert, who was a far stricter Calvinist. Vaughan's only original prose, *The Mount of Olives* (1652), helps to clarify his theological position on the necessity of private devotion. It was probably written after he had pub-

17. John Bunyan, *Grace Abounding to the Chief of Sinners,* pp. xxvii–viii. See also George A. Starr, *Defoe & Spiritual Autobiography,* pp. 3–50.

18. For a discussion of covenant theology, see Richard Strier, *Love Known: Theology and Experience in George Herbert's Poetry,* pp. 84–113, and Perry Miller, *Errand into the Wilderness,* pp. 48–98. We may also learn something of Vaughan's attitude toward the doctrine of election from his gibe against those *"who assume to themselves the glorious stile of Saints"* (*The Mount of Olives,* p. 140). He was evidently uneasy with the smug self-righteousness of the "elect."

lished the first part of *Silex* and while he was completing the second part, so it serves as a useful companion to his devotional poetry. Vaughan offered this practical treatise to his readers as an aid to the devout life, because he believed that sacramental grace is received in proportion to one's spiritual preparation: "This Sacrament is of an infinite vertue, having in it the *Wel-spring* of all graces, even *Jesus Christ* . . . they that come unto this glorious Sacrament, receive onely so much grace as their preparation and holines makes them capable of" (p. 155). As Christ went to Olivet to prepare himself, so too must the believer engage in preparation to receive Christ. The admonition to the disciples after the last supper—"Watch ye therefore, and pray always, that ye may be accompted worthy to escape all these things that shall come to passe, and to stand before the Sonne of Man" (Luke 21:36)—is used as the epigraph on the title page. Although the first section of *The Mount of Olives* begins with morning prayers and includes evening prayers, the work as a whole centers on the preparation to recapitulate Christ's salvation drama through the sacraments. Since the *Book of Common Prayer* had been proscribed by the Puritans, Vaughan probably used his manual to reemphasize the mystical communion of the priest and the faithful, who by grace can participate in Christ.[19] His choice for the title emphasizes the typological connection between the garden on the Mount of Olives as the place of Christ's agony and the place of his final glorification on earth (Acts 1:12): through devotion and grace the locus of regeneration can be transformed into the locus of glory.

Not only does *The Mount of Olives* underscore Vaughan's commitment to the sacramental typology, it also employs the two most significant metaphors for spiritual growth in *Silex*, the garden of the soul as locus of regeneration and the waters from the rock that will descend and return to God. The garden as a motif harkens back to Eden, with its fountain making fertile the entire created world, and especially to the garden of the Canticles. As Barbara Lewalski has pointed out, the Song of Songs was usually interpreted by Protestant commentators as an allegory of the Christian life, presenting the beginnings of regeneration, the many spiritual failures and triumphs that mark the progress toward sanctification, and the intense longing for the return of the bridegroom to the paradisal

19. See *The Book of Common Prayer, 1559: The Elizabethan Prayer Book*, pp. 368–72.

garden.[20] For Vaughan, then, the heart was a garden made fruitful with the dew of grace. But he also brought to the foreground the complex typology of the waters of life in his devotional treatise in much the same way as he did in *Silex*. For example, he wrote:

> Take away, O my God! this heart of stone, and give me a heart of flesh, renew a right spirit within me. . . . . O thou that didst cause the waters to flow out of the stonie rock, and gavest to *Magdalen* such store of teares that she washed thy feet with them, give to me true remorse, and such a measure of repentance as may become a most miserable sinner! (p. 159)

He believed that his flinty heart could only be transformed because of Christ's atonement—when Christ became the true rock. But he also hoped that, with grace, he could reenact the splitting of the rock so the waters of life will return to their heavenly source: "[Grant] that this drink which I drank out of the spiritual rock may become a Well of living waters, springing up in me to eternal life" (p. 165). Vaughan's manual for the devout life thus is predicated on the complex relationship that events in Christ's life have for the believers. By spending time in devotion, the believers can prepare themselves for a more complete sacramental participation in this mystery. As Vaughan wrote in the Preface to *Silex*,

> It is true indeed, that to give up our thoughts to pious *Themes* and *Contemplations* (if it be done for pieties sake) is a great *step* towards *perfection*; because it will *refine*, and *dispose* to devotion and sanctity. And further, it will *procure* for us . . . some small *prelibation* of those heavenly *refreshments*, which descend but seldom, and then very sparingly, upon *men* of an ordinary or indifferent *holyness*. (pp. 391–92)

Most recent critics have argued for some form of typological perspective in *Silex*, especially in the relationship between Parts I and II. Though Lewalski attributed the unity of the volume to Vaughan's development of the Christian pilgrimage as a controlling metaphor, she found that the painful awareness of darkness and the longing to escape, which characterize *Silex* 1650, give way to the speaker's assurance in *Silex* 1655 that his pilgrimage is nearing its successful completion.[21] Post has articulated the typological underpinnings of *Silex* more carefully. In his reading, *Silex* moves metaphorically from Genesis to Revelation. "For the most part," he

20. Lewalski, *Protestant Poetics*, pp. 59–69, 323–24.
21. Lewalski, *Protestant Poetics*, pp. 317–26.

wrote, "Silex 1650 is grounded in 'Bethlehem and Golgotha,' birth and suffering, the two principal events in the early phases of the individual Christian life."[22]

In Part II, "Ascension-day" initiates a sequence of poems that reassures us of the speaker's election and that prepares us for the concluding sequence on the last things, in which "the speaker's present experience becomes a type of his perfected life at the Apocalypse."[23] Though it is tempting to relate Silex 1650 to Silex 1655 in terms of promise and fulfillment, doing so obscures the dynamics of the speaker's progress toward sanctification, which is still as much a struggle in Part II as it is in Part I. There is considerable evidence, as I hope to demonstrate shortly, that the same rhythm of elation and despair can be found in Silex 1655 near the end of the pilgrimage. Just as Herbert's speaker in "Love (III)" replays the familiar scene in which he asserts his unworthiness and yet his desire to participate in the eschatological feast, Vaughan's speaker, in a poem placed just before the sequence on the last things, reminds us of his "troubled soul" and "foul heart" ("Anguish," ll. 3–4). In other words, we are not presented with a wholly regenerated speaker in Part II. While the speaker may be more assured of his salvation, his identity has not yet merged mystically with Christ's.

On the other hand, it would be equally untenable to argue that the speaker makes no progress toward his sanctification, for clearly he has. His many devotions and meditations—presented in such poems as "Vanity of Spirit," "Midnight," "The Evening-watch," and "The Water-fall," for example—offer evidence of a deepening understanding of his faith, and we find evidence of the extraordinarily restorative powers of the grace he receives through the sacraments, as well. As Vaughan explained in The Mount of Olives, one can receive grace only in proportion to one's spiritual preparation and holiness. His sacred poems and private ejaculations show his gradual progress and his increased capacity to receive "the Welspring of all graces, even Jesus Christ" (p. 155). It is significant that Vaughan chose to omit the emblem of the flinty heart struck by sudden force in the completed edition of 1655. As Thomas Calhoun has explained, when Vaughan was writing the second part, this emblem was no longer entirely appropriate.[24] By 1662, Vaughan had adopted as his personal signet the emblem of a heart pierced by an arrow, with drops (of blood or water) nourishing a flower. This image of a flower in bloom, according to Calhoun's argument, better represents the imagery of the regenerate in *Silex* 1655. Vaughan's speaker has certainly experienced spiritual growth during his pilgrimage; however, we should also recall that the epigraph on the title page to the 1655 edition is uttered by the Bible's prototypic sufferer: "*Where is God my Maker, who giveth Songs in the night? / Who teacheth us more then the beasts of the earth, and maketh us wiser then the fowls of heaven?*" (Job 35:10–11). Vaughan asked the same question of God as Job: is his suffering a sign of favor or indifference?[25] While the contorted faces of the sufferers inscribed on the flinty heart no longer introduce us to the volume, the speaker nevertheless gives voice to their anguish even as he nears the end of his pilgrimage.

Under the aegis of the New Criticism, earlier readers studied *Silex* in terms of its image-clusters. Critics such as Molly Mahood, Ross Garner, E. C. Pettet, and R. A. Durr all noted the dew and water imagery, usually under the general head of "images of fructification."[26] My enterprise is not simply to catalogue these images or to identify their typological heritage; rather, I wish to demonstrate that Vaughan, using the same sophisticated typology available to Herbert through contemporary biblical commentary, set forth his speaker's struggle toward sanctification through the resources of typology. That is, the progress of the narrative is measured by the success or failure of the speaker's imitation of the archetypal patterns of the Christian salvation drama. Simply put, the presence or absence of the waters of life discloses his spiritual condition; more importantly, however, the haunting, other-worldly quality of Vaughan's poetry is achieved through this regenerative imagery, which points to an action to be completed in heaven—sanctification and glorification. The interplay between Christological, sacramental, and eschatological types, finally, articulates the distance the speaker feels between promise and fulfillment. *Silex Scintillans* is thus structured significantly by the central experi-

24. Calhoun reprinted his article, "Henry Vaughan's *Silex Scintillans*, 1655: The Missing Emblem," *Library*, 5th Series, 30 (1975), 48–51, as an appendix to his book, pp. 220–26.

25. Post, *Unfolding Vision*, pp. 172–73, made this point.

26. The phrase is Mahood's; see *Poetry and Humanism*, pp. 276–78.

ence set forth in its emblematic preface in 1650, water from the rock springing into everlasting life. The pilgrim's narrative ought to be read, in part, by his reenactment of this typological drama.

The Waters of Life in *Silex Scintillans*

In a tribute to his native Brecknockshire, the Silurist confesses that poets have always "Haunted the *bubling Springs* and *gliding streams*" ("To the River *Isca*," l. 12). While Vaughan may have enjoyed the flowing waters as a natural phenomenon, and while the sacred spring has a long tradition as a source of inspiration—the Arethusa of Theocritus or the Mincius of Virgil, for example—the waters that Vaughan truly longed for in *Silex* are biblical. Using images drawn from the complex typology of the waters of life, Vaughan depicted the stony heart made fleshy by an outpouring of Christ's "dew" and the consequent "river of living water" that will flow from the heart of the believer (as promised in John 4:14 and 7:38). Unlike Herbert, as we have seen, Vaughan believed that through devotion one could prepare oneself to receive grace. Hence, in *Silex* the circularity of the waters of life returning to their source is a far more prominent trope. As a metaphor it describes the reciprocal motion of love and grace downward or outward from God and the movement back to God from the believers in reciprocation of divine love. This metaphor gives expression to the speaker's greatest hope, and as such it forms one of the central metaphoric structures in the volume.[27]

The imagery associated with the Christological types of the waters of life is introduced by the emblem and the explanatory verses that remind the reader the rocks were once made to flow and the crags gush for the chosen people. The metaphors associated with the Christological types of the waters of life—Christ as fountain, as dew, as the true rock, and so forth—are so common in the devotional literature that they have almost a propositional value. About their meaning, we have little doubt. Herbert used them in the same conventional way, as did a host of commentators and authors of

27. Other critics have remarked on Vaughan's use of the divine circularity, though none has argued for its centrality to Silex or for its typological underpinnings. On the notion of the Neoplatonic ascent of the soul, see Florence Sandler, "The Ascents of the Spirit: Henry Vaughan on the Atonement," *JEGP* 73 (1974): 209–26.

guides to godliness. In *Silex*, it is worth observing how Vaughan has employed them for two reasons. First, because the constituent images of the waters of life were perceived as part of a unifying narrative in Scripture (as outlined in Chapter 3 above), the individual images appear separately, so we tend to lose sight of their relationship to one another. More importantly, the narrative of regeneration outlined through the Christological typology of the waters of life serves as a framing narrative against which the speaker because of sacramental recapitulation can understand, measure, and give form to his own life's story.

Christ as the fountain of living waters derives its power as a metaphor from the commonplace that God is "The Circle, Center and Abyss / Of blessings."[28] Or, as Vaughan wrote in "Resurrection and Immortality," at death the soul returns to God, "that spring, / And *source* of spirits" (ll. 42–43). Before the fall of man, the Edenic fountain provided living waters as nourishment; after the fall, the chosen people had to wait for the fulfillment of the promise for a new fountain of life. As the true rock and as the unsealed fountain of the Canticles, Christ is that fulfillment. He is "the great eternal Rock," who can unlock his "waters to a soul that pines" ("White Sunday," ll. 45–48). The watered garden is always a holy place for Vaughan, as we can judge from the opening poem "Regeneration" or from any of a number of such references in *Silex*.

The most prominent metaphor for grace in *Silex* involves the dew-cycle. Grace falls from Christ as dew or as a shower, either to soften the stony heart or to nurture the seed growing secretly in the garden of the soul. Grace is the "Soul-quickning rain, this living water" that must be poured on dead hearts to bring them back to life ("Jesus weeping [I]," l. 10). Perhaps the best-known reference to the dew of grace is Vaughan's homage in "The Morning-watch":[29]

> O joyes! Infinite sweetnes! with what flowres,
> And shoots of glory, my soul breakes, and buds!
>> All the long houres
>> Of night, and Rest

28. These lines are from a poem published in *Thalia Rediviva*, "The World," ll. 64–65, p. 671.

29. Some other examples that can be cited are: "Love, and Discipline," ll. 1–2; "Providence," ll. 25–30; and "The Feast," ll. 19–24.

> Through the still shrouds
> Of sleep, and Clouds,
> This Dew fell on my Breast.
> > (ll. 1–7)

Sometimes Vaughan will liken the abundance of grace to "a showr / Of healing sweets" ("Misery," ll. 49–50), the source of which is "Thy upper river, which abounds / With fertil streams, makes rich all grounds" ("Psalm 65," ll. 29–30).[30]

Another frequently used image for grace is Christ's blood, an image that connects the waters of life with sacrificial propitiation and that foreshadows the affliction each individual can also expect to recapitulate. In many poems Vaughan identified the waters of life flowing from the wound in Christ's side as his blood, "the worlds all-healing *Balm*."[31] Christ's heart is therefore the spring or fountain of life, a fitting metonymy that links the emanation and return of life with love and sacrifice. In "Repentance" the speaker asks for "those streams . . . Whose spring is in my Saviours heart" to revivify his own (ll. 55–56); in "The Feast" he acknowledges that Christ's heart is "The well, where living waters spring" (l. 33). An image from "Mans fall, and Recovery" strengthens the association of the waters of life with Christ's suffering, when the speaker says, "His saving wound / Wept bloud" (ll. 24–25). Christ's *tears* thereby become an image of the suffering that makes regeneration possible:

> Dear *Jesus* weep on! pour this latter
> Soul-quickning rain, this living water
> > On their dead hearts.
> > > ("Jesus weeping [I]," ll. 9–11)

> O holy groans! Groans of the Dove!
> O healing tears! the tears of love!
> Dew of the dead! which makes dust move
> And spring . . .
> > ("Jesus weeping [II]," ll. 9–12)

30. See also "Psalme 104," ll. 37–39: "Thou from thy upper Springs above . . . Doest water the parch'd hills"; and "The Shower," ll. 1–2, ff., published in *Thalia Rediviva*, p. 661: "Waters above! eternal Springs! / The dew, that silvers the *Doves* wings!"

31. "St. Mary Magdalen," l. 40. Christ's blood and grace are likened to the "*Balsam* of Soules" ("The Search," l. 44) and to a "Cordial" ("The Sap," l. 27), and in "The Feast" the speaker apostrophizes the spear that wounded Christ as "the key / Opening the way" (ll. 64–65).

When the imagery of the waters of life drawn from Christological types is viewed as a whole, it forms the complete narrative of Christ's salvation: the splitting of the rock at Calvary is the consummation of many Old Testament foreshadowings. Because this imagery is so traditional, Vaughan used it somewhat allusively. But it is used so ubiquitously and consistently, that we can reconstitute the entire structure of images and relationships from a single element of it.[32]

Like most Protestants of his time, Vaughan conceived of his spiritual life in the terms established by Christ's own. Thus, to appreciate the spiritual dynamics of *Silex*, we must be attuned to the "application" of the Christological types outlined above. In one of the most significant early poems, "The Search," the speaker fails to understand the relationship of "The skinne, and shell of things" (l. 81) to the spiritual kernel within, which is to say, he fails to understand the fundamental typological relationship of promise and fulfillment. In his "roving Extasie," the speaker journeys throughout the external landscape of the Holy Land to find his savior. But he does not find Christ at Jacob's well, even though it was here that Jesus told the Samaritan woman about the well of living waters (John 4:6–15)—nor will he find him in any exterior place. The measure of his failure is that he has not yet understood the full importance of Christ as the *antitype* to such promissory events. The biblical landscape has been interiorized, as the epigraph from Acts makes clear; the heart is the new temple of the Lord. He only discovers his error when someone else tells him to

> Search well another world; who studies this,
> Travels in Clouds, seeks *Manna*, where none is.
>
> (ll. 95–96)

32. Vaughan also referred to other, related Christological types. Notably, in "Religion" the Bible was likened to the waters of life because it is the means of spiritual nourishment (ll. 29–32). Iconographically, the Bible was often depicted as the wellspring of life with Christ as the fountain and the evangelists as the four rivers. The epigraph, Song 4:12, also recalls the typology of the *fons signatus*. "The Rain-bow" celebrates God's promise never to detroy the world by inundation again—"Rain gently spends his honey-drops, and pours / Balm on the cleft earth" (ll. 11–12). The rainbow, as a type of the new covenant, reminds us that Christ is its fulfillment, and yet the speaker knows that a final regeneration must take place: i.e., the flood as type of baptism and of the waters of life has an eschatological antitype: "Yet I know well, and so our sins require, / Thou dost but Court cold rain, till *Rain* turns *Fire*" (ll. 41–42).

Because of Christ's sacrificial atonement, the new dispensation will require activity of another kind: sacramental recapitulation. Regenerating the soul now means, metaphorically, drinking the water of the true rock, the blood of Christ's heart, so that the stony heart of the believer can flow with living waters. By elaboration and repetition, Vaughan developed the metaphor of water out of the rock springing to life everlasting as a central conceit in *Silex*. Even if the speaker's heart is among the "lively stones" in the regenerating fountain, he later confesses that he is imperfectly sanctified—he "kills" Christ daily—and hence he needs a daily infusion of the waters of life ("The Incarnation, and Passion," ll. 13–16). Thus, a pattern of elation and despair inevitably characterizes his spiritual state as he tries to transform his heart of stone into a fit temple for the Lord.

In a poem placed almost at the end of the completed *Silex*, "Jacobs Pillow, and Pillar," Vaughan clearly spelled out the complex typology of the new temple, the heart of stone revivified. As such, this poem explicates the emblem of the flinty heart and clarifies its metaphoric usage in *Silex*. The stone Jacob uses as a pillow and then anoints as an altar (after his dream-vision of the promised land) foreshadowed the New Testament temple of the heart.

> A heart is that dread place, that awful Cell,
> That secret Ark, where the milde Dove doth dwell
> When the proud waters rage. . . .
>
> (ll. 27–29)

The rock that is sanctified has as its basic antecedent a Christological type, "the great eternal Rock" that gives living water to souls that pine ("White Sunday," ll. 45–48); the speaker's hope is that his heart will also be an antitype to the true rock. Other typologically significant events are notable in these lines. As a "secret Ark" the stony heart is manifestly associated with the flood, a type of baptism; furthermore, the ark foreshadows the church and its sacraments as a sanctuary from annihilation. The reference to the "milde Dove" suggests that the speaker's regeneration is a reenactment of the flood, when the earth was re-created out of the waters of life. But the speaker's heart has become "that dread place, that awful Cell," and once again the dove must pacify its proud and raging waters. Much of the tension in *Silex* is created by the speaker's fear that his heart will remain a "dread place" instead of a "secret

Ark."[33] When viewed in light of the drama of typological recapitulation, two patterns of imagery can be discerned that depict this
hope and fear: the desiccated heart vivified by Christ's dew and the
circulation of natural water-cycles.

In order to represent the degenerative effects of the speaker's
spiritual decay, Vaughan exploited, just as Herbert had done, the
metaphoric possibilities of the desiccated heart that does not flow
with living water. Either the vital "spirits" produced in the heart
are so negligible that they cannot perform necessary bodily functions, or his inability to produce them has caused his heart to "pet-
rify." In either case his desiccated heart (the seat of his unregenerate
soul) only serves to emphasize his need for the revivifying waters of
grace.[34] In "The Showre," Vaughan characterized the speaker's
ineffectual prayers as "The smoke, and Exhalations of the brest,"
which he likened to the mists and fogs that ascend from standing
pools (perhaps also echoing Herbert's "Lent" and "Even-song");
these are "Too grosse for heaven" and quickly sink back to earth (ll.
5, 12). The poem that follows begins with the plea that God bring
him back to life.

> O knit me, that am crumbled dust! the heape
> Is all dispers'd, and cheape.
> ("Distraction," ll. 1–2)

Because of his defective will, the distractions of the world have
caused the speaker's soul to dissipate, and he is only capable of
forming dry *blasts* instead of vital "spirits": "I am sadly loose, and
stray / A giddy blast each way," he laments elsewhere ("And do
they so?" ll. 17–18). He likens this condition to the body's dissolution at death (when the bodily "spirits" no longer have the power
to preserve the corpse from disintegration), at which time he will
scatter to the wind like dust.

> Though then (thus crumm'd) I stray
> In blasts,

---

33. Ira Clark, *Christ Revealed: The History of the Neotypological Lyric in the English
Renaissance*, pp. 115–18, has offered a more extensive analysis of this poem.

34. Vaughan translated parts of Henry Nollius's *Systema generale* in 1655 as *Her-
metical Physick*, a treatise predicated on the doctrine that health depends on the
strength and virtue of the "radical Balsame." As we have seen, though, this principle
was also held by Galenists. For a discussion on this point, see Calhoun, *The Achievement of "Silex,"* pp. 122–30.

> Or Exhalations, and wasts
> Beyond all Eyes . . .
> ("Buriall," ll. 25–28)

Similarly, he characterizes the impurity of his heart as "a thick, Egyptian damp" that is as malodorous, as unhealthy as "a stench or fog."[35] And, finally in "The Stone," he contrasts the stone tablets of the law with the stony hearts of those who refuse to accept the law of grace. Without God "whose spirit feeds / All things with life," the heart will be harder than any stone; at the last judgment, God "Will by loose *Dust* that man arraign, / As one then dust more vile and vain" (ll. 25–26, 58–59).

The grace that quickens is sometimes imaged as a refining fire (as in "Love-sick" or "Dressing"), but most often it is the dew that inspirits the heart. "When first I saw true beauty, and thy Joys," he writes, a "balm in one rich floud / O'r-ran my heart, and spirited my bloud" ("Mount of Olives [II]," ll. 1, 7–8). The mystical operation of grace in the recesses of the heart is the subject of one of Vaughan's most enigmatic poems, "Midnight," a nocturnal meditation on the creatures (here, the powerful influences of the stars). It should also be read in light of its guiding text, Matthew 3:11 (or even as a meditation on that text), which places the poem squarely in line with other poems involving the complicated typology of baptism that so fascinated Vaughan. He used Matthew 3:11 as the epigraph to the poem: "*I indeed baptize you with water unto repentance, but he that commeth after me, is mightier than I, whose shooes I am not worthy to beare, he shall baptize you with the holy Ghost, and with fire.*" Most Renaissance commentators believed that this passage established the difference between the "outward ordinance" and the actual grace of the sacrament. John the Baptist was only the "minister," while Christ was its "author."[36] The commentators, moreover, agreed that the Holy Spirit empowered the baptismal act. Just as the dove had hovered over the waters so many times in sacred history, so it hovered over the font during baptismal regeneration. Augustin Marlorat, for example, explained this passage from Matthew on the regeneration by fire and water as follows:

35. "The Relapse," ll. 13–16; and "Unprofitablenes," ll. 17–18. See also "Distraction," ll. 28–34; "The Pursuite," l. 9.; and especially "Church-Service," where the dust of his stony heart is merely "A heap of sand" or a "blast" of dry wind that requires God's intercession to bring it back to life (ll. 11, 16).

36. Richard Ward, *Theologicall Questions, Dogmaticall Observations, and Evangelicall Essays, upon . . . Matthew*, p. 74.

But the name of fyer is applied to the spirite, because he doth purge away our filthines, even, as golde is purified in the fyer. He is called fier metaphorically, as he is called water. Therefore, he shal baptyse you with the holy ghost, and with fier, that is he shal ad unto it, his holy spirite, which hath the propertie & nature of fier: he shal regenerate, renovate, and make cleane your hartes, & shal consecrate you into the adoption of the sonnes of God.[37]

Baptism will thus regenerate the heart of the believer, so that living waters can flow from it, as we see in "Midnight."

The poem opens with the speaker surveying the fixed stars and wishing that his soul always "streamed" with similar, active or vital "Emanations":

> When to my Eyes
> (Whilst deep sleep others catches,)
> Thine hoast of spyes
> The starres shine in their watches,
> I doe survey
> Each busie Ray,
> And how they work, and wind,
> And wish each beame
> My soul doth streame,
> With the like ardour shin'd;
> What Emanations,
> Quick vibrations
> And bright stirs are there?
> What thin Ejections,
> Cold Affections,
> And slow motions here?
>   (ll. 1–16)

In contrast to their constant, bright, and lively influences, the emanations of his heart are "thin Ejections" and "Cold Affections." The second stanza points to the remedy for his condition, regeneration by grace.

> Thy heav'ns (some say,)
> Are a firie-liquid light,
> Which mingling aye
> Streames, and flames thus to the sight.
> Come then, my god!
> Shine on this bloud,

---

37. Augustin Marlorat, *A Catholike and Ecclesiasticall exposition of the holy Gospell after S. Mathewe*, p. 51.

> And water in one beame,
>   And thou shalt see
>   Kindled by thee
> Both liquors burne, and streame.
>   (ll. 17–26)

He needs the metaphoric fire of the Holy Spirit to enkindle the water and blood of his heart, to regenerate it so that the "thin Ejections" are revitalized. These are the "spirits" of the heart that make possible spiritual affections such as joy or love. The stony heart thus gushes with living water, which flows mystically back to its source in the heavens.

> O what bright quicknes,
>   Active brightnes,
> And celestiall flowes
>   Will follow after
>   On that water,
> Which thy spirit blowes!
>   (ll. 27–32)

This poem dramatizes the emblem Vaughan chose for his preface by connecting the notion of the waters out of the rock with the vital "spirits" that imbue the heart with life.[38]

In a number of poems, Vaughan represented the anticipated interchange between human and divine in terms of waters returning to their source. The notion of circularity had a powerful appeal to Vaughan because it imaged not only the descent of grace, the transformation of the stony heart, and the consequent ascent of living water, but also the entire rhythm or motion of the created universe. The circularity of water conveys the idea of the emanation and return of goodness from God, which Vaughan took as evidence of what he called the world's "*Hymning Circulations.*"[39] A passage he

---

38. "Trinity Sunday" uses the terms water, blood, and spirit in a slightly different way to describe the regenerating effects of grace. "Spirit" in this poem refers to the power of God inherent in Christ, the Holy Spirit, not to the bodily "spirits." Christ's atonement involved a triunity of water and blood from the heart and the divine spirit that validated the event (in the way that John the Baptist foretold, Matt. 3:11). The speaker recognizes that the spirit, water, and blood can have "Antytypes" (l. 7) in the individual through sacramental recapitulation. Hence he pleads that this regeneration will occur in him. For a different reading of "Trinity Sunday" and "Midnight," see Pettet, *Of Paradise and Light,* pp. 42–44.

39. "The Morning-watch," l. 10. Simmonds, *Masques of God,* pp. 149–54, has also noted that "The great moving circle composed by the return of the creature to God was a perennial symbol of ideal harmony and perfect order." See also, Leona Spitz, "Process and Stasis: Aspects of Nature in Vaughan and Marvell," pp. 135–47.

translated from Boethius explains his reverence for rings, circles, and the like as emblems of reciprocal exchange:

> Thus all things long for their first State,
> And gladly to't return, though late.
> Nor is there here to any thing
> A *Course* allow'd, but in a *Ring*;
> Which, where it first *began*, must *end*:
> And to that *Point* directly tend.
>
> (p. 651, ll. 43–48)

All life and goodness flows from God where it will eventually return, like waters circulating, unless somehow it is perverted.

In "The Sap," Vaughan expressed the mysterious descent and ascent of grace figuratively as falling and rising dew. Though the poem obviously makes use of the soul-as-blossom metaphor, it also places the typology of the waters of life in its foreground. The soul's nourishment must drop from "an hil of myrrh . . . beyond the Stars" where the Prince of Peace (Melchisedec, a type of Christ as the minister of the sacraments) bestows "his sacred bloud / By wil our sap, and Cordial" (ll. 11–12, 26–27). This "sap" falls as the dew to sustain the spiritual blossom, but it has the power of restoring the "spirits" that already lie within the blossom. Because he used the tag-word "spirits," Vaughan seems to be coordinating the metaphor of soul—as blossom—with the waters out of the rock.

> Such secret life, and vertue in it lies
>   It wil exalt and rise
> And actuate such spirits as are shed
>   Or ready to be dead,
> And bring new too. Get then this sap, and get
>   Good store of it, but let
> The vessel where you put it be for sure
>   To all your pow'r most pure;
> There is at all times (though shut up) in you
>   A powerful, rare dew,
> Which only grief and love extract; with this
>   Be sure, and never miss,
> To wash your vessel wel . . .
>
> (ll. 31–43)

The "sap," or the "balm for souls that ake," descends as the dew and has the power of extracting a "powerful, rare dew" from the purified heart. Grace has the power to first "actuate," then "exalt" and "rise" these "spirits," thus causing them to be sublimed as the morning dew returning to the heavens. This poem expresses exactly the operation of grace on the heart, enabling it to produce the living water that controls the affections of the soul. As he wrote in one of his grandest celebrations of this spiritual interchange, "The Morning-watch," all night long,

> This Dew fell on my Breast;
>   O how it *Blouds*,
> And *Spirits* all my Earth! heark! In what Rings,
> And *Hymning Circulations* the quick world
>   Awakes, and sings . . .
>   (ll. 7–11)

In much the same fashion that Herbert's "The H. Communion" celebrates the inner workings of grace on the heart's blood and "spirits," this poem gives thanks for the sacrifice of Christ whose "dew" *Blouds* and *Spirits* the earth with grace so that it can be restored and redeemed.

Vaughan made the dew- or water-cycle the subject of a series of occasional meditations on the creatures. While he was no doubt a keen observer of the natural world, as a Protestant his meditations were determined by the way nature was used in the Bible. Protestants were suspicious of Jesuit meditative practices, as U. Milo Kaufmann has asserted, because of their reliance on the senses and the imagination.[40] At the heart of the matter is the issue of authority: the reformers were uneasy with any practice that gave credence to the independent interpretation of a text—either from the Book of Scripture or the Book of the Creatures—that the imagination alone might produce. They tried to control the use of reason and imagination in their meditations by focusing on a biblical text or a religious topic grounded on a text, using commonly agreed upon principles of interpretation. As Lewalski has explained, the sermon method and the Protestant meditation were essentially the same: each began with the presentation and explication of a text, was followed by the exposition of the doctrine derived from that text, and concluded with the forceful application of these materials to the self.[41] Joseph Hall in *The Arte of Divine Meditation* (1606), the most influential of the English meditative trea-

40. U. Milo Kaufmann, *"The Pilgrim's Progress" and Traditions in Puritan Meditation*, pp. 41–60.
41. Barbara K. Lewalski, *Donne's "Anniversaries" and the Poetry of Praise: The Creation of a Symbolic Mode*, pp. 73–107.

tises, observed that meditation "begins in the understanding, end-eth in the affection; it begins in the brain, descends to the heart."[42] This procedure, as Lewalski noted, is the reverse of the Jesuit prac-tice of immersing oneself imaginatively in the *compositio loci*. "In-stead of the application of the self to the subject, the Protestant theory in regard to both sermons and deliberate meditation calls for the application of the subject to the self, indeed for the location of the subject in the self."[43] In practice, then, the meditator had to attempt to bend the will to accommodate the spiritual message under consideration. The imagination, in other words, was not simply given free rein to wander about a given "scene"—such as Christ's passion—to re-create the suffering and somehow share in it. Instead, the primary concern of both Protestant meditation and sermon was to find in the Bible a pattern of events based on Christ's life for the individual Christian's experience.[44]

Oftentimes Vaughan's meditations on the water-cycle are used to point up the speaker's insufficiencies, as is the case in "The Showre." In the midst of a rain shower, he notes how similarly his own attempts to "ascend" have failed. The shower is formed by the vapors "breath'd" from the "faint bosome" of a "drowsie Lake," a detail that implies the waters are still and not running; these vapors fall in the late afternoon when the sun's rays are weaker because they are "Too grosse for heaven." In fact, he calls them "the disease [or, the dis-ease] / Of her sick waters, and Infectious Ease." The waters fall like tears, lamenting their return to the earth (ll. 1–6).

> Ah! it is so with me; oft have I prest
> Heaven with a lazie breath, but fruitles this
> Peirc'd not; Love only can with quick accesse
> Unlock the way,
> When all else stray

42. Frank Livingston Huntley, *Bishop Joseph Hall and Protestant Meditation in Seven-teenth-Century England: A Study with the Texts of "The Arte of Divine Meditation (1606)" and "Occasional Meditations (1633),"* p. 87.

43. Lewalski, *Donne's "Anniversaries,"* p. 103.

44. Louis L. Martz, *The Poetry of Meditation: A Study in English Religious Literature of the Seventeenth Century*, is the classic study of Ignatian meditation and Renaissance poetry. In *The Paradise Within*, pp. 17–19, Martz has argued that Augustinian medi-tation is more characteristic of Vaughan, who learned to read nature in terms of the revelation given in the Bible. On Vaughan's use of nature, see Christopher's article in *SP* and Robert Duvall, "The Biblical Character of Henry Vaughan's Silex Scin-tillans," pp. 13–19.

> The smoke, and Exhalations of the brest.
>
> (ll. 7–12)

From his own breast arise dry exhalations, not the living water of
the heart. Quite properly, he sees his own insufficiencies in the
figure of the earth weeping for its mistakes. The resolving image in
the poem is that of the sun/Son, whose tears provide the model of
contrition and whose subliming power can draw the speaker heavenward.[45]

> Yet, if as thou doest melt, and with thy traine
> Of drops make soft the Earth, my eyes could weep
> O're my hard heart, that's bound up, and asleep,
> Perhaps at last
> (Some such showres past,)
> My God would give a Sun-shine after raine.
>
> (ll. 13–18)

The interplay between the implied Christological typology and the
speaker's attempts to recapitulate it defines his insufficiency and
hence his complex dependence on Christ. That is, Christ's atonement, an act of contrition for all mankind, makes the descent and
ascent of grace possible. The speaker's own efforts, his "lazie
breath," at this point have no real effect: "Love only can . . .
Unlock the way." So he ends with the hope that God will send the
sun/Son. His meditation on the creatures is thus typically Protestant in the way that it is conditioned by his prior understanding of
biblical metaphor.

Similarly, in a lyric that looks forward to the return of the bridegroom, "The Dawning," the speaker uses the water-cycle to express his fear that he will be unprepared for the feast.

> Grant, I may not like puddle lie
> In a Corrupt securitie,
> Where, if a traveller water crave,
> He finds it dead, and in a grave;
> But as this restless, vocall *Spring*
> All day, and night doth run, and sing,

45. Since the power of the sun draws the dew back to the heavens, Vaughan made
use of the sun: Son homonym just as Marvell did in "On a Drop of Dew." E.g., in
"Dressing" it is the power of the sun's rays that effectually seals the "mysticall
Communion," melting the frozen waters of the heart; or in "Easter-day," the sun
disperses the mists or "cold damps" that arise from his "sad heart" and "Cloudy
brest."

And though here born, yet is acquainted
Elsewhere, and flowing keeps untainted;
So let me all my busie age
In thy free services ingage . . .

(ll. 29–38)

He fears he will be like a stagnant pool rather than a stream flowing
in God's service. Because of the reference to the bridegroom of the
Canticles, Vaughan probably intended that his readers connect the
water imagery to the *fons signatus* and hence to the waters of life in
general, but the desire to be in "thy free services" also alludes to his
poetry and the waters of inspiration. In his "Jordan" poems, Herbert had announced the waters of the Jordan (with their complex
typological lineage) as the source of his own inspiration. Vaughan
in fact characterized Herbert as "The first, that with any effectual
success attempted a *diversion* of this foul and overflowing *stream* [of
debased poetry]" (p. 391). Herbert's poetry flows like a pure stream
in service to God and Vaughan hoped to follow his example.

Vaughan provided a perfect emblem of the interchange between
the human and the divine in "*Isaacs* Marriage." This poem, as one
critic has noted, is a paradigm for Vaughan's various meditative
practices: a meditation on biblical texts (Gen. 22:1–19, 24:1–67), an
occasional meditation upon a particular marriage, and a meditation
upon Isaac's service to God.[46] Significantly, too, it is an occasional
meditation on the perfumed showers from Lahai-roi's well, which
serve as the emblem of heartfelt prayer since they ascend to the
heavens. As Isaac ponders his approaching marriage with Rebecca,
his soul

> . . . in her piercing flight perfum'd the ayer
> Scatt'ring the *Myrrhe*, and incense of thy pray'r.
> So from *Lahai-roi's* Well some spicie cloud
> Woo'd by the Sun swels up to be his shrowd,
> And from his moist wombe weeps a fragrant showre,
> Which, scatter'd in a thousand pearls, each flowre
> And herb partakes, where having stood awhile
> And something coold the parch'd, and thirstie Isle,
> The thankful Earth unlocks her self, and blends,
> A thousand odours, which (all mixt,) she sends
> Up in one cloud, and so returns the skies
> That dew they lent, a breathing sacrifice.

(ll. 51–62)

46. Lewalski, *Protestant Poetics*, pp. 336–37.

The exquisite imagery conveys an appropriate sense of the numinous, yet a difficulty remains for Vaughan's speaker since this perfect moment of prayer is attributed to Isaac, who, as a figure for Christ, attains a degree of spirituality beyond normal capabilities. Furthermore, Vaughan's marginal note indicates that *Lahai-roi* in Hebrew means "the well of him that liveth," thus linking it with living water even more clearly. As Ira Clark has rightly observed, the irony of the opening lines (which contrast Isaac's marriage with current practices) helps establish Vaughan's true theme in the poem, "faithless man's displacement from types."[47] The irony of the poem is mainly conveyed through the speaker's wide-eyed admiration, a kind of nostalgia or intense longing that expresses the distance he feels from a successful reenactment of Isaac's meditative experience. The perfection of Isaac's prayer serves as a marker of difference against which we can gauge the speaker's less successful meditative experiences.

More typical of the speaker's spiritual life are poems such as "The Storm," "Disorder *and* frailty," or "The Tempest," which represent his attempts to return love and prayer to God as violent meteorologic cycles, requiring God's forceful participation (as in the emblem of the flashing flint). Isaac's experience with God may represent Vaughan's ideal; the reality, however, is the metaphoric storm of affliction that he must suffer to force his stony heart to flow with waters that can ascend like Isaac's prayers to the heavens. In "Affliction," Vaughan wrote that unless "God / Doth use his rod, / And by a fruitfull Change of frosts, and showres / Cherish, and bind thy *pow'rs*" (ll. 11–14), mankind would be lost. The necessity for affliction is firmly inscribed in Christian dogma, on which Vaughan drew to explain his emblem: "Moriendo, *revixi*." The ritual death of the old and rebirth of the new, effected in baptism, is of course the predication for this paradox. These poems on affliction also can be called occasional meditations on watercycles, and they all have the complex typology of the waters of life as part of their contextuality.

"I see the use," the opening half-line of "The Storm," indicates that Vaughan's speaker is applying the lesson provided by the occasion of a dark, violent storm for our edification. He recognizes in the billowing waters, boiling streams, and potent winds an emblem of his own "inner weather": "Yet have I flows, as strong" (l. 5); and he recognizes the purgative effects of such affliction.

47. Clark, *Christ Revealed*, p. 121.

> Lord, then round me with weeping Clouds,
>   And let my mind
> In quick blasts sigh beneath those shrouds
>   A spirit-wind,
> So shall that storme purge this *Recluse*
>   Which sinfull ease made foul,
> And *wind*, and *water* to thy use
>   Both *wash*, and *wing* my soul.
>   (ll. 17–24)

From within the shroud of weeping clouds and heartfelt sighs, the water and spirit will effect his rebirth. As Alan Rudrum has noted, "*Recluse*" in line 21 probably involves a pun on an obsolete meaning of the word, "a reservoir for water" (*OED* 3b).[48] If he has become merely a reservoir instead of a spring of flowing waters, this pun helps to justify the necessity of God's violent action to "wash" and then "wing" his soul toward the heavens.[49]

In "Disorder *and* frailty" Vaughan deployed both of his favorite metaphors for spiritual growth, the seedling nurtured in the heart and the waters that flow from the rock, to portray the difficulties mankind has in emulating Christ's life. Typological recapitulation is clearly evoked in the opening, where the speaker's soul is beckoned from "the grave / And womb of darknes" by Christ who becomes "both guide, and Scout" (ll. 1–4). (We should recall that the baptismal font is also both a tomb and a womb.) Quickly, though, he is beset with storms of affliction: "tost / By winds, and bit with frost" (ll. 6–7). He is the frail plant that buds, "Touch'd by thy fire, and breath; Thy bloud / Too, is my Dew, and springing wel" (ll. 18–19); but while he stretches his branches toward God, he is blighted by earthly travails. Such spiritual activity is linked to the notion of dew rising in the third stanza:

> Thus like some sleeping Exhalation
> (Which wak'd by heat, and beams, makes up
> Unto that Comforter, the Sun,
> And soars, and shines; But e'r we sup
>   And walk two steps

48. Alan Rudrum, ed, *Henry Vaughan: The Complete Poems*, p. 551.

49. Vaughan made use of the related notion of tears ascending in the pilcrow poem, "Thou that know'st for whom I mourne": "A silent teare can peirce thy throne, / When lowd Joyes want a wing, / And sweeter aires streame from a grone, / Than any arted string" (ll. 49–52). And in "The Palm-tree" we learn that the tree of life "Is water'd by their [the saints'] tears, as flowers are fed / With dew by night" (ll. 21–23).

Cool'd by the damps of night, descends,
    And, whence it sprung, there ends,)
        Doth my weak fire
        Pine, and retire,
And (after all my hight of flames,)
In sickly Expirations tames
        Leaving me dead
        On my first bed
Untill thy Sun again ascends.
        Poor, falling Star!

                                    (ll. 31–45)

He at first soars into the sky under the influence of the heat of the
sun, but as day recedes his spiritual ardor is too weak ("my weak
fire") to propel the exhalation very far. It then descends, recon-
denses, and waits for the sun to dissolve and sublime it at a later
time. This metaphor effectively expresses his complex dependency
on Christ. Because Christ is the source of all "living water," the
speaker's descent and ascent as dew represents his participation in
the mystery of God as the source from which all life emanates and
to which it returns (that is, God is both fountain and abyss). Yet
Christ is also the agent (as the subliming sun) by which the speaker
can hope to rise and flow; this dependency renders the notion of
typological recapitulation. As Vaughan put it, Christ is "both
guide, and Scout." While the speaker strives to produce tears of
contrition as "Fresh as the dew" ("Ascension-day," l. 20), or to
extract the "powerful, rare dew" from his heart ("The Sap," l. 40)
in imitation of the scout who has blazed the way for him, he is
finally unable to do so. Thus, he must rely on his guide for help,
who frequently provides the storms of affliction that promote spiritual growth.[50]

Emanation and return, then, is a potent metaphor that Vaughan
exploited to represent the reciprocal interchange between the human and the divine. Since the essential rhythm of the created universe could be characterized as a "hymning circulation," the circulation of living water was an especially appropriate metaphor.
Through the resources of typology, Vaughan developed a sophisticated structure of imagery and metaphor that helps to generate and

50. Vaughan used the metaphoric storms of affliction in other poems, most
notably in "The Tempest." Simmonds, *Masques of God*, p. 157, wrote of this meditation on the water-cycle, "The emblem expresses the ascent of prayer and the
answering descent of grace. It is an exemplary model of the spiritual life, a representation of the ideal form of human response to human sinfulness" (see pp. 156–60).

unify the unfolding narrative of *Silex Scintillans*. The speaker articulates his own narrative as a sacramental recapitulation of Christ's
salvation drama. Because of his imperfect sanctification and natural
insufficiencies, his despair at times seems to outweigh his elation.
Vaughan's typological structure, however, has an eschatological
dimension that resolves the dilemma, for the sacramental imagery
points beyond itself to an action that can only be completed in the
fulness of time, when the waters out of the rock spring into life
everlasting.

The Eschatology of *Silex Scintillans*

Renaissance theologians recognized that the promise fulfilled
temporally through Christ's propitiatory suffering would have a
more perfect fulfillment in the new age to come. As the period
under the law had given way to the period of grace, so the faithful
could anticipate an age of glory. In the mid-seventeenth century,
interest in the second coming of Christ was particularly keen. The
Thirty Years' War and the Civil Wars in England seemed to be the
bitter prelude to the apocalyptic struggles, heralding the last judgment and the new age. Vaughan, as did many of his contempo-
raries, believed the dissolution and regeneration of the universe to
be imminent. In his meditation on death, *Man in Darkness*, he
wrote:

> Suddenly do the high things of this world come to an end, and their
> delectable things passe away, for when they seem to be in their *flowers*
> and full strength, they perish to astonishment; And sure the ruine of
> the most goodly peeces seems to tell, that the dissolution of the whole
> is not far off. (p. 171)

It is therefore not surprising that Vaughan made significant use of
the eschatological antitype of the waters, the crystal fountain of the
New Jerusalem, to achieve emotional and narrative closure in *Silex*.
    The eschatological images of the waters of life are used both *in
malo* and *in bono* to convey the speaker's greatest fear and greatest
hope. If the speaker's pilgrimage toward sanctification has only just
begun in "Regeneration," then the two dialogues on death and
salvation that follow it are especially important in establishing the
spiritual condition of the speaker. In each poem, the disjunction
between the positions held by the "*Body*" and the "*Soule*" expresses
the speaker's fear of the land of darkness and of his fate. The

"*Soule*" in the second dialogue chides this "Poore, querulous hand-full" of dust because of the hesitant reading the "*Body*" makes of a text from the Book of the Creatures (that is, the rebirth of the "drowsie silk-worme"). The "*Soule*" then offers a powerful reading of a natural text to comfort the "*Body*."

> For a preserving spirit doth still passe
> > Untainted through this Masse,
> Which doth resolve, produce, and ripen all
> > That to it fall;
> > Nor are those births which we
> > Thus suffering see
> Destroy'd at all; But when times restles wave
> > Their substance doth deprave
> And the more noble *Essence* finds his house
> > Sickly, and loose,
> > He, ever young, doth wing
> > Unto that spring,
> And *source* of spirits, where he takes his lot
> > Till time no more shall rot
> His passive Cottage.
> > ("Resurrection and Immortality," ll. 31–45)

This depiction of the cycle of birth and death, in terms of the emanation and return of the waters of life, is intended to reassure him:

> For no thing can to *Nothing* fall, but still
> > Incorporates by skill,
> And then returns, and from the wombe of things
> > Such treasure brings
> > As *Phenix*-like renew'th
> > Both life, and youth.
> > (ll. 25–30)

But such reassurance is of little moment to the speaker who feels the awful gulf between himself and the "spring / And *source* of spirits." His disgust for the body he inhabits is registered in this passage through the contrast between the grossness of the world and the preserving spirit that flows "Untainted" through it; as soon as this poor handful of dust, compacted into a body, begins to decay, the soul wings its way back to its source as quickly as it can. His preoccupation with his body's fetidness is the measure of his fear that it is somehow beyond restoration. Indeed, the next poem, "Day of Judgement," is a horrific description of the destruction that must be wrought to cleanse and restore the earth. What sets the emotional tone for this series of poems, beginning with "Regeneration," is the interplay between the sacramental and eschatological recapitulation of baptismal regeneration. By reminding us of the speaker's insufficiencies, Vaughan emphasized both the desperate fear the speaker has of damnation and his need for continual infusions of grace until such time as he can drink freely of the waters at their source.

As the speaker makes progress in this pilgrimage, allusions to the upper waters as a source of comfort and hope begin to emerge. One notable example is from "The Timber," in which the speaker acknowledges that his afflictions produce a few drops of the upper waters (by way of sacramental reenactment):

> Blest showers they are, and streams sent from above
> Begetting *Virgins* where they use to flow;
> And trees of life no other waters love,
> These upper springs and none else make them grow.
>
> But these chaste fountains flow not till we dye;
> Some drops may fall before, but a clear spring
> And ever running, till we leave to fling
> Dirt in her way, will keep above the skie.
>
> (ll. 49–56)

The reiteration of such comforting images as these gradually amplifies the speaker's hope that he will be among the faithful at the fountain of life in the New Jerusalem. The eschatological antitype, the upper waters of the crystal fountain, provides the consummating or resolving image that gives emotional closure to this pilgrimage.

The speaker's progress toward sanctification is marked by moments of elation, when he feels the joys of sacramental grace, and by moments of despair, when he feels estranged from God because of his own insufficiencies. The first part of *Silex* plainly features this pattern. As Calhoun and Post have both argued, at the center of *Silex* 1650 is a liturgical and typological sequence on Christ's passion, beginning with "Dressing" and culminating with "The Holy Communion."[51] In the latter, Vaughan linked typologically the restorative effect of sacramental grace with the original act of

---

51. See Calhoun, *The Achievement of "Silex,"* pp. 139–41; and Post, *Unfolding Vision*, pp. 143–44.

creation when all life was shaped out of the dark chaos of the
waters.

> Welcome sweet, and sacred feast; welcome life!
> Dead I was, and deep in trouble;
> But grace, and blessings came with thee so rife,
> That they have quicken'd even drie stubble;
> Thus soules their bodies animate,
> And thus, at first, when things were rude,
> Dark, void, and Crude
> They, by thy Word, their beauty had, and date.
>
> (ll. 1–8)

Vaughan emphasized that the warrant for sacramental palingenesis
derives from typological recapitulation, which effectively reminds
his readers that this reenactment will recur again and again to restore the image of God in mankind. The final poem in *Silex* 1650
begs God to "Perfect what thou hast begun" ("Begging," l. 3), but
the rising and falling action never ceases for the weary pilgrim.

While the second part of *Silex* begins with the speaker claiming a
share in Christ's glorification on the Mount of Olives ("I / Feel me
a sharer in thy victory," "Ascension-day," ll. 7–8), this joyous
moment is not sustained. The same pattern characterizes the second
book as the first, though there is more elation than despair. For
example, after the initial sequence following "Ascension-day," we
find a cluster of poems ("The Garland," "Love-sick," and "Trinity-
Sunday") that describe the speaker's fall back into sin and the
"mountains of cold Ice" in his heart ("Love-sick," l. 12). Similarly,
the cluster consisting of "Fair and yong light," "The Stone," and
"The dwelling-place" replays the same drama as does a cluster just
before the sequence of poems on the last things ("Anguish,"
"Tears," and "Jacobs Pillow, and Pillar"). The speaker is finally
incapable of true linear progress in his pilgrimage. To borrow the
image of the winding stair from W. B. Yeats, typological recapitulation takes the believer up a seemingly endless spiral stair-
case, always covering the same ground as before. Though the journey is arduous, Vaughan's speaker at last begins to make some
progress upward.

The companion poems on the last judgment, for instance, clearly
measure his progress; in the 1650 poem, the utter destructiveness of
the impending cosmic dissolution startles us:

> When all shall streame, and lighten round
> And with surprizing flames

> Both stars, and Elements confound
> And quite blot out their names . . .
> ("Day of Judgement [I]," ll. 5–8)

But at the end of his journey, the pilgrim-speaker hails the moment of the great instauration as the "day of life, of light, of love!" ("The day of Judgement [II]," l. 1). In the second part of *Silex* he "dreams of Paradise and light" with greater frequency, and thus the eschatological imagery of the waters of life also recurs more often, which helps to give closure metaphorically and structurally to the pilgrimage being narrated.[52]

His longing for paradise is rendered using the familiar imagery of biblical eschatology. Since the prototypical garden of Eden will be restored and perfected in the pastoral New Jerusalem, Vaughan's speaker longs to be

> Where freed souls dwel by living fountains
> On everlasting, spicy mountains!
>   Alas! my God! take home thy sheep;
>   This world but laughs at those that weep.[53]

Between the primal and eternal images of paradise stand other important types, as we have seen: the garden of the bridegroom in the Canticles, the garden atop Olivet, and Golgotha itself (where the pierced side represents the fountain and the cross represents the tree of life). But as the pilgrim-speaker moves up the spiral stairs, his thoughts turn increasingly toward the "upper springs." In "The Seed growing secretly," he hopes the dove will bring him "One living drop" of the waters of life to regenerate him, for only those who wear "spotless *white*" can approach "thy eternal, living wells" (ll. 14, 21–24).[54] The crystal fountain is referred to frequently in

---

52. The references to the upper waters are approximately three times more numerous in Part II than in Part I. The notable references from *Silex* 1650 are: "Resurrection and Immortality," ll. 41–43; "Corruption," ll. 23–24; and "The Constellation," ll. 1–4. In the second part: "The Palm-tree," ll. 21–23; "The Timber," ll. 49–56; "The Seed growing secretly," ll. 21–24; "Fair and yong light," ll. 49–50; "The Ass," ll. 59–64; "Tears," ll. 9–12; "Psalm 65," ll. 29–32; and "The Water-fall," ll. 23–40.

53. "Fair and yong light," ll. 49–52. Similarly, in "Corruption," ll. 23–24, he wrote that *"Paradise* lay / In some green shade, or fountain."

54. In some verses on the baptismal font he translates as part of *Primitive Holiness*, Vaughan elaborated on the connection between the Holy Spirit, baptismal water, and the upper waters: "Here the great well-spring of wash'd Soules, with beams / Of living light quickens the lively streams; / The Dove descends, and stirs them with her wings, / So weds these waters to the upper springs, / They strait conceive:

Silex: it is "a clear spring / And ever running" ("The Timber," ll. 55–56); he hopes the Lord will lead him to the "living springs" to restore him to health and perfect peace ("The Ass," l. 60); and, at times, he is granted a foretaste of

> those true Joys
> Whose spring is on that hil where you [the stars] do grow
> And we here tast sometimes below.
> ("The Constellation," ll. 2–4)

In the Preface, Vaughan had described the waters of a grace as a "small *prelibation* of those heavenly *refreshments*" (p. 392), and at the end of his journey, the speaker anticipates drinking unreservedly from "Thy upper river, which abounds / With fertil streams, makes rich all grounds" ("Psalm 65," ll. 29–30).

Silex concludes with a series of poems on the last things.[55] Beginning and ending the sequence are poems on the apocalypse, "The day of Judgement" and "L'Envoy," that look beyond to the new age. Two poems offer thanksgiving in anticipation of the joys of paradise ("Psalm 65" and "The Queer"); two are given to Christ's death and resurrection ("Death" and "The Obsequies"); one is devoted to "The Throne" and one to "The Feast"; and two are paeans to the Logos. The focus of these poems is obviously sacred history as it is prophesied in Revelation. In contrast to the uncertainties and afflictions characteristic of Part I, the sequence on the last things looks beyond the vagaries of time to the new age to come. Midway through this sequence stands "The Water-fall," a poem featuring the complex typology of the waters of life. Not only is this one of Vaughan's most beautiful lyrics, it is also one of the most significant in terms of the metaphoric structure of *Silex*. It incorporates a central motif of Part I (the garden of the Canticles and the stony heart that must be split open) into the greater scheme of sacred history: like the waters that plunge from a rocky gorge to the deep beneath only to be recirculated endlessly, the waters of life, "quickned by this deep and rocky grave, / Rise to a longer course more bright and brave" (ll. 11–12). In addition to the familiar sacramental and Christological implications of the recirculation of the waters of life, "The Water-fall" extends its frame of

---

A new birth doth proceede / From the bright streams by an immortall seed" (p. 365).

55. Lewalski, *Protestant Poetics*, p. 323, and Post, *Unfolding Vision*, pp. 151–56, have discussed this sequence.

reference to a more encompassing typological dimension. Not only the typical Christian life but all sacred history can be imaged in terms of water returning to its source—the creation out of the waters of the deep, the purification of the waters through Christ's intercession in time, and the perfection of the waters in the fulness of time. The source of the solitary figure's comfort, as he meditates beside the falls, lies in his full understanding of the way the crucial events in his life are closely mirrored in Christ's.

The opening line of the poem—"With what deep murmurs through times silent stealth"—seems to locate the speaker's meditation in just the perspective we should expect from a Protestant meditation on a "text," be it from the Book of Scripture or the Book of the Creatures.[56] The lesson of the speaker's meditation derives from his understanding of the circularity of water, which the speaker emphasizes by examining three aspects of this emblematic waterfall: the fall from the precipice (ll. 9–12), the stream that forms and flows again below (ll. 15–16), and the "streaming rings" that are engendered on the surface of the pool beneath the falls (ll. 33–36).[57] What guides the speaker through his meditation, and what becomes the real source of his joy, is his understanding as a believer that this natural water-cycle expresses a more profound circulation. Just as all water streams from the fountain of living waters and then flows into the abyss where it must be purified before it can return to its source, so must mankind be born and then redeemed before resurrection into eternal life.

In the water flowing endlessly through the falls, the speaker recognizes the pattern of three different biblical events that involve "living" water and the mystery of his faith. The waters flowing from "this deep and rocky grave" (l. 11), first of all, offer an ob-

56. The poem has been usually read as classic Ignatian meditation. See, for example, Wulf Datow, "*The Water-fall* von Henry Vaughan (1621–1695)," pp. 410–20, who found in the first twelve lines a *compositio loci*, then exposition, and finally colloquy. I believe that the poet does not discover these truths during his meditation, but rather he reveals what his reading of the Book of Scripture has already taught him.

57. In lines 33–36, Vaughan described the expanding rings that gradually disappear when they reach the bank of the pool. As Rudrum, *Complete Poems*, p. 639, has explained, "restagnates" (l. 34) refers to "the characteristic motion of water in process of regaining stillness." A passage from Vaughan's translation of *The World Contemned*, p. 322, clarifies the point: "As streames of water falling from high, the one still following the other, doe in successive circles break and terminate at the banks; so the appointed times and successions of men are cut off at the boundary of death." As the "streaming rings" seem to disappear in their circular return to their source, so too do men disappear to an "invisible estate."

vious parallel to the sacramental waters of baptism, which plunge
the catechumens into a watery grave only to restore them to eternal
life. The speaker acknowledges this when he identifies the water in
the falls as "My sacred wash and cleanser here" (l. 24). (The water
flowing from the rocks also recalls the rock of Horeb.) Second, he
acknowledges that baptismal water is his "consigner" (l. 25) or the
"seal" (which recalls the language of the Anglican article on the
sacraments) that will enable him to partake of the fountains of life
in the New Jerusalem. What follows these commonplace associations of springing water with "living" baptismal water and the
"river of water of life" is an association with a third biblical event,
which suggests that the speaker understands these "mystical, deep
streams" (l. 28) as part of the complex typology of the waters of
life.[58] For the speaker links baptismal and apocalyptic waters to the
waters of the deep of Genesis, the material out of which the universe was created.

> O useful Element and clear!
> My sacred wash and cleanser here,
> My first consigner unto those
> Fountains of life, where the Lamb goes?
> What sublime truths, and wholesome themes,
> Lodge in thy mystical, deep streams!
> Such as dull man can never finde
> Unless that Spirit lead his minde,
> Which first upon thy face did move,
> And hatch'd all with his quickning love.
>   (ll. 23–32)

In the circulating waters, the speaker finds the decisive moments in
each Christian's life (birth, baptism, redemption) connected in
terms of promise and fulfillment. In explicating this "text" he underscores the fact that these personal moments are also mirrored in
the broader course of sacred history (creation, redemption, apocalypse): the waters that flow through this cataract are those upon
which the Holy Spirit hovered to "hatch" the universe (l. 32, a
word strongly reminiscent of the Vulgate's *incubabat* in Genesis
1:2); they are the cleansing waters of baptism; and ultimately they

58. Other scholars have noted these biblical echoes, but none to my knowledge
has pointed out the typological connections. See W. Nelson Francis, "Vaughan's
'The Waterfall,'" p. 57; Michael Murrin, *The Veil of Allegory: Some Notes toward a
Theory of Allegorical Rhetoric in the English Renaissance*, pp. 135–41; and Simmonds,
Masques of God, pp. 17–19.

will become the fountains of life in the New Jerusalem. The speaker, in other words, understands the waterfall in terms of a pattern of biblical events that links his own life to the course of sacred history—which is progressing "through times silent stealth" from creation, to redemption, and inexorably to the new age.

Vaughan's recognition that "times silent stealth" is delimited by the emanation and return of the waters of life from God was traditional. The river of time is an archetypal metaphor that found expression in many seventeenth-century sources. Vaughan made special use of it in *The Mount of Olives*, in which he pointed out that "by the *river* we may understand *time,* upon whose brink we are always pearching" (p. 174); later he referred again to "that *deepest* and *smoothest current* of *time*" (p. 187).[59] The metaphor commonly used to depict the ultimate reintegration of time with eternity was derived from the same sources on which Vaughan appears to have based his meditation: Genesis 1:2, Ecclesiastes 1:7, and Revelation 22:1. John Swan clearly recognized that the mysterious circularity of water provided a metaphoric equivalent to the mystery of God's essence and a key to understanding the correspondence of the temporal and eternal in his cosmographic *Speculum Mundi*:

> *Time*, by whose revolutions we measure houres, dayes, weeks, moneths and years, is nothing else but (as it were) a certain space borrowed or set apart from *eternitie*; which shall at the last return to eternitie again: like the rivers, which have their first course from the seas; and by running on, there they arrive, and have their last: for before *Time* began, there was *Eternitie*, namely GOD: which was, which is, and which shall be for ever: without beginning or end, and yet the beginning and end of all things.[60]

Vaughan also exploited the implicit circularity of the river of time in his translation of Nierembergius's *Of Temperance and Patience*: "*Time* is a sacred thing: it flowes from Heaven. . . . It is an emanation from that place, where eternity springs. The right use of it, is to reduce it to its Original: If we follow time close, it will bring us to its Fountain" (p. 261).

The waterfall is then a natural hieroglyph, but the hidden message that the speaker shares with us is one that he has gleaned from his study of the complex typology of water imagery found in

59. In *Silex* he also used the river of time in "Resurrection and Immortality," ll. 35–45, and "The Dawning," ll. 33–44.

60. John Swan, *Speculum Mundi, or, a Glasse representing the Face of the World. . . . Whereunto is joyned an Hexameron*, p. 39.

Scripture. More importantly, he has verified the pattern expressed through the imagery, in part, by his own experience. The pilgrimage recorded in *Silex Scintillans* is metaphorically nearing its completion. "The Water-fall" is perhaps best understood as the complement, or "antitype," to certain poems from Part I, "Regeneration" and "Vanity of Spirit" in particular. As Lewalski has argued, the latter is really an enactment of the speaker's failure to meditate successfully on the creatures.[61] Just as he would do in "The Water-fall," he sits alongside a spring to rifle its secrets, relying on his ability to reason. Though he "beg'd here long, and gron'd to know" (l. 3), his insufficiencies prevent him from reading this text; for as Lewalski explains, he has not learned to use the Book of Scripture as his guide. His meditation is a vain exercise. In some ways, this parallels his situation in the opening poem, where he discovers that the living water is collecting into a cistern instead of flowing freely. Both poems help us gauge the spiritual condition of the speaker, using the circularity of water as a marker; as imperfect "types," they prepare us for the transcendent insights at the waterfall. Through his long nights of devotion and meditation, as the full record of his hardships will attest, he prepares himself to receive the dew of grace that will transform his flinty heart into a living one. Gradually, allusions to sacramental and Christological types of the waters of life give way to more frequent allusions to the perfected garden of the New Jerusalem with its rivers of living waters, signaling a change in his thinking from type to antitype. Post is surely right in arguing that "The Water-fall" ought to be seen as the measure of Vaughan's development: "The ability of his speaker to be able to interpret the waterfall allegorically—as a fountain of life—exactly reverses the situation in 'Regeneration' where the poet-pilgrim is only a figure in an allegory, pondering, without really understanding."[62] "The Water-fall" thus provides emotional, metaphoric, and structural closure to *Silex*.

The concern with time in "The Water-fall," introduced by the allusion to "times silent stealth" in the opening line, is thus not limited to the lifetime of any single individual. For in its fullest sense typology is not simply a matter of the recapitulation of Old Testament types in Christ's life by each believer; rather, typology, the underpinning of the Protestant reading code in the Renaissance,

61. Lewalski, *Protestant Poetics*, pp. 335–36.
62. Post, *Unfolding Vision*, p. 154.

revealed the essential unity of time, whether it be the lifetime of the Christian or the full span of sacred history.[63] To use the metaphor of the water-cycle to express this notion: time will once again flow into eternity for the individual and the cosmos. That this day will soon be forthcoming is the speaker's fervent hope, for he ardently longs to taste the upper waters at their source—the crystal fountain.

> O my invisible estate,
> My glorious liberty, still late!
> Thou art the Channel my soul seeks,
> Not this with Cataracts and Creeks.
>   (ll. 37–40)

63. On this point see Fredson Bowers, "Henry Vaughan's Multiple Time Scheme," pp. 291–96.

❧[VI]❧

THE SOUL AS FOUNTAIN
AND ABYSS IN
THE DOBELL *POEMS*

Man is a Great and Wonderfull Miracle. . . . A Messenger between the
Creatures, Lord of Inferior things, and familiar to those abov; by the
Keeness of his sences, the Peircing of his Reason, and the Light of
Knowledg, the Interpreter of Nature, A seeming Intervall between Time
and Eternity and the Inhabitant of both, the Golden link or Tie of the
World, yea the Hymenaeus Marrying the Creator and his Creatures
together; made as David witnesseth a little lower then the Angels.

Traherne's optimistic claim for the place of man in the universe has
its roots in the Platonism that flourished at Cambridge in the mid-
seventeenth century.[1] This quotation, in fact, is a paraphrase of
Pico's *Oratio de dignitate hominis*, and scholars have traced most of
his philosophy to similar sources.[2] The keystone to his world view,
as it is outlined in "The Circulation" and developed throughout his
writings, is no doubt indebted to the Ficinian idea of the *circuitus
spiritualis*, the uninterrupted current of spiritual energy and essence
flowing from the godhead to the universe and reverting back to it.[3]
Though Traherne certainly would have been familiar with the
fountain as metaphor for God's immanence and dynamism from

1. IV.74. Quotations are taken from Thomas Traherne, *Centuries, Poems, and
Thanksgivings*; each meditation will be identified by *Century* number in upper case
Roman and its individual number in Arabic. Quotations from Traherne's *Christian
Ethicks* will be indicated by the abbreviation CE, followed by a page number.

2. See Rosalie L. Colie, "Thomas Traherne and the Infinite: The Ethical Com-
promise"; S. Sandbank, "Thomas Traherne on the Place of Man in the Universe";
Carol L. Marks, "Thomas Traherne and Cambridge Platonism," "Thomas Tra-
herne and Hermes Trismegistus," and "Traherne's Ficino Notebook"; Malcolm M.
Day, "Traherne and the Doctrine of Pre-existence"; and Gerard H. Cox,
"Traherne's *Centuries*: A Platonic Devotion of 'Divine Philosophy.'"

3. The expression is from Marsilio Ficino, *Theologica Platonica*, I. fol. 211. For an

Neoplatonic sources, he would not have found one of the central images in his work there: the notion of the individual soul as an abyss receiving and a fountain returning the divine essence. To account for this powerful, recurring motif in the Dobell Folio *Poems*,[4] we need to recognize that Traherne was also drawing from the symbolic riches of the Bible.

In the Dobell *Poems*, the same metaphor—the circulation of the waters of life that flow ceaselessly from the fountain to the abyss and back again—is employed to depict both God's mode of being in the universe and the soul's. This relationship between the individual soul and God is essentially typological; the soul, in its purest state of being (the act that Traherne called *thinking*), recapitulates the emanation and return of the godhead. The biblical imagery of the waters of life is thus central to Traherne's system of belief because it expresses the "marriage" of the creator with his creatures. As we have seen, the circularity of the waters of life was fully understood by the interpreters of Scripture and used by such poets as Herbert and Vaughan. As other seventeenth-century poets before him had also done, Traherne simply adopted it for his own creative purposes in the Dobell *Poems*.

Typological Strategies in Traherne's Thought

Though it has become a critical commonplace to regard Traherne primarily as a Platonist, let us remember that he was ratified for the living at Credenhill in 1657 by the Commissioners for the Approbation of Public Preachers under the Commonwealth and served later as a good Anglican divine and chaplain for over a decade after the Restoration. It is thus natural for us to expect that

---

account of Ficino's doctrine of love, see Paul O. Kristeller, *The Philosophy of Marsilio Ficino*, especially pp. 110–15; and Ernst Cassirer, *The Individual and the Cosmos in Renaissance Philosophy*, pp. 131–36.

4. Those poems found in the Dobell manuscript (Bodleian MS. Eng. poet, c. 42) are generally accepted as an ordered sequence written in the poet's own hand. Most modern editions, including the Oxford *Traherne*, preserve the arrangement and considerable emendation of Philip Traherne as they are found in the *Poems of Felicity* manuscript (Burney MS. 392). Some of Traherne's best poems unfortunately exist only in Philip's emended version. Because of these textual difficulties, I have confined my study only to what seems definitely to be Thomas's final intentions, the so-called Dobell Folio. For an account of the textual history of Traherne's poems, see Margoliouth's introduction to *Centuries, Poems, and Thanksgivings*, 1:xii–xvii.

his Anglicanism would exert a strong influence over what he would borrow in his readings among the Platonists.[5] Hence, the language and the symbolic modes of the Bible ought to be recognized for their formative influences on his thinking. With few exceptions, there has been little critical interest in Traherne's use of typology, despite the open discussion of typology in the *Centuries* and *Christian Ethicks*.[6] Not only did he mention some of the prominent types of Christ and ceremonies of the old law—such as the brazen serpent (I.57), the stony heart (I.88 and III.83), or the tabernacle (*Church's Year-Book*, fols. 49ᵛ–50ʳ)—but he also offered complete "readings" of several major types; the typology of the old temple (CE, pp. 129–30) and of the Canticles (III.77) are two notable examples. When the many separate references are considered together, we must admit that Traherne was as familiar with the typological commonplaces of his era as we would expect an Anglican divine to be.[7]

More importantly, Traherne's interest in typology is evident in the structure of the Dobell *Poems*. Critics have labored over naming the parts of the sequence, but nearly all agree that the paradigm for the spiritual life presented follows the classic pattern of innocence, a fall into sin, redemption, and glorification.[8] Since Traherne discussed the spiritual life in terms of the four "estates" in *Christian Ethicks* (chapter 4) and the *Third Century*, it is appropriate to use his own terminology to plot this pattern. In general, Traherne viewed

5. Carol L. Marks, in "Thomas Traherne's Early Studies," has demonstrated that he read selectively and recorded in his Early Notebook only those ideas he found congenial.

6. See Ira Clark, *Christ Revealed: The History of the Neotypological Lyric in the English Renaissance*, pp. 133–59; and Richard D. Jordan, *The Temple of Eternity: Thomas Traherne's Philosophy of Time*, pp. 58–73.

7. For a more complete listing of typological references, see Clark, *Christ Revealed*, pp. 139–45.

8. John Malcolm Wallace, "Thomas Traherne and the Structure of Meditation," was the first to describe the *Poems* as a sequence, arguing that they followed the pattern of an Ignatian meditation. Louis L. Martz, *The Paradise Within: Studies in Vaughan, Traherne, and Milton*, pp. 35–102, has argued instead for an Augustinian pattern of meditation. A. L. Clements, *The Mystical Poetry of Thomas Traherne*, found the pattern of innocence, fall, and redemption set against a backdrop of the mystical path. Stanley Stewart, *The Expanded Voice: The Art of Thomas Traherne*, pp. 170–207, also saw a progression from birth to the New Jerusalem; his reading is perhaps the most acute. Finally, Barbara K. Lewalski, *Protestant Poetics and the Seventeenth-Century Religious Lyric*, pp. 373–82, has argued for a three-part meditation on man's felicity.

life as a pilgrimage, an "Estate of Trial," which follows the basic
Christian paradigm, the "fourfold Estate of Innocency, Misery,
Grace and Glory" (III.43). The Dobell *Poems* seem to follow the
same division. In the first group of poems (from "The Salutation"
to "The Preparative"), in Traherne's words, "we are to Contem-
plate the Nature and Maner of His Happiness, the Laws under
which He was governed, the Joys of Paradice, and the Immaculat
Powers of His Immortal Soul"; the next group (from "The Instruction" to "Speed") deals with the Estate of Misery, "his Fall the
Nature of Sin Original and Actual, His Manifold Punishments Ca-
lamity Sickness Death &c."; the third group (from "The Designe"
to "Another") renders the Estate of Grace, "the Tenor of the New
Covenant . . . the Conditions of it Faith and Repentance"; and the
last poems (from "Love" to "Goodness") look forward to the Estate of Glory, "the Nature of Seperat Souls, their Advantages Excellencies and Privileges, the Resurrection of the Body, the Day of
Judgment and Life Everlasting" (III.43). Having the "estates" as a
structural schema emphasizes the same typological pattern evident
in the poetry of Herbert and Vaughan, the paradigm for the spiritual life based on a typological understanding of the relationship of
the individual to Christ set forth in Scripture, whereby the individual recapitulates the pattern of salvation made possible by Christ's
perfect experience of it: creation, fall, redemption, and glorification.

Though the *Centuries of Meditation* places the crucifixion at the
heart of Traherne's faith—see, for example, his meditation on the
cross (I.86) or his embracing the doctrine of imputed righteousness
(II.35)—the suffering of Christ has curiously little role in the *Poems*.
The focus instead is on celebrating God's presence in the life of the
speaker. Ira Clark has observed that Traherne transcended the usual
form of the typological lyric by blurring the distinctions between
Christological and sacramental types.[9] This is most clearly seen in
Traherne's use of Adamic typology. Since Adam is the *forma futuri*,
"the figure of him that was to come" (Rom. 5:14) and Christ is the
"last Adam" (1 Cor. 15:45), the fulfillment of the prototypic man,
Traherne pronounced that each believer is capable of becoming
another Adam, a typological everyman. "Certainly Adam in Paradice had not more sweet and Curious Apprehensions of the World,
then I when I was a child" (III.1). Throughout the Dobell *Poems* he
assumed this prototypic identity:

9. Clark, *Christ Revealed*, pp. 133–39, did not use the terms *Christological, sacramental*, and *eschatological*, preferring instead a term of his own, *neotypological*.

> I was an Adam there,
> A little Adam in a Sphere
>
> Of Joys!
>   ("Innocence," ll. 51–53)

That Traherne perceived himself to be the son of God (III.29), "the Sole Heir of the whole World" (I.29), is the fundament upon which he grounded his system of beliefs. For Traherne, however, the most attractive form of expression for this relationship was not in the figure of Adam, but rather in the metaphoric annihilation of the self in the abyss—in the flowing of the abyss of the self back into the abyss of the godhead. Consequently, the typology of the waters of life is quite prominent. The "Enlarged Soul," as he designated it in the *Centuries* (III.84), is made expansive by sacramental recapitulation whereby the soul is transformed into a fountain returning praise and love to God—the source and end of love. At the very center of Traherne's hope lay the implicit typological fusion of the identities of Christ, Adam, and the soul. As Stanley Stewart has put it, love annihilates the distinctions between self and others.[10] Traherne's belief in this annihilation of the boundaries of the self gives his work its characteristic optimism.

Fortunately for readers of his poetry, Traherne was something of a systematic philosopher who, in his *Centuries of Meditation* and *Christian Ethicks*, explained the pattern of thought informing his poems. At the center of his philosophy is his conception of God: "GOD is not a Being compounded of Body and Soul, or Substance and Accident, or Power and Act but is All Act, Pure Act, a Simple Being. Whose Essence is to be, Whose Being is to be Perfect, so that He is most Perfect towards all and in all" (III.63). God's essence, in other words, is to manifest himself through the act of love that begat (or is begetting) the universe. The most pervasive and most important metaphor Traherne used for the manifestation of God's essence is the mystery of waters flowing from and returning to their source, the *circuitus spiritualis*:[11] "He is the Fountain, Governor, and End" (III.43). So insistent is his work upon the notion of

---

10. Stewart, *Expanded Voice*, p. 154.

11. God is frequently described in the Dobell *Poems* as both "fountain" and "end"; see, for example, "The Vision," "Silence," "Nature," "The Circulation," "The Anticipation," "Thoughts. IV," and "Goodnesse." Traherne noted the paradox of fountain and end in the *Centuries of Meditation* (II.40, 41, 46, 62; III.43; and V.1) and in *Christian Ethicks* (pp. 70, 152, and 251). This paradox was familiar to other Neoplatonists. Theophilus Gale, for example, one of the writers Traherne featured

God as fountain, means, and end that it becomes almost a refrain that unifies the *Centuries*, recurring nearly every tenth one.[12] The endless circulation of divine essence, furthermore, offers a way of understanding the mystery of the trinity.

> In all Lov there is some Producer, som Means, and som End: all these being Internal in the Thing it self. Lov Loving is the Producer, and that is the father; Lov produced is the Means, and that is the Son: for Lov is the Means by which a Lover loveth. The End of these Means is Lov: for it is Lov, by loving: and that is the H. Ghost. The End and the Producer being both the same, by the Means attained. for by Loving Lov attaineth it self and Being. The Producer is attained by Loving, and is the End of Himself. That Lov is the End of it self, and that GOD loveth that He might be lov, is as evident to him that considers spiritual Things, as the Sun. Becaus it is impossible there should be a Higher End, or a Better proposed. . . . Since GOD therfore chuseth the most Perfect Life, what can be more Perfect, then that Life and that Being which is at once the fountain, and the End of all Things? There being in it the Perpetual Joy of Giving and Receiving infinit Treasures. To be the Fountain of Joys and Blessings is Delightfull. And by being Lov GOD is the fountain of all Worlds. (II.46)

The consummate manifestation of the triune nature of God was the creation: when *"first He thought upon Angelical and Celestial Vertues, and that Thought was the Work, which he wrought by the WORD, and fulfilled by the Spirit"* (III.65). The Father provides the essence, the Son the informing intellect or Logos, and the Holy Spirit both means and end. Though the fountain of life as a representation of the creation is a traditional Neoplatonism, it also has its roots in Christian orthodoxy: the Father is the fountain of life, who effects the creation by means of the Son with the agency of the Holy Spirit, hovering over the waters of the abyss.

Two crucial postulates follow from Traherne's basic conception of God and of the typological relationship suggested by it. The

---

most prominently in his *Commonplace Book*, stated that the "*Grandeur* and sovereign *Perfection* of God consists principally in his being the *first principle* and *last end* of all things: from whom all things at first flow as from the *Plentitude of Being*: to whom they again have their *refluxe*, as rivers to the Ocean." The quotation is from Theophilus Gale, *The Court of the Gentiles,* Part I, p. 2, cited in Marks's General Introduction, CE, p. xlv.

12. The fountain metaphor is ubiqitous in the *Centuries*; in addition to the implicit use he made of the metaphor throughout his meditations, the explicit references include I.23, 42, 45, 48, 59, 91, 95; II.7, 19, 23, 25, 40, 41, 46, 58, 62, 68, 78, 83, 92; III.27, 43, 76, 78, 82, 94, 100; IV.43, 44, 46, 49, 51, 81, 84, 85; and V.1, 9.

individual, first of all, has the infinite capacity to receive the plenitude emanating from God. Metaphorically, Vaughan rendered this
relationship by likening the soul to an ocean or abyss that is filled
by this divine fountain of living water.

> He was an Ocean of Delights from Whom
> The Living Springs and Golden Streams did com:
> My Bosom was an Ocean into which
> They all did run. And me they did enrich.
> A vast and Infinit Capacitie,
> Did make my Bosom like the Deitie,
> In Whose Mysterious and Celestial Mind
> All Ages and all Worlds together shind.
> Who tho he nothing said did always reign,
> And in Himself Eternitie contain.
>
> ("Silence," ll. 71–80)

Furthermore, because this living water returns to its source, the
speaker imagines the soul as a fountain returning spiritual essence
back to God. Throughout his meditations and his poetry, he be-
seeches God to "send down the Holy Ghost upon me: Breath upon
me, Inspire me, Quicken Me, Illuminat me, Enflame me, fill me
with the Spirit of GOD; that I may *overflow* with Praises and
Thanksgivings as they did" (I.95, italics added). More confident
than either Herbert or Vaughan in the human capability to overflow with praise and love for God, Traherne conceived of the soul
in the same paradoxical terms as God—as both fountain and abyss:
"the Soul is a Miraculous Abyss of infinit Abysses, an Undrainable
Ocean, an inexhausted fountain of Endles Oceans, when it will
exert it self to fill and fathom them" (II.83). By using the same
metaphor for God and the individual, Traherne adhered to a basic
typological strategy to show how the soul participates in the godhead. Some readers, in fact, have gone so far as to argue that
Traherne identified God with the human soul in essence.[13] While
this may overstate the case, it is clear that both God and the soul
were for him conduits in the ceaseless flux and reflux of spiritual
essence in the universe. Much of the exclamatory quality of the
Dobell *Poems* derives from the speaker's exuberance over the astonishing fact of this potential: "My Soul a Spirit infinit! / An Image of
the Deitie!" ("My Spirit," ll. 71–72).

As a Christian Neoplatonist, Traherne viewed the corporeal
world as a less perfect (because material) manifestation of the pure

---

13. See, e.g., Day, "Traherne and the Doctrine," p. 86.

intelligibility of God's mind. By enabling God to enjoy his universe intellectually, the individual, in effect, "marries" the creator with his creatures. Thus, Traherne attributed a central role to mankind in this dynamic cosmos as "A Messenger between the Creatures . . . the Hymenæus Marrying the Creator and his Creatures together" (IV.74). Traherne's position, S. Sandbank has explained, is that "man's ascent to his origin in God spells, beyond his own perfection, the perfection of Being itself through its restoration to its origin. The human soul, knowing the lower in terms of the higher world, collects it, purifies it, and lifts it up to universality, thus restoring the unity of Being itself."[14] Yet Traherne took an even bolder step by claiming that God needs the soul to return these thoughts to him: "GOD is the Spring whence Things came forth / Souls are the fountains of their Real Worth" ("The Demonstration," ll. 59–60). His warrant for this staggering claim is offered in the *First Century*:

> This is very strange that GOD should Want. for in Him is the Fulness of all Blessedness: He overfloweth Eternaly. His Wants are as Glorious as Infinit. . . . He is from Eternity full of Want: Or els He would not be full of Treasure. Infinit Want is the very Ground and Caus of infinit Treasure. It is Incridible, yet very Plain: Want is the Fountain of all His Fulness. Want in GOD is a Treasure to us. For had there been no Need He would not hav Created the World, nor Made us, nor Manifested his Wisdom, nor Exercised his Power, nor Beautified Eternity, nor prepared the Joys of Heaven. But He Wanted Angels and Men, Images, Companions. And these He had from all Eternitie. (I.42)

In Traherne's thought, God, as the fountain of spiritual essence, needs the individual to receive infinitely (as an abyss) in order to return this essence to God who is paradoxically the end (as well as the beginning) of all. Thus, the notion of the fountain in all its metaphoric complexity—especially the relationship of fountain to abyss implied in the doctrine of circularity—is the key to understanding the mystery of Traherne's dynamic, infinite universe. Moreover, it also explains the importance for Traherne of learning to know or esteem the universe rightly. The soul's potential, its boundless capacity to receive, must be transformed into actuality through the intellectual act Traherne called *thinking*, an act that turns the soul into a fountain returning love to God to satisfy his own infinite wants.

14. Sandbank, "Traherne on the Place of Man," p. 122.

The *thoughts* with which Traherne was concerned are not simply the products of the ordinary, rational mind; when the intellectual faculty truly contemplates the intelligible world, it resembles the mode of thinking characteristic of the mystics. For Traherne thinking, Malcolm Day has explained, is "a direct perception in which the existential condition of the Mind is changed when we set our Minds in frame in such a way as to view everything as God does, when we rise to the point of view of the Intellect, which is our real Self, and view all from the dimensionless point of eternity."[15] Knowledge, therefore, is quite important in Traherne's philosophy, especially self-knowledge, for one "knows and loves the infinite by knowing and loving the infinite in himself."[16] By thinking, one can expand one's being ("Yea by Loving Thou Expandest and Enlargest thy self" I.73), thereby allowing love to flow from the fountain of the soul. "Lov is the true Means by which the World is Enjoyed. Our Lov to others, and Others Lov to us. We ought therfore abov all Things to get acquainted with the Nature of Lov. . . . Lov in the fountain, and Lov in the End is the Glory of the World, and the Soul of Joy" (II.62). When the world is perceived rightly, *thoughts* flow back to the abyss of the godhead.

Ultimately, though, it is love rather than *thinking* that glorifies the universe for God; consequently, love enables the human soul to manifest itself in its most perfect being: "Lov is your tru Self when you are in Act what you are in Power" (IV.67). Just as the emanation of God's love is expressed in the mystery of the trinity as it emanates and returns from the godhead, the lover must direct the affections outward to objects:

> the Soul without Extending, and living in its Object, is Dead within it self. an Idle Chaos of Blind and confused Powers. for which when it loveth, it gaineth Three Subsistences in itself by the Act of Loving. A Glorious Spirit that Abideth within: a Glorious Spirit that floweth in the Stream. A glorious Spirit that resideth in the Object. Insomuch that now it can Enjoy a Sweet Communion with it self: in contemplating what it is in it self, and to its Object. (II.56).

The love of the self thus is a mystical analogue to the love of God for himself, a relationship given powerful expression through the paradox of the soul as fountain and abyss.[17]

The cogency of this metaphor is even more remarkable when we

15. Day, "Traherne and the Doctrine," p. 92.
16. Stewart, *Expanded Voice*, p. 64.
17. K. W. Salter, *Thomas Traherne: Mystic and Poet*, p. 97.

recognize that through the intellectual act of *thinking*—the emanation and return of God's essence—mankind recapitulates the primal act of creation. Without thinking, the soul would resemble the waters of the deep before the creation. According to Traherne, *thinking* fills an otherwise empty space through its creation of "Amiable Ideas": "Your Soul being naturaly very Dark, and Deformed and Empty when Extended through infinit but empty Space: the World servs you in Beautifying and filling it with Amiable Ideas; for the Perfecting of its Stature in the Ey of GOD" (II.84). The language in this passage echoes the very description of the watery chaos before the creation in Genesis 1:2. The world is dark, unformed, chaotic, unless the soul perceives the Ideas inherent in it and returns them as *thoughts* to God. Moreover, since *thoughts* approximate the true intellectual nature of God, *thoughts* are in fact superior to things. "For God hath made you able to Creat Worlds in your own mind, which are more Precious unto Him then those which He Created: And to Give and offer up the World unto Him, which is very Delightfull in flowing from Him, but much more in Returning to Him" (II.90). The human soul truly recapitulates the godhead through *thinking* by becoming a fountain that returns praise and love to God for his enjoyment. Love, *thinking*, and enjoyment thus constitute a trinity that describes mankind's participation in the universe, based on his understanding of the typological relationship of the soul to God: "We are to be Conformed to the Image of His Glory . . . For then shall we be *Mentes* as He is *Mens*" (II.84). Such an intense optimism is supported by the typological promise of John 7:38, which with only a slight metaphoric transformation can describe *thoughts* flowing back to God: "He that believeth on me out of his belly shall flow rivers of living water."

The "Enlarged Soul" Flowing into the Abyss

Traherne celebrated, as no other poet in the seventeenth century, the correspondence between the act of the expansive soul in receiving and bestowing love to God and that of God in bestowing and receiving love. This confluence of love between God and man expresses, essentially, a recapitulative relationship using one of the fundamental biblical types, the waters of life. The biblical waters of life thus provide a controlling metaphor for the Dobell *Poems*. "The

Circulation" outlines the twin notions of confluence and interdependence at the heart of Traherne's system of beliefs.

> All things do first receiv, that giv.
>   Only tis GOD above,
> That from, and in himself doth live,
>   Whose All sufficient Love
> Without Original can flow
> And all the Joys and Glories shew
> Which Mortal Man can take Delight to know
> He is the Primitive Eternal Spring
> The Endless Ocean of each Glorious Thing.
>   The Soul a Vessel is
> A Spacious Bosom to Contain
> All the fair Treasures of his Bliss
> Which run like Rivers from, into the Main,
> And all it doth receiv returns again.
>   (ll. 71–84)

The idea of God as the origin, "The Endless Ocean of each Glorious Thing," evokes one of the most basic Old Testament types. Moreover, the notion that God can receive again what he gives from the "Vessel" of the human soul is predicated on a sacramental recapitulation of this typology. Just as all the rivers run into the sea only to return again as pure waters, so does God's plenitude flow into the depth of the soul, only to return to God in an expression of love. Mankind needs God to fill the vessel of the soul; God delights in the love that mankind returns. The water-cycle renders this interdependence perfectly: "And as the spacious Main / Doth all the Rivers, which it Drinks, return, / Thy Love receivd doth make the Soul to burn" ("The Estate," ll. 40–42).

Traherne occasionally used the full range of typological water imagery involving the sacramental recapitulation of the basic type (God as fountain of life) in his writing. In his *Meditations on the Six Days of the Creation*, he asked God to sanctify "all the Waters of Tribulation that are in my Soul," and described his heart as dry and needing the "celestial Waters of Repentance" to revive him.

> Rain down, I beseech thee, upon my Soul, the celestial Waters of *Repentance*, that those Vapours which arise from those Sighs and Sobs of my Heart, for having offended thee, may be converted into Clouds of Fear and Care that I never offend thee more, but weep Showers of Tears for what I have already offended thee in.[18]

18. Thomas Traherne, *Meditations on the Six Days of the Creation*, pp. 12, 19.

In the Dobell *Poems* Traherne made a few allusions to conventional
aspects of sacramental typology: the speaker admits that his heart is
"hard" when he is without God ("The Approach," ll. 20–22); and
he likens his soul to a "stone" when he is without *thoughts* ("Ye
hidden Nectars," l. 25). The *Third Century* also describes the Bible
as "the Spring of Life, and a fountain of Happiness" (III.27). For the
most part, though, Traherne's interest lay in eschatological typology, rather than Christological or sacramental; therefore, his writings present a different emphasis than the typology of the waters of
life in *The Temple* or *Silex Scintillans*. Given Traherne's optimistic
view of human potential, the images he found most engaging were
those of the confluence of the fountain of the soul with the abyss of
the godhead.

"My Spirit" gives a comprehensive account of the soul's mode of
being, how it perceives, *thinks*, and loves.[19] The first stanza identifies the "Essence" of the soul as its "Capacitie" to perceive all things
in their unity, without the limitations imposed by custom or con-
tingency (l. 8). The experience outlined in this poem is unlike the
kind depicted in the "Estate of Innocency" poems, in which the
speaker describes a naïveté soon lost through contact with the fallen
world. To be able to manifest its true being, the soul must suffer
the travails of the "Estate of Misery" and gain God's grace (following the traditional Pauline paradigm). "My Spirit" portrays a mature experience of "oneness" with God, from which springs *thoughts*.

> My Naked Simple Life was I.
> That Act so Strongly Shind
> Upon the Earth, the Sea, the Skie,
> That was the Substance of My Mind.
> The Sence it self was I.
> I felt no Dross nor Matter in my Soul,
> No Brims nor Borders, such as in a Bowl
> We see, My Essence was Capacitie.
> That felt all Things,
> The Thought that Springs
> Therfrom's it self. It hath no other Wings
> To Spread abroad, nor Eys to see,
> Nor Hands Distinct to feel,
> Nor Knees to Kneel:
> But being Simple like the Deitie

19. For a more complete analysis of "My Spirit," see Malcolm M. Day, " 'Naked
Truth' and the Language of Thomas Traherne," pp. 305–25.

> In its own Centre is a Sphere
> Not shut up here, but evry Where.
>   (ll. 1–17)

The "Essence," which in Traherne's metaphysics actually *is* the expansive soul as it is "present" with the object it views, manifests itself in a "perfect Act"—*thinking*.

> It Acts not from a Centre to
>   Its Object as remote,
> But present is, when it doth view,
>   Being with the Being it doth note.
>   Whatever it doth do,
> It doth not by another Engine work,
> But by it self; which in the Act doth lurk.
>   Its Essence is Transformed into a true
>   And perfect Act.
>   (ll. 18–26)

That act is *thinking*, as Traherne defined and presumably experienced it—for the complete absence of irony in his poems has eliminated any of the traditional barriers between author and speaker. And the speaker surely has experienced such *thoughts*.

"My Spirit" also gives readers of Traherne perhaps the most memorable image in his poetry, the one he employed to depict the soul in its essential state of being. The active soul, able to dissolve the habitual distinctions between subject and object ("Being with the Being it doth note"), is described as a dilating sphere.

> A Strange Extended Orb of Joy,
>   Proceeding from within,
> Which did on evry side convey
>   It self, and being nigh of Kin
>   To God did evry Way
> Dilate it self even in an Instant, and
> Like an Indivisible Centre Stand
>   At once Surrounding all Eternitie.
>   Twas not a Sphere
>   Yet did appear
> One infinit. Twas somwhat evry where.
>   And tho it had a Power to see
>   Far more, yet still it shind
>   And was a Mind
> Exerted for it saw Infinitie

> Twas not a Sphere, but twas a Power
> Invisible, and yet a Bower.
>
> (ll. 86–102)

This "Orb of Joy" is able to engulf the entire universe in its expansiveness. Traherne adapted the well-known scholastic definition of God (as a circle whose center is everywhere and whose circumference nowhere) to imply the affinities between God's nature and the soul's.[20] In Traherne's world view, the soul plays a role that is imitative of God's role in creating the universe. *Thinking* recreates the order and beauty of the universe by recognizing the unity of subjects and objects, the unity of the creation. To value all things as God does, to be actually "present" with them, is to dissolve distinctions imposed by the contingencies of the fallen world and to view the universe in its oneness. As Traherne explained in the *First Century*:

> An Object Seen, is in the Faculty seeing it, and by that in the Soul of the Seer. . . . Dead Things are in a Room containing them in a vain maner; unless they are Objectivly in the Soul of a Seer. The Pleasure of an Enjoyer, is the very End why Things placed are in any Place. The Place and the Thing Placed in it, being both in the Understanding of a Spectator of them. Things Dead in Dead Place Effect nothing. But in a Living Soul, that seeth their Excellencies, they Excite a Pleasure answerable to their value, a Wisdom to Embrace them, a Courage not to Forsake them, a Lov of their Donor, Praises and Thanksgivings; and a Greatness and a Joy Equal to their Goodness. And thus all Ages are present in my Soul, and all Kingdoms, and GOD Blessed forever. (I.100)

Seeing the "Excellencies" of all created things amounts to what Sandbank has called "the spiritualization of 'things.'"[21] It represents an addition of value to what God has already created, without

---

20. For an account of how the Renaissance valued the notion of the circle of perfection, see Marjorie Hope Nicolson, *The Breaking of the Circle: Studies in the Effect of the "New Science" upon Seventeenth-Century Poetry*, and Georges Poulet, *The Metamorphoses of the Circle*.

21. Sandbank, *Traherne on the Place of Man*, p. 129, explained: "The spiritualization of 'things,' turning them into 'thoughts,' means that they are set against a background of infinity, or seen *sub specie aeternitatis*. This is the meaning of 'right esteem,' the attitude to things repeatedly recommended by Traherne. To know things is to see them as parts of a whole, thus realizing the value of everything and giving it the 'right' or 'true' esteem, 'prizing' it (I.7–8)." See also John E. Trimpey, "An Analysis of Traherne's 'Thoughts I.'"

which the world would be filled with "Dead Things." Rightly apprehended, the world is laden with the pleasure God intended the soul to enjoy. Perception, as it is outlined in "My Spirit" and developed in the "Thoughts" poems, is an active process that results in an expansion of the soul as it recognizes the unity of the creation. The soul thus receives spiritual influences and, by recognizing and enjoying them, adds to what it receives.

The metaphor usually used to describe *thinking* is the watercycle. In the first "Thoughts" poem he writes that "Thoughts and Apprehensions are / The Heavenly Streams which fill the Soul with rare / Transcendent Perfect Pleasures" (11. 25–27). *Thoughts* are thus associated in the Dobell *Poems* with the rich tradition of living water; as we have seen above, the Logos has often been associated with a pure stream of flowing water, the Bible with the well of life, "Whose streams we got by the Apostles sluce" (Herbert's "The Jews," l. 3). Because Traherne evoked the Renaissance commonplace of the water-cycle, *thoughts*, as living waters or "Heavenly Streams," flow back to God for his enjoyment.

> Ye hidden Nectars, which my GOD doth drink,
>   Ye Heavenly Streams, ye Beams Divine,
>   On which the Angels think,
>   How Quick, how Strongly do ye shine!
>   ("Ye hidden Nectars," ll. 1–4)

Thoughts are openly extolled here as the "Nectar" that the soul returns to God in an endless circulation as all things flow back to their source. Through *thinking*, the individual participates fully in the *circuitus spiritualis* as both fountain and abyss.

The water-cycle is probably the only metaphor that can express Traherne's particular beliefs on the infinite expansiveness of the soul through thinking. Since mankind not only receives but adds to what God bestows, if not in substance at least in the point-of-view offered, a dilation and exchange occurs that becomes progressively more immense. Even a concept as powerful as that of the abyss does not convey the magnitude of Traherne's version of the *circuitus spiritualis* (which amounts to abysses infinitely expanding into other abysses). Portraying both God and the soul as fountain and abyss, infinitely receiving and augmenting, does manage to capture some sense of what is finally ineffable. We should properly think of his notion of interdependence as a doctrine of "amplified circulation," the implications of which Traherne found astounding.

First of all, he was dazzled both by God's magnificence and by mankind's ability to contribute to his magnificence.

> My Contemplation Dazles in the End
> Of all I comprehend.
> And soars abov all Heights,
> Diving into the Depths of all Delights.
> Can He becom the End,
> To whom all Creatures tend?
> Who is the Father of all Infinites!
> Then may He Benefit receiv from Things,
> And be *not Parent only* of all Springs.
>   ("The Anticipation," ll. 1–9)

This notion led Traherne to the more startling concept of God's dependence on mankind.

> And what then this can be more Plain and Clear
> What Truth then this more Evident appear!
> The GODHEAD cannot prize
> The Sun at all, nor yet the Skies,
> Or Air, or Earth, or Trees, or Seas,
> Or Stars, unless the Soul of Man they pleas.
>   ******
> The Joy and Pleasure which his Soul doth take
> In all his Works, is for his Creatures sake.
> So great a certainty
> We in this Holy Doctrine see
> That there could be no Worth at all
> In any Thing Material Great or Small
> Were not som Creature more Alive,
> Whence it might Worth Derive.
> GOD is the Spring whence Things came forth
> Souls are the fountains of their Real Worth.
>   ("The Demonstration," ll. 41–46, 51–60)

God, in other words, needs the expansive thoughts of the regenerate soul to take joy or pleasure from the creation, just as the spring feeds the fountains and in turn is fed by them in the recirculation of flowing water ("unto the place from whence the rivers come, thither they return again," Eccles. 1:7). Using a homophonous pun on *eye/I* as part of a spatial metaphor (*eye/sphere*), Traherne argued for the special place of the soul in the universe.

> But neither Goodness, Wisdom, Power, nor Love,
> Nor Happiness it self in things could be,
> Did not they all *in one fair Order* move,
> And joyntly by their Service End in *me*.
>   Had he not made an *Ey* to be the Sphere
>   Of all Things, none of these would e're appear.
>   ("The Improvement," ll. 19–24)

That God actually needs mankind to act as "a Glorious Spring of Joys and Riches" is so engaging an idea that Traherne devoted the five poems immediately following "The Circulation" to it (a sequence that closes out those poems on the estate of grace): "Amendment," which shows that God's works are more pleasing after they have been amended by the soul; "The Demonstration," which argues that the idea of amending the creation is a logical demonstration of the mystery and love of God; "The Anticipation," which tries to explain the mystery of the godhead in terms of Aristotelian causality ("He is the Means both of Himself and all, / Whom we the Fountain Means and End do call," ll. 116–17), a mystery the individual can comprehend by recognizing that the soul too is a means and end in this *circuitus spiritualis*; "The Recovery," which asserts that in one voluntary act of love God is repaid for his efforts; and "Another," which jubilantly urges the soul to return this love to God.

This notion of "amplified circulation" fulfilling God's needs lies at the heart of Traherne's theory of circulation. The individual's responsibility to God is to value the world rightly, to sound God's praises. From the soul that is properly animated by the magnificence of itself and of God's kingdom, praise will "arise and ascend" from an interior fountain (II.92). This praise should be as continuous and inexhaustible as a fountain because such praise glorifies God as nothing else can.

> It is evident that Praises are infinitly more excellent then all the creatures becaus they proceed from Men and Angels. for as streams do they derive an Excellency from their Fountains, and are the last Tribut that can possibly be paid to the Creator. Praises are the Breathings of interior Lov, the Marks and Symptoms of an Happy Life, Overflowing Gratitud, returning Benefits, an Oblation of the Soul, and the Heart ascending upon the Wings of Divine Affection to the Throne of GOD. GOD is a Spirit and cannot feed on Carcases: but He can be Delighted with Thanksgivings, and is infinitly pleased with the Emanations of our Joy, becaus His Works are Esteemed, and Himself is Admired. (III.82)

Since *thoughts* constitute God's gratification in Traherne's anthropocentric universe, *thinking* represents the highest mode of being for the soul. In that the right apprehension of the universe through *thinking* imitates the creative act of God, this relationship is essentially typological, thus underscoring the importance of the paradox that runs like a current throughout his writing: "By Him, the Fountain of all these Things is the End of them: for He can return to their Author deserved Praises" (II.23). The pronominal ambiguity in this statement—the capitalization of "He" and "Author" merges the identity of God and the soul—also emphasizes that through *thinking* the speaker makes himself the true image of God.

Traherne did exploit another metaphor, the mirror, to depict certain aspects of his doctrine of circulation. We should note, however, that he carefully distinguished between the essentially static reflection of the "mirror" and the dynamic activity of the fountain.[22] The distinction hinges on the difference between the capabilities of the child and those of the adult. It is a mistake to regard his fascination with the child's heavenly mindedness as a desire to return to the innocence of childhood; the adult's perspective is far more glorifying to God and hence is more to be desired. The child, with its pure but "empty" powers, simply has the ability to reflect naively every impression that it perceives and is not hampered by any of the limitations that the fallen world imposes on thinking.

> Pure Empty Powers that did nothing loath,
>   Did like the fairest Glass,
>   Or Spotless polisht Brass,
> Themselvs soon in their Objects Image cloath.
>   Divine Impressions when they came,
>   Did quickly enter and my Soul inflame.
>   Tis not the Object, but the Light
> That maketh Heaven; Tis a Purer Sight.
>   Felicitie
> Appears to none but them that purely see.
>   ("The Preparative," ll. 51–60)

The child can only mirror what it receives (though the purity of its reflection is at first astonishing), while the redeemed soul can add to

---

22. In Hebrew, as Marks has pointed out ("Traherne and Cambridge Platonism," p. 533), one root for the word *fountain* is related to the word for *eye,* a connection the Cambridge Platonist Peter Sterry noted. Nonetheless, Traherne seems to have differentiated between the passivity of the mirrored reflection and the activity of the fountain (as he made clear in *Century* IV.85). See also Joan Webber, *The Eloquent "I": Style and Self in Seventeenth-Century Prose,* p. 224.

what it receives like a fountain swelling into a river as it empties into the abyss of the godhead.

Traherne characterized the special joys and limited abilities of the child quite precisely in a poem about the praise that the mature soul can offer God. The central idea of "The Improvement" is expressed in its opening line: "Tis more to recollect, then make." One who can perceive evidence of God's wisdom, goodness, and power in the universe allows the creation to shine as brightly as possible through recollection, through *thinking*.

> His Wisdom, Goodness, Power, as they unite
> All things in one, that they may be the *Treasures*
> Of one *Enjoy'r*, shine in the utmost Height
> They can attain; and are most Glorious *Pleasures*,
>   When all the Univers conjoynd in one,
>   Exalts a Creature, as if that alone.
>   (ll. 25–30)

Because only the human soul can act to please the creator, its potential for expansiveness is limitless, but so too is its obligation to offer "*Endless Prais*." Traherne's awareness of his special responsibilities is clearly retrospective in this poem, as indicated by the handling of time in it. The idea of "amplified circulation" is simply beyond the child's abilities:

> But Oh! the vigor of mine Infant Sence
> Drives me too far: I had not yet the Eye
> The Apprehension, or Intelligence
> Of Things so very Great Divine and High.
>   But all things were *Eternal* unto me,
>   And *mine*, and *Pleasing* which mine Ey did see.
>   (ll. 67–72)

Traherne viewed childhood from a mature retrospect that enabled him to evaluate what he could only experience naively as a child.[23] Like a mirror, the child can only reflect passively; as an adult, the redeemed soul can add to what it receives.

In a passage in the *Centuries* in which Traherne was meditating on the occasional inconstancies of the soul's love for God, he declared the "fountain" to be a better metaphor than the "mirror" for his purposes.

---

23. Stewart, *Expanded Voice*, pp. 145–55, made the same point in his analysis of "Shadows in the Water."

That the Soul shineth of it self is equaly manifest. for it can lov with a lov distinct from GODs. It can lov irregularly. And no irregular Lov is the Lov of GOD. It can forbear to lov while GOD loveth. It can lov while GOD forbeareth. It can lov a Wicked Man, Wickedly, and in his Wickedness. This shews plainly that it can lov regularly, with a Lov that is not meerly the Reflexion of Gods. for which caus it is not called a Mirror, but esteemed more, a real fountain. (IV.85)

He then explicated a familiar verse from the Canticles—"A garden inclosed is my sister, my spouse; a spring shut up, a fountain sealed" —as evidence of the perfected love to be experienced in the New Jerusalem, when the fountain of the soul will flow into the crystal fountain. Thus Traherne himself seemed to insist that the "fountain" metaphor ought to be distinguished, therefore, from the "mirror" that he usually employed in conjunction with childhood. That difference also serves to emphasize Traherne's optimism over the human potential for typological recapitulation; the soul of the pilgrim in the estate of grace, who has moved beyond the child's capacity, can actively imitate the godhead by flowing with love and praise, augmenting what it has already received. Usually, Traherne called the soul a fountain,[24] even designating it at one point "the very Throne of Blessedness" since it offers purer "Nectars" than it receives:

> They Drink in Nectars, and Disburs again
> In Purer Beams, those Streams,
> Those Nectars which are causd by Joys.
> And as the spacious Main
> Doth all the Rivers, which it Drinks, return,
> Thy Love receivd doth make the Soul to burn.
> ("The Estate," ll. 37–42)

The "hidden Nectars, which my GOD doth drink" are, as we have seen, *thoughts.*

The last group of poems in the Dobell Folio, those describing the "Estate of Glory," contains a series of four poems, all entitled "Thoughts," which Margoliouth has numbered for convenience. The four are framed by poems on "Love" and "Goodnesse," the former showing the perfect love of God, the latter foreseeing the apocalyptic fellowship of souls in love with God and each other.

---

24. Like most poets, though, Traherne did not follow this distinction slavishly. Late in the Dobell sequence he called the soul a fountain of riches and a glorious mirror in the same stanza; see "Amendment," ll. 29–35.

This group on *thinking* and loving provides the appropriate climax
to the Dobell *Poems* because it defines the perfect mode of being for
the soul that has gained the "Estate of Glory," the endless circulation of love and praise.

Traherne clearly associated thinking with that which makes the
soul "An Image of the Deitie!" in the opening lines of "Thoughts.
I":

> Ye brisk Divine and Living Things,
> Ye great Exemplars, and ye Heavenly Springs,
>   Which I within me see;
>   Ye Machines Great,
>   Which in my Spirit God did Seat,
>   Ye Engines of Felicitie;
>   Ye Wondrous Fabricks of his Hands,
> Who all possesseth that he understands;
>   That ye are pent within my Brest,
>   Yet rove at large from East to West,
> And are Invisible, yet Infinite;
> Is my Transcendent, and my Best Delight.
>   (ll. 1–12)

Thoughts are created by God (that is, the soul can only reproduce
thoughts that God has already created), yet the soul is infinite in its
capacity to re-create or imitate the order of the universe. Such
thoughts are the praise that mankind returns to God:

> Thoughts are the Wings on which the Soul doth flie,
> The Messengers which soar abov the Skie,
> Elijahs firey Charet, that conveys
> The Soul, even here, to those Eternal Joys.
>   ("Thoughts. IV," ll. 1–4)

Thoughts constitute the praise returned to God because through
thinking the soul can re-create in the eternal realm of *being* what
would otherwise exist only in the realm of *becoming*.

> This Sight which is the Glorious End
> Of all his Works, and which doth comprehend
>   Eternity, and Time, and Space,
>   Is far more dear,
>   And far more near,
> To him, then all his Glorious Dwelling Place.
>   It is a Spiritual World within.
> A Living World, and nearer far of Kin
>   To God, then that which first he made.

> While that doth fade
> This therfore ever shall Endure,
> Within the Soul as more Divine and Pure.
> ("Thoughts. II," ll. 37–48)

In the re-creation of "a Spiritual World within," the individual can imitate God.

Moreover, such *thoughts* consummate what God began in the original act of creation.

> A Delicate and Tender Thought
> The Quintessence is found of all he Wrought.
> It is the fruit of all his Works,
> Which we conceive,
> Bring forth, and Give,
> Yea and in which the Greater Value lurks.
> ("Thoughts. II," ll. 1–6)

Only the soul, a being formed in the image of God, is capable of this glorifying act. For Traherne, *thoughts* take on almost an independent existence as they recapitulate the eternal Ideas.

> Thoughts are the highest Things,
> The very Offspring of the King of Kings.
> Thoughts are a kind of Strange Celestial Creature,
> That when they're Good, they're such in evry Feature,
> They bear the Image of their father's face,
> And Beautifie even all his Dwelling Place . . .
> ******
> A Thought can Clothe it self with all the Treasures
> Of GOD, and be the Greatest of his Pleasures.
> It all his Laws, and Glorious Works, and Ways,
> And Attributs, and Counsels; all his Praise
> It can conceiv, and Imitate, and give:
> It is the only Being that doth live.
> Tis Capable of all Perfection here,
> Of all his Love and Joy and Glory there.
> ("Thoughts. III," ll. 27–32, 49–56)

Thinking, loving, or praising are all essentially the same mode of being for Traherne. Just as he can speak of God as the fountain of bliss, or the fountain of love, so does he conceive of him as the fountain of knowledge:

> THE Original of our Knowledge is his Godhead, His Essence and his will are the Fountain of it; and the stream so excellent, that in all

> Estates it is for ever to be continued, as the Light and Glory of the
> whole Creation. (CE, p. 36)

Whether God is conceived of as the fountain of love, of bliss, or of
knowledge, the water-cycle is still the metaphor used most cogently and frequently to characterize God's magnificence and the
soul's participation in it.

In the Dobell *Poems*, the speaker participates in the *circuitus spiritualis* (the emanation of God's wisdom, goodness, and power and
the return of *thoughts* of love and praise) through his essentially
unitive perceptions. As Clements has explained, "Our finite minds,
our conventionalizing eye and conceptualizing psyche, perceive
disordered plurality, but the timeless and spaceless Spirit seizes all
things in their unity; in God's mind everything is eternally now."[25]
Thoughts allow the soul to enter into this eternity with God.

> Could we but justly, wisely, truly prize
> These Blessings, we should be above the Skies,
> And Praises sing with pleasant Heart and Voice,
> Adoring with the Angels should rejoyce.
>   ("Thoughts. IV," ll. 53–56)

There, with God at the fountainhead, the soul will join the saints
who already are "one" with God.

> All these are in his Omnipresence still
> As Living Waters from his Throne they trill.
> As Tokens of his Lov they all flow down,
> Their Beauty Use and Worth the Soul do Crown.
>   ("Thoughts. IV," ll. 67–70)

At last, in the concluding poem in the Dobell Folio, "Goodness," in
his mind's eye Traherne foresaw the eventual annihilation of the
soul, immersed and absorbed into the source of all as one of the
millions bathing in the crystal fountain:

> The Bliss of other Men is my Delight:
>   (When once my Principles are right:)
>   And evry Soul which mine doth see
>   A Treasurie.
> The Face of GOD is Goodness unto all,
> And while he Thousands to his Throne doth call,
>   While Millions bathe in Pleasures,
>   And do behold his Treasures

25. Clements, *The Mystical Poetry*, p. 165.

    The Joys of all
    On mine do fall
And even my Infinitie doth seem
A Drop without them of a mean Esteem.

                 (ll. 1–12)

❧[VII]❧

AFTERWORD

If the typology of the waters of life was discernible to poets such as Herbert, Vaughan and Traherne, then we ought to find other writers using its resources. Reading with typological "spectacles" (and with some diligence), we can locate and identify many references to the types and antitypes of the waters of life as well as to the circularity of the waters. But nowhere can we discover writers exploiting the resources of this typology quite so successfully as these three poets. For example, many readers of seventeenth-century literature may recall Bishop Joseph Hall's occasional meditation, "Upon the Rain and Waters," which finds in the phenomenon of circularity—as set forth in Ecclesiastes 1:7, Hall's biblical countertext—the same profound lesson that many before him had (and as Vaughan's speaker in "The Water-fall" would later).

> What a sensible interchange there is in nature betwixt union and division! Many vapors rising from the sea meet together in one cloud; that cloud falls down divided into several drops; those drops run together and in many rills of water meet in the same channels; those channels run into the brook, those brooks into the rivers, those rivers into the sea. One receptacle is for all, though a large one, and all make back to their first and main original. So it either is or should be with spiritual gifts. O God, Thou distillest Thy graces upon us not for our reservation but conveyance. Those manifold faculties Thou lettest fall upon several men Thou woudst not have drenched up where they light but wouldest have derived, through the channels of their special vocations, into the common streams of public use for Church or Commonwealth. Take back, O Lord, those few drops Thou hast rained upon my soul and return them into that great ocean of the glory of Thine own bounty, from whence they had their beginning.[1]

1. Frank Livingston Huntley, *Bishop Joseph Hall and Protestant Meditation in Seventeenth-Century England: A Study with the Texts of "The Arte of Divine Meditation (1606)" and "Occasional Meditations (1633),"* pp. 132–33.

Hall's reading of the water-cycle is broader than those we have
heretofore considered; he found in the emanation and return of the
waters a natural hieroglyph to instruct us in making use of all God's
gifts, not simply a figure for the descent of grace and the reascent of
the soul. Nonetheless, "Upon the Rain and Waters" clearly oper-
ates within the same general tradition as Herbert, Vaughan and
Traherne: the Book of the Creatures presents emblematic texts to
be read by God's other Book; the mystery of the circularity of the
waters illustrates the correspondence between the microcosm and
the macrocosm; though God is the origin of the waters, the soul
too plays its part in receiving and returning them (a complex relationship that has decided typological overtones). Such examples,
however, are comparatively rare, and it may be of interest in these
last pages to try to account for the ebbing of this literary tradition
by examining a few poems of some forgotten Caroline poets.

Thomas Philipott was the author of a small collection in the
metaphysical mode, *Poems* (1646). Though he wrote elegies on
George Sandys and Francis Quarles and commendatory verses for
William Cartwright and Edward Benlowes, many of his religious
poems show the influence of Donne in their use of irony, complexity, and ingenuity. His best poem, "A divine Hymńe," uses imagery associated with the typology of the waters of life. Since it is not
well known, I quote in full.

> "A divine Hymne"
> O Thou who art all light, from whose pure beames
>   The infant day-light streames,
> And to whose Lustre all the throng of stars
>   Those mystick Characters,
> Writ in the dusky volumne of the Night,
>   Do owe their stocke of the Light;
> Who when the Sun, i'th nonage of the yeare,
>   Like a Bridegroom does appeare,
> Sweet with the Balmy Perfumes of the East,
>   With Lights Embroidery drest,
> And spangled o're with brightnesse, does array
>   That Planet with each Ray
> He glitters with, a powerfull spark inspire
>   Of thy Celestiall fire
> Into my frozen heart, that there may be
>   A flame blowne up in me,
> Whose light may shine like the meridian sun
>   In the dark horison

Of my benighted soul, and thence distill
　　　Into a pious rill
Of contrite tears, those clouds which do controule
　　　The prospect of my soule,
That so the beams of faith may clearly shine
　　　Amidst its Christalline,
That I may by th'infusion of their light
　　　Learn to spell Christs Crosse aright.
And as one touch from *Moses* did unlock
　　　The casquet of the rock,
And thaw'd its liquid treasures to repell
　　　The thirst of Israel;
So let this flame dissolve that masse of sin
　　　That lies wrapt up within
The chambers of my heart, that there may rise
　　　Two fountaines in my eyes,
Which may put out those scorching flames, which were
　　　First fed and kindled there,
By that same hot Artillery which lust
　　　Into my eye-balls thrust;
And as when Feavers blaze within the blood,
　　　And parch that purple flood,
The sparks and embers of them, are by heat
　　　Still'd from the pores in sweat;
So when sin flames within me and does roule
　　　Its heat about my soule,
And sparkles in each facultie, my eyes
　　　Being lusts Incendiaries,
Oh let this inward sicknesse by that fire
　　　Devotion does inspire,
Be still'd out, at those pores o'th soule, my eies,
　　　In a liquid sacrifice,
Which gathering into one heap, may swell
　　　Into a holy well,
Wherein when the old Dragon wounds me, I
　　　May bath incessantly,
And having wash'd my festred wounds, may be
　　　Sure both at once of cure and victorie.[2]

Though the poem begins with a paean to the God of light, the
conceit around which it is framed involves the complexities of the
waters of life. The poet invokes the "Celestiall fire" only so that it
will distill the noxious vapors of the speaker's frozen heart "Into a

2. Thomas Philipott, *Poems (1646)*.

pious rill / Of contrite tears" (ll. 20–21). Philipott's hope is based on his understanding that Moses' striking of the rock of Horeb has already provided the warrant for such a recapitulation (ll. 27–30). Making use of the physiology of the heart, the poet states that this "Celestiall fire" will dissolve the sin "within / The chambers of my heart, that there may rise / Two fountaines in my eyes . . . Which gathering into one heap, may swell / Into a holy well" (ll. 32–34, 51–52). The echo of John 4:14 is unmistakable ("the water that I shall give him shall be in him a well of water springing up into everlasting life"), and this well will provide a bath in which the speaker can continue to heal the wounds of the "old Dragon" (ll. 53–56).

Nearly every flourish in this hymn is used to develop the conceit involving the unlocking of "The casquet of the rock" (l. 28)—itself an elaborate pun on life from death, as well as a reference to sacramental recapitulation involving the typological relationship among the rock of Horeb, the true rock at the crucifixion, and the speaker's stony heart. A later poem, "On Christs Passion, a Descant," makes further use of this pun by noting that Israel, in recompense to Christ, "who did unlock / The stony Casquet of the barren Rock," offered only ignominy—"The Rock it selfe is laid beneath a Stone" (ll. 112, 164). But Philipott only rarely achieved such focus. His other poems, some fifty in all—a hodgepodge of elegies, occasional pieces, school-boy exercises, and a few voguish amatory poems—are often ingenious but never so intensely realized. While he was familiar with the complexities of typological imagery and fully capable of employing it in his poetry, he seems to have spent his force in these few poems. The appearance of a poem as typologically witty as "A divine Hymne" in such a heterogeneous collection is indicative of the changing literary tastes at mid-century.

Since Mildmay Fane, Second Earl of Westmorland, apparently learned much from *The Temple*, we might also expect to find some evidence of Herbert's penchant for biblical typology in *Otia Sacra* (1648).[3] But when Fane turned to the creatures, he produced only trite moralizations on God's goodness. "My Observation at Sea" has none of the profound understandings of the confluence of the upper and lower waters or the manifold significance of divine circularity; instead, he remarked on God's wisdom in economically

---

3. Mildmay Fane, *Otia Sacra (1648)*; in his introduction, Donald M. Friedman, has noted some of Herbert's influences, pp. vii–ix.

fashioning the universe: "Though every thing we see or hear may raise / The Makers Praise . . . Yet amongst Those there's none / Like to the Oceon" (ll. 1–2, 5–6). His best known poem, "Annus annulus," uses the same typological conceit as Herbert's "The Agonie" and "The Bunch of Grapes," Christ in the *torcular* of his passion as a wine press producing balm; but he seldom exploited such conceits. One poem, "Contemplatio Diurna," offers the opportunity to develop the traditional association of rising dew with the dew of grace and the subliming Son—as Marvell did in "On a Drop of Dew." But Fane's poem simply moralizes on the rising and setting sun as a reminder of the passage of time and the inevitability of death:

> "Contemplatio Diurna"
> When we behold the Morning Dew
> Dissolve ith' rising Sun: What would it shew?
> But that a Sun to us did rise,
> Our Fathers hoary sin to Atomise.
> And when the Flowers display'd appear,
> To entertain the mounting Charettier:
> What would they speak in that fair dress?
> But Man's redemption out of wretchedness.
> For the shade-shortning Noon can tell
> The Proud, and such as with Ambition swell;
> That whilst upon Opinions wing
> They seek to sore, they work their lessening.
> And the Prognostick Western set,
> May Our Conditions rightly counterfeit;
> For if we rise, shine, and set Cleer,
> The Day-Star from on high's our Comforter:
> If Sin beclowd us as we fall,
> Our next dayes rise will prove our Funerall:
> *Et quid lachrymabilius?*

This is not a forgotten poem because Fane chose to neglect the resources of biblical typology, but rather because he abandoned the figure of the dewdrop with which the poem opens, so it never quite achieves closure. He seems to have devoted himself mainly to displaying his learning and his talent for bizarre verse forms. *Otia Sacra* is little more than a miscellany of divine acrostics, anagrams, pattern poems, and emblematic designs, befitting its title. Fane's problem is neatly summarized by Hobbes in his "Answer" to D'Avenant, when he said, "Judgment begets the strength and structure, and Fancy begets the ornaments of a Poem."[4] Fane had the facility for invention but lacked the judgment to give strength and structure to his poems.

One final example helps us see more clearly the metaphysical mode of poetry in its dotage. Edward Benlowes is chiefly remembered now as the object of Butler's ridicule in the character of "A Small Poet."[5] Benlowes' *Theophila* (1652) is a rare example of a literary form justly forgotten—the heroic poem on spiritual warfare. The heart of the work is "Theophila's Love Sacrifice," in nine cantos, one hundred stanzas each, written in an awkward triplet, which Saintsbury in a flash of wit calls a "'cross-gartered' triplet."[6] Since Benlowes' intention was to write a poem on the mystical ascent of the way-faring soul, it seems likely that the typology of the waters of life would be of some help in his work. And, indeed, the constituent elements of this metaphoric commonplace are evident in *Theophila*. The second canto begins with an invocation that recognizes in the traditional spring of the muses a figure of grace, much as Herbert in the "Jordan" poems before him (and Milton in the invocation of *Paradise Lost* after):

> ALMIGHTY Power, who didst all souls create:
>   Who didst redeem their fall'n estate;
> Who still dost sanctify, and them redintegrate.
>
> Source, river, ocean of all bliss, instil
>   Spring-tides into my low-ebb'd quill:
> Each graceful work flows from (what works all grace) Thy Will.
>   (II. 1–2)

Benlowes also made use of the typological relationship of the stony heart to the rock of Horeb—by this time a literary commonplace—in describing the deformities of the soul before contrition and sanctification:

4. Thomas Hobbes, "Answer to D'Avenant's Preface to *Gondibert*," in *Critical Essays of the Seventeenth Century*, J. E. Spingarn, ed., 2:59.

5. Samuel Butler, *Characters*, p. 89, attacked Benlowes for his literary thievery and fantastic wit: "There is no Feat of Activity, nor Gambol of Wit, that ever was performed by Man, from him that vaults on *Pegasus*, to him that tumbles through the Hoop of an Anagram, but *Benlows* has got the Mastery in it, whether it be high-rope Wit, or low-rope Wit. He has all Sorts of *Echoes*, *Rebus's*, *Chronograms*, &c. besides *Carwitchets*, *Clenches*, and *Quibbles*."

6. Edward Benlowes, *Theophila*, in *Minor Poets of the Caroline Period*, George Saintsbury, ed., 1:313.

> Perplex'd in crime's meand'ring maze, GOD'S law,
>   And guilt, that does strict judgement draw,
> And her too carnal, yet too stony heart she saw.
>
> Yet rocks may cleave,' she cries. Then weeps for tears,
>   And grieves for grief; fears want of fears;
>   She hell, Heav'n's prison, views; distress, for robe, she wears.
>
> (II.55–56)

Early in the poem, Theophila ascends to the empyrean and we are treated with long, ecstatic descriptions of paradise, mostly involving the deity as the source of light. Occasionally, Benlowes continued with the imagery of the waters of life to depict God or Theophila, "by limpid spring of life-joy, where / Crystal is limbeck'd all the year" (III.96):

> O prodigy of great and good! Faith, sound
> This Love's abyss, that does so strangely bound
> Almightiness Itself! From whose veins, see,
> Unsluic'd, Love's purple ocean, when His free
> Red-streaming life did vanquish Death and Hell!
> That thou might'st live, He died! That thou might rise, He fell!
>
> (IV.11–12)

Benlowes's defenders might very well object that he was unconcerned with developing such typological conceits. While such a defense is unassailable on its own grounds, one might well ask in return what other kind of unity—either in the central narrative line or in a coherent imagistic structure—is offered in its stead. For the poem clearly suffers from its lack of such a unity; in the words of his modern biographer,

> It is not possible to attempt any sort of narrative synopsis of the poem. Benlowes moves from ecstasy to ecstasy without coherence of incident. Such order as the poem has is the artificial symmetry produced by cantos with matching titles and equal length.[7]

There is simply a welter of detail in displaying his far-fetched learning. As Douglas Bush has remarked, he has "something of Crashaw's baroque lusciousness."[8] A poet more interested in a tightly structured narrative, even one told through lyrics such as *The Temple* or *Silex Scintillans*, could have done much with Benlowes' sub-

---

7. Harold Jenkins, *Edward Benlowes (1607–1676): Biography of a Minor Poet*, p. 193.

8. Douglas Bush, *English Literature in the Earlier Seventeenth Century*, p. 159.

ject. In "An Execration Upon Vulcan," when Ben Jonson decried
"the strong lines that so the times do catch" (l. 78) of those who
clumsily imitate Donne, he surely had versifiers like Benlowes in
mind. Straining to show his own learning and wit, Benlowes could
multiply conceits in his "strong lines," but he did not learn that the
real secret of Donne's art was making the conceit the poem—as in
"Valediction: Forbidding Mourning" where the circle of perfection, as an emblem of their love, is made to bear the burden of the
entire poem.

So what accounts for this lost tradition? First and foremost
among the reasons for this decline is the change in the dominant
poetic mode. Though the term "metaphysical poetry" is a conten-
tious one, it is still useful in describing a style that exhibits complexity of thought, as well as a corresponding complexity in rhetorical strategy and poetic form, a love of paradox, and a love of
obscurity through *discordia concors*. As Earl Miner has argued in a
series of books on the subject, the "private" mode of the meta-
physicals was replaced with a more "public" one.[9] While the metaphysical conceit did not disappear entirely—witness the number of
"strong-lined" poems among the Cavaliers—a reaction did set in
against the obscurity and erudition of poets such as Donne. And the
lyric was no longer the dominant poetic genre; such forms as the
ode, the verse epistle, the occasional poem, the heroic poem, the
epic, and above all verse satire succeeded the lyric as the primary
vehicles for sharing the poet's values and interests with others. The
example of Philipott demonstrates that some devotional poets in
the metaphysical mode continued to develop the traditional associations of the waters of life in their work. More typically, however, we find such religious miscellanies as Fane's *Otia Sacra*, where
poetic wit—sometimes involving typology—and formal ingenuity
are displayed for their own sake. Because Benlowes used a narrative rather than a lyric form, he can be seen as something of a
transitional figure. While occasional references to the waters of life
appear, they are lost amid the general profusion that mars *Theophila*. The difference between structured, unified works such as
Herbert's, Vaughan's, and Traherne's and the poems of these
minor Caroline poets is very great indeed.

9. Earl Miner, *The Metaphysical Mode from Donne to Cowley*, pp. 3–47, and *The
Restoration Mode from Milton to Dryden*, pp. 3–50, has discussed the public world and
the private mode in the seventeenth century.

In the mid-seventeenth century, writers were still keen observers of natural phenomena, as a poem such as Fane's "My Observation at Sea" will attest. Interest in meditation on the creatures, however, is supplanted in large measure by an interest in natural theology. Works such as John Ray's *The Wisdom of God* came to enjoy an enormous popularity by century's end.[10] Advances in quantitative science gradually were beginning to undermine the foundations of the older world view that would eventually demystify such natural hieroglyphs. Even by the end of the century, the notion of divine circularity was no longer universally accepted. And, too, with the publication of Denham's *Cooper's Hill* a new genre of poem emerged, the topographical poem, that sees in nature an emblem of moral, political, philosophical or aesthetic values.

As a crucial element in St. Paul's view of the relationship of the testaments, biblical typology itself could not easily fade to insignificance in the later part of the seventeenth century. Indeed, as Paul Korshin has so ably demonstrated, despite the general distrust of mystery that set in after 1650, interest in typology as a figural mode remained strong throughout the next century.[11] Korshin has pointed out that typology was taken out of its theological context and used for other purposes precisely because it provided a figurative language that could be readily understood.

Since typology was familiar even to an unsophisticated audience, it provided the late seventeenth-century writer a shorthand of allusion with which the common reader was acquainted and which therefore required a minimum of explanation or self-exegesis. Mystical obscurity withered because it was difficult; typology, potentially equally mysterious, resisted figural change because it required very little knowledge of hermeneutics to use it or to decipher its meaning.[12]

If Renaissance antiquarianism suffered at the hands of Butler and Pope—both of whom burlesqued the pedantry centered on etymological and mythological interpretation in *Hudibras* and *The Dunciad*—the tendency to view the world symbolically by drawing parallels and making analogies persisted. Anglican rationalists continued to read Scripture figuratively while seeking a balance be-

10. Yi-Fu Tuan, in *The Hydrologic Cycle and the Wisdom of God: A Study in Geoteleology*, has an excellent summary of the natural theology of the late seventeenth century.

11. The following discussion is much indebted to Paul J. Korshin, *Typologies in England, 1650–1820*.

12. Korshin, *Typologies in England*, p. 66.

tween the mysteries of the faith and "the one sense of Scripture."[13] Keach's typological compendium, *Tropologia* (1682), after all, dates from this period. While the excesses of millenarian "readings" of the Civil War were eschewed, writers still regarded Charles I as the martyr king and Cromwell the Davidic king.[14] Dryden and Marvell both were important in popularizing this kind of secularized typological imagery.

But it was Milton, more than any other figure, who advanced the scope of typology, as many scholars have observed.[15] The waters of life are quite prominent in *Paradise Lost*; we find their typological resonance, for example, in the relationship between poetic creation and the creation itself (I.21), in the waters of the deep as the *prima materia* of the creation (VII.211 ff.), in the upper waters and the Sea of Jasper (III.520, VII.619), in the fountain of Eden that waters the garden (IV.222 ff.), in the Satanic connection with the abyss at the fall (when Satan "involv'd in rising Mist" descends into the waters to ascend into Eden, IX.75), in Michael's purging of Adam's visual nerve with water from the Well of Life (XI.416), and in the vision of the New Jerusalem (XII.546 ff.). But as his epics are concerned with the prototypic act of disobedience and its complementary act of obedience in *Paradise Regained,* Milton did not feature the sacramental recapitulation of the waters of grace in the way that Herbert's lyrics do, for example. Thus, the "application" of these types remains submerged. After Milton's day, typology became even more secularized and more broadly construed, and thus the tradition waned until others discovered figural significance in the mysterious waters of life.

13. Korshin, *Typologies in England*, pp. 42–43.

14. Steven N. Zwicker, *Dryden's Political Poetry: The Typology of King and Nation*, pp. 48–55.

15. The most important typological studies of Milton are William G. Madsen, *From Shadowy Types to Truth: Studies in Milton's Symbolism*; Barbara K. Lewalski, *Milton's Brief Epic*; and Mary Ann Radzinowicz, *Toward "Samson Agonistes": The Growth of Milton's Mind*.

BIBLIOGRAPHY

Primary Works

Agricola, Georg. *De ortu et causis subterraneorum libri V.* Basel, 1546.
————. *De Re Metallica.* Translated by Herbert Hoover and Lou Hoover. London: Salisbury House, 1912.

Albertus Magnus. *Meteora.* Vol. 4. In *Opera omnia.* Edited by August Borgnet. 38 vols. Paris, 1890–1899.

Ambrose, Isaac. *Prima & ultima: The First & Last Thinges; or, Regeneration and Meditation Sermons.* London, 1640.

Aquinas, St. Thomas. *Summa Theologiae.* Translated and edited by Thomas Gilby, et al. 60 vols. New York: McGraw-Hill; London: Eyre & Spottiswoode, 1964.

Aristotle. *Meteorologica.* Translated by H. D. P. Lee. Cambridge, Mass.: Harvard University Press, and London: Heinemann, 1952.

Attersoll, William. *The New Covenant, or, a Treatise of the Sacraments.* 2d ed. London, 1614.

d'Aubigné, Agrippa. *Les Tragiques.* Edited by A. Garnier and J. Plattard. Société des Textes Français Modernes. 4 vols. Paris: Droz, 1932–1933.

Babington, Gervase. *Certaine Plaine, briefe and comfortable Notes upon every Chapter of Genesis.* 2d ed. London, 1596.

Bale, John. *The Ymage of Bothe Churches after the . . . Revelacioun of Saincte John the Evangelyst.* London, 1550.

Bartholomaeus Anglicus. *On the Properties of Things.* Translated by John Trevisa. Edited by M. C. Seymour, et al. 2 vols. Oxford: Clarendon Press, 1975.

Berry, Lloyd E., introduction. *The Geneva Bible: A Facsimile of the 1560 Edition.* Madison: University of Wisconsin Press, 1969.

Booty, John E., ed. *The Book of Common Prayer, 1559: The Elizabethan Prayer Book.* Charlottesville: University Press of Virginia for the Folger Shakespeare Library, 1976.

Brocardo, Giacopa. *The Revelation of S. Jhon reveled.* Translated by James Sanford. London, 1582.

Broughton, Hugh. *The Works of the Great Albionean Divine . . . Hugh Broughton.* London, 1662.

Bunyan, John. *Grace Abounding to the Chief of Sinners.* Edited by Roger Sharrock. Oxford: Clarendon Press, 1962.

Butler, Samuel. *Characters.* Edited by Charles W. Davis. Cleveland and London: Press of Case Western Reserve, 1970.

Charles, R. H., et al., trans. and ed. *The Apocrypha and Pseudepigrapha of the Old Testament*. 2 vols. Oxford: Clarendon Press, 1913.

Cosmas Indicopleustes. *Christian Topography*. Translated and edited by J. W. McCrindle. Hakluyt Society, No. 98. London: Hakluyt, 1897.

Cowper, William. *The Workes of Mr. William Cowper late Bishop of Galloway*. 2d ed. London, 1629.

Crashaw, Richard. *The Poems, English, Latin and Greek*. Edited by L. C. Martin, 2d ed. Oxford: Clarendon Press, 1957.

Crooke, Helkiah. *Mikrokosmographia: A Description of the Body of Man*. London, 1615.

Cuningham, William. *The Cosmographical Glasse*. London, 1559.

Donne, John. *The Complete Poetry*. Edited by John T. Shawcross. Garden City, NY: Doubleday Anchor, 1967.

Downame, John. *The Christian Warfare against the Devill, World, and Flesh*. London, 1634.

Dryden, John. *The Poems*. Edited by James Kinsley. 4 vols. Oxford: Clarendon Press, 1958.

Dyke, Daniel. *The Second and Last Part of the Works . . . viz. Sixe Evangelical Histories*. 2d ed. London, 1633.

Elyot, Sir Thomas. *The Castel of Helth*. 1541. Reprint. New York: Scholars' Facsimiles, 1936.

Fane, Mildmay. *Otia Sacra (1648)*. Introduction by Donald M. Friedman. Delmar, NY: Scholars' Facsimiles, 1975.

Ficino, Marsilio. *Theologica Platonica*. In *Opera omnia*. 2d ed. 2 vols. Basel, 1576.

Flacius, Matthias Illyricus. *Clavis Scripturae Sacrae; seu de sermone sacrarum literarum*. 2 vols. Jena, 1567.

Fulke, William. *A Goodly Gallerye . . . to behold the naturall causes of all kynde of Meteors*. London, 1563.

―――. *Praelections upon the Sacred and holy Revelation of S. John*. Translated by George Gyffard. London, 1573.

Gale, Theophilus. *The Court of the Gentiles,* Part I. Oxford, 1669.

Galen. *On the Usefulness of the Parts of the Body*. Translated and edited by Margaret T. May. 2 vols. Ithaca: Cornell University Press, 1968.

Gell, Robert. *Noah's Flood Returning*. Edited by W. P. London, 1655.

Gibbens, Nicholas. *Questions and Disputations concerning the holy scripture*. London, 1602.

Glass, Salomon. *Philologiae Sacrae . . . libri quinque*. 2d ed. 3 vols. in 1. Jena: 1636–1645.

Guild, William. *Moses Unvailed; or, those figures which served unto the patterne and shaddow of heavenly things*. 2d ed. London, 1623.

Hall, John. *Emblems with Elegant Figures, 1658*. Edited by John Horden. Menston, Yorkshire: Scolar Press, 1970.

Harvey, William. *The Works of William Harvey*. Translated by Robert Willis. London, 1847.

Heidel, Alexander, trans. and ed. *The Babylonian Genesis*. 2d ed. Chicago: Phoenix, 1963.

Herbert, George. *The Works of George Herbert*. Edited by F. E. Hutchinson. Corr. ed. Oxford: Clarendon Press, 1945.

Hesiod. *Theogony*. Translated by Hugh G. Evelyn-White. 2d ed. Cambridge: Harvard University Press, and London: Heinemann, 1959.

Homer. *Iliad*. Translated by A. T. Murray. 2 vols. Cambridge: Harvard University Press, and London: Heinemann, 1924.

Huntley, Frank Livingstone. *Bishop Joseph Hall and Protestant Meditation in Seventeenth-Century England. A Study with the Texts of "The Art of Divine Meditation (1606)" and "Occasional Meditations (1633)."* Medieval & Renaissance Texts & Studies, vol 1. Binghamton, N.Y.: Center for Medieval & Early Renaissance Studies, 1981.

Hutcheson, George. *An Exposition of the Gospell of Jesus Christ according to John.* London, 1657.

Jackson, Thomas. *The Works . . . of Thomas Jackson.* Edited by D. D. Barnabas Oley. 3 vols. London, 1673.

Jorden, Edward. *A Discourse of naturall Bathes and Minerall Waters.* 2d ed. London, 1632.

Keach, Benjamin. *Tropologia: A Key to Open Scripture Metaphors.* 3 pts. London, 1682.

———. *Troposchemalogia: Tropes and Figures.* London, 1682.

Kircher, Athanasius. *Mundus subterraneus.* 2 vols. in 1. Amsterdam, 1664–1665.

———. *The Vulcano's.* London, 1669.

Lee, Samuel. *Orbis miraculum; or, The Temple of Solomon.* London, 1659.

Lightfoot, John. *A few, and new, observations upon the Booke of Genesis.* London, 1642.

Lukin, Henry. *An Introduction to the Holy Scriptures.* London, 1669.

Lydiat, Thomas. *Disquisitio physiologica de origine fontium* (pub. with *Praelectio Astronomica de Natura Coeli*). London, 1605.

Marlorat, Augustin. *A Catholike and Ecclesiasticall exposition of the holy Gospell after S. John.* Translated by Thomas Tymme. London, 1575.

———. *A Catholike and Ecclesiasticall exposition of the holy Gospell after S. Mathewe.* Translated by Thomas Tymme. London, 1570.

———. *A Catholike exposition upon the Revelation of Saint John.* Translated by Arthur Golding. London, 1574.

Marvell, Andrew. *The Poems and Letters.* Edited by H. M. Margoliouth. Revised by Pierre Legouis with E. E. Duncan-Jones. 3d ed. 2 vols. Oxford: Clarendon Press, 1971.

Mayer, John. *Ecclesiastica Interpretatio: or, the expositions upon . . . the seven Epistles called Catholike, and the Revelation.* London, 1627.

Milton, John. *The Complete Prose Works of John Milton.* Edited by Don M. Wolfe, et al. Vol 6. *Christian Doctrine.* Translated by John Carey. Edited by Maurice Kelley. New Haven: Yale University Press, 1973.

Paradin, Claude. *The Heroicall Devises of M. Claudius Paradin.* Translated by P. S. London, 1591.

Pareus, David. *A Commentary upon the Divine Revelation.* Translated by Elias Arnold. Amsterdam, 1644.

———. *In Genesin Mosis commentarius.* Geneva, 1614.

Pererius, Benedict. *Commentariorum et disputationum in Genesim tomi quatuor.* Cologne, 1601.

Perkins, William. *The Works of that famous and worthie Minister of Christ.* 3 vols. London, 1616–1618.

Philipott, Thomas. *Poems* (1646), Edited by L. C. Martin. Liverpool Reprints, No. 4. Liverpool: University Press of Liverpool, 1950.

Place, Josue de la. *Opuscula nonnulla.* Saumur, 1656.

Plato. *Phaedo.* Translated by H. N. Fowler. London: Heinemann, and New York: Macmillan, 1913.

———. *Timaeus.* Translated by R. G. Bury. London: Heinemann, and Cambridge: Harvard University Press, 1929.

———. *Timaeus: a Calcidio translatus commentarioque instructus.* Edited by Jan Hendrik Waszink. Corpus Platonicum Medii Aevi, vol. 4. London: Warburg Institute, 1962.

Pliny. *Natural History.* Translated by Horace Rackham, et al. 10 vols. Cambridge: Harvard University Press, and London: Heinemann, 1947–1962.

Plotinus. *The Enneads.* Translated by Stephen MacKenna. Revised by B. S. Page. 3d ed. London: Faber and Faber, 1962.

Primaudaye, Pierre de la. *The Second Part of the French Academy.* Translated by T. B[owes]. 2d ed. London, 1605.

Raleigh, Sir Walter. *The History of the World.* London, 1614.

Ray, John. *The Wisdom of God.* 8th ed. London, 1722.

Saintsbury, George, ed. *Minor Poets of the Caroline Period.* 3 vols. Oxford: Clarendon Press, 1905.

Sedgwick, Obadiah. *The Fountain opened: and the waters of life flowing forth, for the refreshing of thirsty sinners.* London, 1657.

Seneca. *Natural Questions.* Translated by Thomas H. Corcoran. 2 vols. Cambridge: Harvard University Press, and London: Heinemann, 1971.

Spingarn, J. E., ed. *Critical Essays of the Seventeenth Century.* 3 vols. 1908. Reprint. Bloomington and London: Indiana University Press, 1957.

Swan, John. *Speculum Mundi, or, a Glasse representing the Face of the World. . . . Whereunto is joyned an Hexameron.* 2d ed. London, 1643.

Taylor, Thomas. *Christ Revealed; or, The Old Testament explained.* London, 1635.

———. *Meditations from the Creatures.* 2d ed. London, 1629.

Traherne, Thomas. *Centuries, Poems, and Thanksgivings.* Edited by H. M. Margoliouth. 2 vols. Oxford: Clarendon Press, 1958.

———. *Christian Ethicks.* Edited by Carol L. Marks and George R. Guffey. Ithaca: Cornell University Press, 1968.

———. *Meditations on the Six Days of the Creation.* Edited by George R. Guffey. Augustan Reprint Society, No. 119. Los Angeles: William Andrews Clark Memorial Library, 1966.

Trapp, John. *Commentary or Exposition upon the four Evangelists and the Acts of the Apostles.* 3 pts. London, 1647–1646.

Vaughan, Henry. *The Complete Poems.* Edited by Alan Rudrum. New Haven and London: Yale University Press, 1981.

———. *The Secular Poems of Henry Vaughan.* Edited by E. L. Marilla. Essays and Studies on English Language and Literature, vol. 21. Uppsala: Lundequistska Bokhandeln, 1958.

————. *The Works.* Edited by L. C. Martin. 2d ed. Oxford: Clarendon Press, 1957.

Voragine, Jacobus de. *The Golden Legend.* Translated by Granger Ryan and Helmut Ripperger. 1941. Reprint. New York: Arno, 1969.

Walton, Izaak. *The Lives of John Donne, Sir Henry Wotton, Richard Hooker, George Herbert, and Robert Sanderson.* Introduction by George Saintsbury. London: Oxford University Press, 1927.

Ward, Richard. *Theologicall Questions, Dogmaticall Observations, and Evangelicall Essays, upon . . . Matthew.* London, 1640.

Weemes, John. *The Christian Synagogue.* 4th ed. London, 1633.

————. *The Portraiture of the Image of God in Man in His Three Estates, of Creation. Restauration. Glorification.* 2d ed. London, 1632.

Westminster Assembly. *Annotations Upon All the Books of the Old and New Testament.* Edited by John Downame, et al. 2d ed. 2 vols. London, 1651.

Willet, Andrew. *Hexapla in Genesin.* Cambridge, 1605.

Whitaker, William. *Disputatio de Sacra Scriptura contra huius temporis Papistas.* Cambridge, 1588.

White, John. *A Way to the Tree of Life: Discovered in Sundry Directions for the Profitable Reading of the Scriptures.* London, 1647.

Worden, Thomas. *The Types unveiled, or, the Gospel pick't out of the Legal Ceremonies.* London, 1664.

Secondary Sources

Adams, Frank D. *The Birth and Development of the Geological Sciences.* Baltimore: Williams & Wilkins, 1938.

Asals, Heather A. R. *Equivocal Predication: George Herbert's Way to God.* Toronto, Buffalo, and London: University of Toronto Press, 1981.

Auerbach, Erich. "Figura." In *Scenes from the Drama of European Literature.* Translated by Ralph Manheim. New York: Meridian, 1959.

Ball, Bryan W. *A Great Expectation: Eschatological Thought in English Protestantism to 1660.* Leiden: Brill, 1975.

Bedard, Walter M. *The Symbolism of the Baptismal Font in Early Christian Thought.* Catholic University Studies in Sacred Theology. 2d Series. No. 45. Washington: Catholic University Press, 1951.

Bell, Ilona. "'Setting Foot into Divinity': George Herbert and the English Reformation." *MLQ* 38 (1977): 219–41.

Benet, Diana. *Secretary of Praise: The Poetic Vocation of George Herbert.* Columbia: University of Missouri Press, 1984.

Bercovitch, Sacvan, ed. *Typology and Early American Literature.* Amherst: University of Massachusetts Press, 1972.

Berthoff, Ann E. *The Resolved Soul: A Study of Marvell's Major Poems.* Princeton: Princeton University Press, 1970.

Biswas, Asit K. *History of Hydrology.* Amsterdam and London: North-Holland, 1970.

Blacker, Carmen, and Michael Loewe, eds. *Ancient Cosmologies.* London: Allen & Unwin, 1975.

Bloch, Chana. "George Herbert and the Bible: A Reading of 'Love (III).'" *ELR* 8 (1978): 329–40.

————. *Spelling the Word: George Herbert and the Bible*. Berkeley, Los Angeles, and London: University of California Press, 1985.

Booty, John E. "George Herbert: *The Temple* and *The Book of Common Prayer*." *Mosaic* 12 (1979): 75–90.

Bowers, Fredson. "Henry Vaughan's Multiple Time Scheme." *MLQ* 23 (1962): 291–96.

————. "Herbert's Sequential Imagery: 'The Temper.'" *MP* 59 (1961): 202–13.

Bradbury, Malcolm, and David Palmer, eds. *Metaphysical Poetry*. Bloomington and London: Indiana University Press, 1971.

Bush, Douglas. *English Literature in the Earlier Seventeenth Century*. 2d ed. Oxford: Clarendon Press, 1962.

Calhoun, Thomas O. *Henry Vaughan: The Achievement of "Silex Scintillans."* Newark: University of Delaware Press, 1981.

Cassirer, Ernst. *The Individual and the Cosmos in Renaissance Philosophy*. Translated by Mario Domandi. New York: Harper & Row, 1964.

Christopher, Georgia B. "In Arcadia, Calvin . . . : A Study of Nature in Henry Vaughan." *SP* 70 (1973): 408–26.

Clark, Ira. *Christ Revealed: The History of the Neotypological Lyric in the English Renaissance*. University of Florida Monographs, Humanities No. 51. Gainesville: University Presses of Florida, 1982.

Clements, A. L. *The Mystical Poetry of Thomas Traherne*. Cambridge: Harvard University Press, 1969.

Colie, Rosalie. *"My Ecchoing Song": Andrew Marvell's Poetry of Criticism*. Princeton: Princeton University Press, 1970.

————. "Thomas Traherne and the Infinite: The Ethical Compromise." *HLQ* 21 (1957): 69–82.

Cox, Gerard H. "Traherne's *Centuries*: A Platonic Devotion of 'Divine Philosophy.'" *MP* 69 (1971): 10–24.

Craze, Michael. *The Life and Lyrics of Andrew Marvell*. London: Macmillan, and New York: Barnes & Noble, 1979.

Crombie, A. C. *Robert Grosseteste and the Origins of Experimental Science, 1100–1700*. Oxford: Clarendon Press, 1953.

Cullen, Patrick. *Spenser, Marvell, and Renaissance Pastoral*. Cambridge: Harvard University Press, 1970.

Daniélou, Jean. *The Bible and the Liturgy*. No translator given. Notre Dame, Ind.: Notre Dame University Press, 1956.

————. *From Shadows to Reality: Studies in the Biblical Typology of the Fathers*. Translated by Wulstan Hibberd. London: Burns & Oates, 1960.

————. "La typologie d'Isaac dans le Christianisme Primitif." *Biblica* 38 (1947): 363–93.

Datow, Wulf. "The Water-fall von Henry Vaughan (1621–1695)." *NS* 15 (1966): 410–20.

Davies, Horton. *Worship and Theology in England from Cranmer to Hooker, 1534–1603*. Princeton: Princeton University Press, 1970.

————. *Worship and Theology in England from Andrewes to Baxter and Fox, 1603–1690*. Princeton: Princeton University Press, 1975.

Day, Malcolm M. "'Naked Truth' and the Language of Thomas Traherne." *SP* 68 (1971): 305–25.

————. "Traherne and the Doctrine of Pre-existence." *SP* 65 (1968): 81–97.

Dickson, Donald R. "The Complexities of Biblical Typology in the Seventeenth Century." *Renaissance and Reformation* 23, 3 (1987).

Dugmore, C. W. *Eucharistic Doctrine in England from Hooker to Waterland.* London: SPCK, 1942.

Duncan, Joseph E. *Milton's Earthly Paradise: A Historical Study of Eden.* Minneapolis: University of Minnesota Press, 1972.

Durr, R. A. *On the Mystical Poetry of Henry Vaughan.* Cambridge: Harvard University Press, 1962.

Duvall, Robert. "The Biblical Character of Henry Vaughan's *Silex Scintillans.*" *PCP* 6 (1971): 13–19.

Elsky, Martin. "George Herbert's Pattern Poems and the Materiality of Language: A New Approach to Renaissance Hieroglyphics." *ELH* 50 (1983): 245–60.

Empson, William. *Seven Types of Ambiguity.* 3d ed. New York: New Directions, 1974.

Fish, Stanley E. *The Living Temple: George Herbert and Catechizing.* Berkeley, Los Angeles, and London: University of California Press, 1978.

————. *Self-Consuming Artifacts: The Experience of Seventeenth-Century Literature.* Berkeley and Los Angeles: University of California Press, 1972.

Francis, W. Nelson. "Vaughan's 'The Waterfall.'" *Expl* 14 (1956), No. 57.

Freccero, John. "The River of Death: Inferno II, 108." In *The World of Dante: Six Studies in Language and Thought.* Edited by S. Bernard Chandler and J. A. Molinaro. Toronto: University of Toronto Press for the Dante Society, 1966.

Frye, Northrop. *The Great Code: The Bible and Literature.* New York and London: Harcourt Brace Jovanovich, 1982.

Galdon, Joseph A. *Typology and Seventeenth-Century Literature.* The Hague: Mouton, 1975.

Garner, Ross. *Henry Vaughan: Experience and the Tradition.* Chicago: University of Chicago Press, 1959.

Gibson, Edgar C. S. *The Thirty-Nine Articles of the Church of England.* 2d ed. London: Methuen, 1898.

Gilbert, Otto. *Die meteorologischen Theorien des griechischen Altertums.* Leipzig: Teubner, 1907.

Ginzberg, Louis. *The Legends of the Jews.* Translated by Henrietta Szold. 7 vols. Philadelphia: Jewish Publications Society, 1909–1938.

Gottlieb, Sidney. "How Shall We Read Herbert?: A Look at 'Prayer' (I)." *GHJ* 1,i (1977): 26–38.

Guibbory, Achsah. *The Map of Time: Seventeenth-Century English Literature and Ideas of Pattern in History.* Urbana and Chicago: University of Illinois Press, 1986.

Guilfoyle, Cherrell. "The 'Paragraph Poems' in *Silex Scintillans.*" *EA* 33 (1980): 296–307.

Halewood, William H. *The Poetry of Grace: Reformation Themes and Structures in English Seventeenth-Century Poetry.* New Haven and London: Yale University Press, 1970.

Hall, Thomas S. *Ideas of Life and Matter.* 2 vols. Chicago: University of Chicago Press, 1969.

Hardison, O. B., Jr. *Christian Rite and Christian Drama in the Middle Ages.* Baltimore: The Johns Hopkins University Press, 1965.

Harman, Barbara Leah. *Costly Monuments: Representations of the Self in George Herbert's Poetry.* Cambridge and London: Harvard University Press, 1982.

Harris, Victor. "Allegory to Analogy in the Interpretation of Scriptures during the Middle Ages and the Renaissance." *PQ* 45 (1966): 1–23.

Hellman, Gustav. *Denkmäler Mittelalterlicher Meteorologie.* Neudrucke von Schriften und Karten über Meteorologie und Erdmagnetismus, no. 15. 1904. Reprint. Liechtenstein: Krause Reprints, 1969.

Heninger, S. K. *A Handbook of Renaissance Meteorology.* Durham: Duke University Press, 1960.

Herlitzius, Erwin. *Georgius Agricola 1494–1555: seine Weltanschauung und seine Leistung als Wegbereiter einer materialistischen Naturauffassung.* Freiberger Forschungshefte, Kultur und Technik, D 32. Berlin: Akademie-Verlag, 1960.

Hunter, A. Mitchell. *The Teaching of John Calvin: A Modern Interpretation.* 2d ed. London: James Clarke, 1950.

Jenkins, Harold. *Edward Benlowes (1607–1676): Biography of a Minor Poet.* Cambridge: Harvard University Press, 1952.

Jordan, Richard D. *The Temple of Eternity: Thomas Traherne's Philosophy of Time.* Port Washington, N.Y.: Kennikat Press, 1972.

Kahn, Charles H. *Anaximander and the Origins of Greek Cosmology.* New York: Columbia University Press, 1960.

Karl, Werner. "Chaos und Tartaros in Hesiods Theogonie." Ph.D. diss. Friedrich-Alexander-Universität. Erlangen–Nürnberg, 1967.

Kaufmann, U. Milo. *"The Pilgrim's Progress" and Traditions in Puritan Meditation.* New Haven and London: Yale University Press, 1966.

King, Bruce. *Marvell's Allegorical Poetry.* New York and Cambridge: Oleander Press, 1977.

Korshin, Paul J. *Typologies in England, 1650–1820.* Princeton: Princeton University Press, 1982.

Kristeller, Paul O. *The Philosophy of Marsilio Ficino.* Translated by Virginia Conant. 1943. Reprint. Gloucester, Mass.: Peter Smith, 1964.

Lampe, George W. H., and Woollcombe, Kenneth J. *Essays on Typology.* London: SCM Press, 1957.

Lewalski, Barbara K. *Donne's "Anniversaries" and the Poetry of Praise: The Creation of a Symbolic Mode.* Princeton: Princeton University Press, 1973.

———. *Milton's Brief Epic.* Providence and London: Brown University Press, 1966.

———. *Protestant Poetics and the Seventeenth-Century Religious Lyric.* Princeton: Princeton University Press, 1979.

———. *"Samson Agonistes* and the 'Tragedy' of the Apocalypse." *PMLA* 85 (1970): 1050–61.

Low, Anthony. *Love's Architecture: Devotional Modes in Seventeenth-Century English Poetry.* New York: New York University Press, 1978.

Lowance, Mason I., Jr. *The Language of Canaan.* Cambridge: Harvard University Press, 1980.

Lundberg, Per Ivar. "La Typologie baptismale dans l'ancienne Église." Diss. Uppsala 1942, Acta Seminarii Neotestamentici Upsaliensis, no. 10. Uppsala, Sweden: Almqvist & Wiksell, 1942.

Madsen, William G. *From Shadowy Types to Truth: Studies in Milton's Symbolism.* New Haven and London: Yale University Press, 1968.

Mahood, Molly M. *Poetry and Humanism.* London: Jonathan Cape, 1950.

Marks, Carol L. "Thomas Traherne and Cambridge Platonism." *PMLA* 81 (1966): 521–34.

————. "Thomas Traherne and Hermes Trismegistus." *RN* 19 (1966): 118–31.

————. "Thomas Traherne's Early Studies." *PBSA* 62 (1968): 511–36.

————. "Traherne's Ficino Notebook." *PBSA* 63 (1969): 73–81.

Martz, Louis L. *The Paradise Within: Studies in Vaughan, Traherne, and Milton.* New Haven and London: Yale University Press, 1964.

————. *The Poetry of Meditation: A Study in English Religious Literature of the Seventeenth Century.* Rev. ed. New Haven and London: Yale University Press, 1962.

Middleton, W. E. Knowles. *A History of the Theories of Rain and other Forms of Precipitation.* 1965. Reprint. New York: Franklin Watts, 1966.

Miller, Perry. *Errand into the Wilderness.* 1956. Reprint. New York: Harper & Row, 1964.

Miner, Earl. *The Metaphysical Mode from Donne to Cowley.* Princeton: Princeton University Press, 1969.

————. *The Restoration Mode from Milton to Dryden.* Princeton: Princeton University Press, 1974.

Miner, Earl, ed. *Literary Uses of Typology from the Late Middle Ages to the Present.* Princeton: Princeton University Press, 1977.

Mulder, John R. *The Temple of the Mind.* New York: Pegasus, 1969.

Murrin, Michael. *The Veil of Allegory: Some Notes toward a Theory of Allegorical Rhetoric in the English Renaissance.* Chicago and London: University of Chicago Press, 1969.

Nicolson, Marjorie Hope. *The Breaking of the Circle: Studies in the Effect of the "New Science" upon Seventeenth-Century Poetry.* Rev. ed. New York: Columbia University Press, 1960.

Novarr, David. *The Making of Walton's "Lives."* Ithaca: Cornell University Press, 1958.

O Hehir, Brendan. *Expans'd Hieroglyphicks: A Critical Edition of Sir John Denham's "Cooper's Hill."* Berkeley and Los Angeles: University of California Press, 1969.

Patrides, C. A. *The Grand Design of God: The Literary Form of the Christian View of History.* London: Routledge & Kegan Paul, Toronto and Buffalo: University of Toronto Press, 1972.

Patrides, C. A., ed. *Approaches to Marvell.* London: Routledge & Kegan Paul, 1978.

Pettet, E. C. *Of Paradise and Light: A Study of Vaughan's "Silex Scintillans."* Cambridge: Cambridge University Press, 1960.

Post, Jonathan F. S. *Henry Vaughan: The Unfolding Vision.* Princeton: Princeton University Press, 1982.

Poulet, Georges. *The Metamorphoses of the Circle.* Translated by Carley Dawson and Elliott Coleman. Baltimore: Johns Hopkins University Press, 1966.

Preus, James Samuel. *From Shadow to Promise: Old Testament Interpretation from Augustine to the Young Luther*. Cambridge: Belknap, 1969.

Quint, David. *Origin and Originality in Renaissance Literature: Versions of the Source*. New Haven and London: Yale University Press, 1983.

Radzinowicz, Mary Ann. *Toward "Samson Agonistes": The Growth of Milton's Mind*. Princeton: Princeton University Press, 1978.

Rahner, Hugo. "Flumina de ventre Christi: Die patristische Auslegung von Joh 7, 37. 38." *Biblica* 22 (1941): 269–302, 367–403.

Rickey, Mary Ellen. *Utmost Art: Complexity in the Verse of George Herbert*. Lexington: University of Kentucky Press, 1966.

Roberts, John R., Jr. *George Herbert: An Annotated Bibliography of Modern Criticism, 1905–1974*. Columbia and London: University of Missouri Press, 1978.

Roberts, John R., Jr., ed. *Essential Articles for the Study of George Herbert's Poetry*. Hamden, Conn.: Archon, 1979.

Roston, Murray. *Biblical Drama in England from the Middle Ages to the Present Day*. Evanston: Northwestern University Press, 1968.

Salter, K. W. *Thomas Traherne: Mystic and Poet*. New York: Barnes & Noble, 1964.

Sandbank, S. "Thomas Traherne on the Place of Man in the Universe." *Scripta Hierosolymitana* 17 (1966): 121–36.

Sandler, Florence. "The Ascents of the Spirit: Henry Vaughan on the Atonement." *JEGP* 73 (1974): 209–26.

———. "'Solomon vbique regnet': Herbert's Use of the Images of the New Covenant." *PLL* 8 (1972): 147–58.

Scheick, William J. "Typology and Allegory: A Comparative Study of George Herbert and Edward Taylor." *ELWIU* 2 (1975): 76–86.

Seelig, Sharon Cadman. *The Shadow of Eternity: Belief and Structure in Herbert, Vaughan and Traherne*. Lexington: The University Press of Kentucky, 1981.

Siegel, Rudolph E. *Galen's System of Physiology and Medicine*. Basel: S. Karger, 1968.

Simmonds, James D. *Masques of God: Form and Theme in the Poetry of Henry Vaughan*. Pittsburgh: University of Pittsburgh Press, 1972.

Singer, Charles. *A Short History of Scientific Ideas to 1900*. Oxford: Clarendon Press, 1959.

Singleton, C. S. *Dante's "Commedia": Elements of Structure*. Dante Studies, no. 1. Baltimore and London: The Johns Hopkins University Press.

Spitz, Leona. "Process and Stasis: Aspects of Nature in Vaughan and Marvell." *HLQ* 32 (1969): 135–47.

Stahl, W. H. *Roman Science*. Madison: University of Wisconsin Press, 1962.

Starr, George A. *Defoe & Spiritual Autobiography*. Princeton: Princeton University Press, 1965.

Stewart, Stanley. *The Enclosed Garden: The Tradition and the Image in Seventeenth-Century Poetry*. Madison: University of Wisconsin Press, 1966.

———. *The Expanded Voice: The Art of Thomas Traherne*. San Marino, Calif.: Huntington Library, 1970.

———. "Time and *The Temple*." *SEL* 6 (1966): 97–110.

Strier, Richard. *Love Known: Theology and Experience in George Herbert's Poetry.* Chicago and London: University of Chicago Press, 1983.

Stroup, Thomas B. "'A Reasonable, Holy, and Living Sacrifice': Herbert's 'The Altar.'" *ELWIU* 2 (1975): 149–63.

Summers, Claude J., and Ted-Larry Pebworth, eds. "Vaughan's Temple in Nature and the Context of 'Regeneration.'" *JEGP* 74 (1975): 351–60.

Summers, Claude J., and Pebworth, Ted-Larry, ed. *"Too Rich to Clothe the Sunne": Essays on George Herbert.* Pittsburgh: University of Pittsburgh Press, 1980.

Summers, Joseph H. *George Herbert: His Religion and Art.* Cambridge: Harvard University Press, 1954.

Temkin, Owsei. *Galenism: Rise and Decline of a Medical Philosophy.* Ithaca: Cornell University Press, 1973.

Tervarent, Guy de. *Attributs et symboles dans l'art profane, 1450–1600: Dictionnaire d'un langage perdu.* Travaux d'humanisme et renaissance. Vol. 29, 3 pts. Geneva: Droz, 1958–1964.

Trimpey, John E. "An Analysis of Traherne's 'Thoughts I.'" *SP* 68 (1971): 88–104.

Tuan, Yi-Fu. *The Hydrologic Cycle and the Wisdom of God: A Study in Geoteleology.* University of Toronto Department of Geography Research Publication, no. 1. Toronto: University of Toronto Press, 1968.

Tuve, Rosemund. *A Reading of George Herbert.* Chicago: University of Chicago Press, 1952.

Underwood, Paul A. "The Fountain of Life in Manuscripts of the Gospels." *Dumbarton Oaks Papers* 5 (1950): 41–138.

Veith, Gene Edward, Jr. *Reformation Spirituality: The Religion of George Herbert.* Lewisburg, Pa.: Bucknell University Press, 1985.

Vendler, Helen. *The Poetry of George Herbert.* Cambridge and London: Harvard University Press, 1975.

Wallace, Dewey D., Jr. *Puritans and Predestination: Grace in English Protestant Theology, 1525–1695.* Chapel Hill: University of North Carolina Press, 1982.

Wallace, John Malcolm. "Thomas Traherne and the Structure of Meditation." *ELH* 25 (1958): 79–89.

Webber, Joan. *The Eloquent "I": Style and Self in Seventeenth-Century Prose.* Madison: University of Wisconsin Press, 1968.

Wensinck, Arendt Jan. *The Ocean in the Literature of the Western Semites.* Verhandelingen der Koninklijke Akademie van Wetenschappen te Amsterdam. Vol. 19, pt. 2. Amsterdam: Johannes Muller, 1918.

Westerweel, Bart. *Patterns and Patterning: A Study of Four Poems by George Herbert.* Costerus, n.s., vol. 41. Amsterdam: Rodopi, 1984.

Wightman, W. P. D. *Science and the Renaissance.* 2 vols. Edinburgh: Oliver and Boyd, 1962.

Williams, Arnold L. *The Common Expositor: An Account of the Commentaries on Genesis, 1527–1633.* Chapel Hill: University of North Carolina Press, 1948.

Wolfson, Harry A. *The Philosophy of the Church Fathers.* 2d ed. Cambridge: Harvard University Press, 1956.

Woods, Susanne. "The 'Unhewn Stones' of Herbert's Verse." *GHJ* 4,ii (1981): 30–46.

Zwicker, Stephen N. *Dryden's Political Poetry: The Typology of King and Nation.* Providence: Brown University Press, 1972.

INDEX